Abraham Lincoln, J. B. (James Baird) McClure

Abraham Lincoln's Stories and Speeches

Abraham Lincoln, J. B. (James Baird) McClure

Abraham Lincoln's Stories and Speeches

ISBN/EAN: 9783337112066

Printed in Europe, USA, Canada, Australia, Japan

Cover: Foto ©ninafisch / pixelio.de

More available books at **www.hansebooks.com**

ABRAHAM LINCOLN'S

STORIES AND SPEECHES,

INCLUDING "EARLY LIFE STORIES;" "PROFESSIONAL LIFE STORIES;" "WHITE HOUSE INCIDENTS;" "WAR REMINISCENCES," Etc., Etc.

—o—

ALSO HIS SPEECHES, CHRONOLOGICALLY ARRANGED, FROM PAPPSVILLE, ILL., 1832, TO HIS LAST SPEECH IN WASHINGTON, APRIL 11, 1865. INCLUDING HIS INAUGURALS, EMANCIPATION PROCLAMATION, GETTYSBURG ADDRESS, Etc., Etc., Etc.

FULLY ILLUSTRATED.

EDITED BY

J. B. McCLURE, A. M.

———:o:———

EDITOR OF "MISTAKES OF INGERSOLL;" "LIFE OF GEN. GARFIELD;" "EDISON AND HIS INVENTIONS;" "MOODY'S ANECDOTES;" "SKETCHES OF GEN. GRANT;" "EVILS OF THE CITIES;" "POETIC PEARLS;" Etc.

CHICAGO.
RHODES & McCLURE PUBLISHING COMPANY.
1895.

Entered according to Act of Congress, in the year 1894, by

RHODES & McCLURE PUBLISHING COMPANY,

In the Office of the Librarian of Congress, at Washington.

All Rights reserved.

In his speeches—and we may add—his stories, the great Lincoln "still lives," with an influence for good among men.

Whatever may attach to his mere biography, that reveals a life of struggle and disadvantage in early years—unparalleled in fact in this respect—the truth is the MAN LINCOLN is not in the "early cabin home," but in "words that never die"—in the compiled utterances of this volume, that reveal and perpetuate the soul life of him who spoke so often, so fully and truly, of life, liberty, and the pursuit of happiness, and of a government "that is of the people, by the people, and for the people."

In this form these stories and speeches, whose radiance lightens all pathways, are dedicated to the world, in the firm faith that in the fulness of time, the knowledge of the truth shall make all people free.

         J. B. McCLURE.

CHICAGO, June 1, 1894.

EARLY LIFE STORIES.

An Honest Boy; Young Lincoln "Pulls Fodder" Two Days for a Damaged Book.............	18
An Incident of Lincoln's Early Hardships and Narrow Escape from Death....................	21
A Pig Story; Lincoln's Kindness to the Brute Creation..	32
A Hard Tussle with Seven Negroes; Life on a Mississippi Flat-boat...........................	33
A Remarkable Story; "Honest Abe" as Postmaster.	40
A Humoros Speech; Lincoln in the Black Hawk War..	46
A Joke on Lincoln's Big Feet..................	50
Baby Footprints.............................	73
"Clarey's Grove Boys"; A Wrestling Match........	57
Elected to the Legislature.....................	47
Gen. Linder's Early Recollections; Amusing Stories.	55
How Lincoln Earned his First Dollar...........	17
How Lincoln Helped to Build a Boat: and How he Loaded the Live Stock....................	28
How Lincoln Resented an Insult................	29

CONTENTS. 7

How Lincoln Piloted a Flat-boat Over a Mill Dam. 42
How Lincoln Became a Captain................. 45
How Lincoln Treated His Early Friend, Dennis
　Hanks, in Washington....................... 62
Incidents Illustrating Lincoln's Honesty.......... 27
Judge Ewing's Story........................... 63
Judge Moses' Early Recollections of Lincoln....... 64
Little Lincoln Firing at Big Game Through the
　Cracks of His Cabin Home................... 20
Lincoln and his Gentle Annie; A Touching Incident 24
Lincoln Splits Several Hundred Rails for a Pair of
　Pants; How he Looked, as Described by a Companion.................................... 35
Lincoln's Story of a Girl in New Salem.......... 35
Lincoln's Mechanical Ingenuity.................. 39
Lincoln's Marriage; Interesting Letters........... 51
Lincoln's Mother; How He Loved Her........... 54
Mrs. Brown's Story of Young Abe; How a Man
　Slept with a President of the United States..... 36
Reminiscences; The Turning Point.............. 59
Splitting Rails and Studying Mathemetics; Simmons,
　Lincoln & Company........................ 42
Senator Cullom's Interesting Reminiscences of Lincoln... 66
"The Long Nine."............................. 49
What Some Men Say About Lincoln; His First
　Meeting with Richard Yates.................. 30
When and Where Lincoln Obtained the Name of
　"Honest Abe."............................. 37
Young Lincoln's Kindness of Heart· He Carries
　Home and Nurses a Drunkard................ 21

CONTENTS.

Young Lincoln and his Books; Their Influence on his Mind.................................... 22

PROFESSIONAL LIFE STORIES.

A Remarkable Law Suit About a Colt............ 75
A Famous Story............................. 78
A letter to His Beloved Stepmother............. 82
An Amusing Story Concerning Thompson Campbell..................................... 85
An Incident Related by one of Lincoln's Clients.... 87
Attention Shown to Relatives................... 91
A Good Temperance Man....................... 94
A Revolutionary Pensioner Defended by Lincoln... 101
Gen. Linder's Account of the Lincoln-Shields Duel. 95
Honest Abe and His Lady Client............... 89
How Lincoln Kept His Business Accounts......... 91
How Lincoln Always Turned a Stury to His Advantage..................................... 103
Hon. Newton Bateman's Thrilling Story of Mr; Lincoln; The Great Man Lookiag to See How the Springfield Preachers Voted................... 106
How Lincoln and Judge B. Swapped Horses...... 75
Lincoln's Story of a young Lawyer as he Told it to Gen. Garfield............................. 79
Lincoln and His Stepmother.................... 80
Lincoln's Story of Joe Wilson and his "Spotted Animals."................................ 86
Lincoln Defends Col. Baker.................... 88
Lincoln in Court............................. 92
Lincoln Defends the Son of an Old Friend Indicted for Murder................................ 97
Lincoln's Pungent Retort...................... 100

CONTENTS. 9

Lincoln Threatens a Twenty Years' Agitation in Illinois.. 101
Lincoln's Visit to Kansas........................ 111
Lincoln and the Little Chicago Girls............ 114
Lincoln's Simplicity............................ 118
One of Lincoln's "Hardest Hits.".............. 93
Some of Lincoln's "Cases" and how He Treated Them.. 99
The Lincoln-Shields Duel...................... 83
The Judge and the Drunken Coachman.......... 88
Why Mr. Lincoln Let His Whiskers Grow........ 115

WHITE HOUSE INCIDENTS.

A Story Which Lincoln Told the Preachers........ 122
An Irish Soldier Who Wanted Something Stronger than Water.................................. 127
A Story About Jack Chase...................... 128
A "Pretty Tolerable Respectable Sort of a Clergyman".. 132
An Apt Illustration............................ 135
A Touching Incident........................... 144
A Praying President........................... 161
"Browsed Around"............................. 136
Bishop Turner's Remiscences................... 164
Common Sense................................ 131
Cutting Red Tape.............................. 136
Comments of Mr. Lincoln on the Emancipation Proclamation................................ 148
Ejecting a Cashiered Officer from the White House. 153
How Lincoln Stood up for the Word "Sugar-Coated.".. 123

CONTENTS.

How Lincoln and Stanton Dismissed Applicants for Office.. 138
How the Negroes Regarded "Massa Lincoln"...... 154
Lincoln's Advice to a Prominent Bachelor......... 124
Looking Out for Breakers....................... 128
Lincoln's Confab with a Committee on "Grant's Whisky.".. 131
Lincoln and the Artist........................... 133
Lincoln and the Preacher........................ 142
Lincoln and Little "Tad."....................... 142
Lincoln Wipes the Tears from his Eyes and Tells a Story.. 147
Lincoln Arguing Against the Emancipation Proclamation that he May Learn all About It......... 149
Lincoln and the Newspapers..................... 150
Lincoln's Bull-frog Story........................ 150
Lincoln's Story of a Poodle Dog.................. 151
Lincoln's Speech to the Union League............ 152
Lincoln and the Wall Street Gamblers............ 154
Lincoln's Habits in the White House............. 157
Lincoln's High Compliment to the Women of America... 158
Lincoln in the Hour of Great Sorrow............. 159
Mr. Lincoln and the Bashful Boys................ 125
Mlnnehaha and Minneboohoo!.................. 133
More Light and Less Noise...................... 135
Mr. Lincoln's Laugh............................. 150
Mr. Lincoln's Remedy for Baldness.............. 168
Opened his Eyes................................. 132
One of Lincoln's Drolleries..................... 137
One of Lincoln's Last Stories................... 156
Philosophy of Canes............................. 130

CONTENTS. 11

Stories Illustrating Lincoln's Memory............ 129
Seward and Chase............................. 167
Trying the "Greens" on Jake.................... 121
Telling a Story and Pardoning a Soldier.......... 162
Where the President's Mind Wandered............ 141

WAR STORIES.

A Soldier that Knew no Royalty................. 173
A Little Soldier Boy........................... 174
A Remarkable Letter........................... 183
A "Henpecked Husband"....................... 185
A Short Practical Sermon....................... 186
A Celebrated Case............................. 186
A Church Which God Wanted for the Union Soldiers.. 190
An Interesting Incident Connected with Signing the Emancipation Proclamation.................. 194
A Dream that was Portentous; What Lincoln said to Gen. Grant Said About It................. 195
A Merciful President........................... 201
A Touching Incident in the Life of Lincoln........ 207
A Joke on Mr. Chase........................... 209
"A Great Deal of Shuck for a Little Nubbin"...... 226
A Position that Lincoln Wanted................. 228
An Inauguration Incident....................... 238
A Lincoln Story About Little Dan Webster's Soiled Hands; How Dan Escaped a Flogging.......... 229
"Borrowing the Army........................... 178
D. L. Moody's Story of Lincoln's Compassion; What a Little Girl Did with Mr. Lincoln to Save her Brother................................. 231
Dr. Edwards Bumping the President............. 236

CONTENTS.

Gen. C. H. Howard's Reminiscences.	221
Getting at the Pass-word.	223
His Visits to the Hospitals.	179
How Lincoln Relieved Rosecrans	192
How a Negro Argued the Point	203
How Lincoln Associated his Second Nomination with a very Singular Circumstance	205
How Lincoln Illustrated what Might be Done with Jeff Davis	208
How Lincoln Told a Secret.	215
Hon. Frederick Douglas' Reminiscences	233
Hon. Leonard Sweet's Reminiscenses	216
Lincoln's Vow	178
Lincoln's Politeness.	179
Lincoln's Curt Reply to a Clergyman	185
Lincoln's Cutting Reply to the Confederate Commission	199
Lincoln and Judge Baldwin	200
Lincoln and the Colored People of Richmond	218
Lincoln's First Convictions of War; His Great Sadness	220
Lincoln and a Clergyman.	224
Lincoln and the Little Baby; A Touching Story	230
Lincoln "Taking up a Collection".	237
Lincoln and Stanton Fixing up Peace Between the Two Contending Armies.	239
Mr. Lincoln and a Clergyman	182
No Mercy for the Man Stealer.	202
Pardons a Soldier.	176
Recollections of the War President by Judge William Johnson.	187
Story of Andy Johnson and his Doubtful Interest in	

CONTENTS. 13

Prayers................................ 171
Sallie Ward's Practical Philosophy............. 175
The Serpent in Bed with Two Children.......... 198
The President's Aversion to Bloodshed.......... 212
The President Advises Secretary Stanton to Prepare for Death............................. 225
"Tad's" Rebel Flag....................... 227
The Brigadier General and the Horses........... 238
Two Hundred and Fifty Thousand Passes to Richmond................................ 216

MISCELLANEOUS STORIES, ETC.

Attending Henry Ward Beecher's Church......... 243
An Amusing Illustration..................... 249
Abraham Lincoln's Death; Walt Whitman's Vivid Description of the Scene at Ford's Theater...... 281
Didn't Know his Own House; How Mrs. Lincoln Surprised her Husband..................... 271
Funeral Services of Lincoln's Mother; The Old Pastor and Young Abraham.................... 251
How Lincoln Took his Altitude; A Prophetic Bowl of Milk............................... 255
Lincoln's Love for Little Tad.................. 244
Lincoln at the Five Points House of Industry in New York.............................. 245
Lincoln and his New Hat.................... 246
Lincoln's Failure as a Merchant; He, However, Six Years Later Pays the "National Debt.".......... 247
Lincoln's Feat at the Washington Navy Yard with an Axe................................ 248
How Lincoln won the Nomination for Congress.... 257
How Lincoln won a Case from his Partner........ 263

Lincoin's Life as Written by Himself; The Whole
Thing in a Nut Shell........................ 265
Lincoln's Foster-Mother; Her Romantic Marriage to
Thomas Lincoln........................... 272
Little Lincoln Stories......................... 275
Lincoln's Last Story and Last Written Words and
Conversation.............................. 279
Lincoln's Favorite Poem...................... 288
Lincoln as a Lover........................... 265
Something Concerning Mr. Lincoln's Religious
Views.................................... 253
Thurlow Weed's Recollections................. 254

LINCOLN'S SPEECHES—1832-1865.

A Great Congressional Speech................. 326
A Fourth of July Speech...................... 446
Douglas' Seven Question's.................... 386
"God Bless the Women of America"............ 449
Exculpating the Whigs....................... 302
Forquer's Lightning Rod is Struck.............. 294
First Talk After Nomination................... 423
First Inaugural Address....................... 429
First Speech After Nomination................. 423
Lincoln's First Political Speech................ 291
Lincoln's First Speech in the Supreme Court...... 301
Lincoln's Temperance Speech.................. 309
Lincoln "Linked to Truth".................... 347
Lincoln's First Speech in the Senatorial Campaign.. 348
Lincoln's Great Cooper Institute Speech......... 393
Lincoln's Rail Splitting Speech................. 422
Lincoln's Speech at Gettysburg................ 448
Lincoln's Second Inaugral.................... 453

CONTENTS.   15

Lincoln's Religious Belief....................... 464
Lincoln's Speech in Washington................. 426
Mr. Lincoln's Debate with Douglas.............. 361
National Bank vs. Sub-Treasury................ 303
President Lincoln's Last Speech................. 458
Showing his Hand............................. 293
Speech After the Battle of the Wilderness......... 450
Speech on the War............................ 451
Speech to 140th Indiana Regiment............... 455
The Perpetuity of Our Free Institutions.......... 295
"The Age is Not Dead"........................ 345
The Ballot vs. the Bullet....................... 345
The Emancipation Proclamation................ 443

ILLUSTRATIONS.

Birthplace of Abraham Lincoln.................. 19
Unforgotten................................... 25
Early Home of the Lincolns in Illinois........... 31
White Pigeon Church.......................... 38
The Old Capitol Building at Springfield, Ill....... 48
Lincoln's Residence at Springfield, Ill............ 73
Abraham Lincoln the Young Lawyer............ 74
Gen. James A. Garfield........................ 79
Mrs. Sarah Bush Lincoln, Lincoln's Stepmother... 81
W. H. Herndon, Lincoln's Law Partner.......... 102
The Republican Wigwam at Chicago, Where Lincoln was Nominated........................ 107
John Hanks, Lincoln's Rail Splitting Companion.. 118
United States Capitol.......................... 120
Lincoln's Family at Home in the White House.... 146
Mrs. John A. Logan........................... 158
The Dawn.................................... 195

ILLUSTRATIONS.

Gen. Grant After his Return from a Tour of the World	196
Birthplace of Gen. U. S. Grant	207
Dwight L. Moody	231
Gen. Grant's Monument at Lincoln Park, Chicago	240
Henry Ward Beecher	242
Lincoln's Father's Monument, near Rockford, Ind.	250
Triumphal Arch	258
The Original Fort Dearborn (as built in 1804)	261
The Lincoln Family Moving from Kentucky to Indiana in 1816	273
The House in Which Lincoln Died, April 15, 1865.	287
Monument of Abraham Lincoln at Lincoln Park, Chicago	292
George Washington, First President of the United States	299
The Fountain	308
Temptation	311
The Dance and the "Gulf"	319
The Waiting Wife	323
Gen. Taylor's Army near Popocataptl, in Mexico	341
Capitol at Springfield	343
The Old Jerasulem Which Fell	369
Half Slave and Half Free	371
Our Savior Performing the Miracle in Cana	384
Lincoln Raising the Flag on Independence Hall, Philadelphia	425
First Inauguration	428
Lincoln's Burial	466
Lincoln's Tomb	470
Bronze Pieces, Etc	471

———:o:———

LINCOLN'S STORIES,

RELATED BY HIMSELF AND BY OTHERS.

─────:o:─────

EARLY LIFE.

How Lincoln Earned His First Dollar.

The following interesting story was told by Mr. Lincoln to Mr. Seward and a few friends one evening in the Executive Mansion at Washington. The President said: "Seward, you never heard, did you, how I earned my first dollar?"

"No," rejoined Mr. Seward.

"Well," continued Mr. Lincoln, "I belonged, you know, to what they call down South, the 'scrubs.' We had succeeded in raising, chiefly by my labor, sufficient produce, as I thought, to justify me in taking it down the river to sell.

"After much persuasion, I got the consent of mother to go, and constructed a little flatboat, large enough to take a barrel or two of things that we had gathered, with myself and little bundle, down to the Southern market. A steamer was coming down the river. We have, you know, no wharves on the Western streams; and the custom was, if passengers were at any of the landings, for them to go out in a boat, the steamer stopping and taking them on board.

"I was contemplating my new flatboat, and wondering

whether I could make it strong or improve it in any particular, when two men came down to the shore in carriages with trunks, and looking at the different boats singled out mine, and asked, 'Who owns this?' I answered, somewhat modestly, 'I do.' 'Will you," said one of them, 'take us and our trunks out to the steamer?' 'Certainly,' said I. I was very glad to have the chance of earning something. I suppose that each of them would give me two or three bits. The trunks were put on my flatboat, the passengers seated themselves on the trunks, and I sculled them out to the steamboat.

"They got on board, and I lifted up their heavy trunks, and put them on deck. The steamer was about to put on steam again, when I called out that they had forgotten to pay me. Each of them took from his pocket a silver half-dollar, and threw it on the floor of my boat. I could scarcely believe my eyes as I picked up the money. Gentlemen, you may think it was a very little thing, and in these days it seems to me a trifle; but it was a most important incident in my life. I could scarcely credit that I, a poor boy, had earned a dollar. The world seemed wider and fairer before me. I was a more hopeful and confident being from that time."

―――:o:―――

An Honest Boy—Young Lincoln "Pulls Fodder" Two Days for a Damaged Book.

The following incident, illustrating several traits already developed in the early boyhood of Lincoln, is vouched for by a citizen of Evansville, Ind." who knew him in the days referred to:

In his eagerness to acquire knowledge, young Lincoln

BIRTH-PLACE OF ABRAHAM LINCOLN.

In what is now LaRue Co., Kentucky, one and a half miles from Hodgenville, and seven miles from Elizabethtown. The three pear trees were planted by Lincoln's father, and mark the spot near where the house stood. Abraham Lincoln was born February 12, 1809. He resided here only a few years.

had borrowed of Mr. Crawford, a neighboring farmer, a copy of Weems' Life of Washington—the only one known to be in existence in that region of the country. Before he had finished reading the book, it had been left, by a not unnatural oversight, in a window. Meantime a rainstorm came on, and the book was so thoroughly wet as to make it nearly worthless. This mishap caused him much pain; but he went, in all honesty, to Mr. Crawford with the ruined book, explained the calamity that had happened through his neglect, and offered, not having sufficient money, to "work out" the value of the book.

"Well, Abe," said Mr. Crawford, after due deliberation, "as it's you, I won't be hard on you. Just come over and pull fodder for me two days, and we will call our accounts even."

The offer was readily accepted, and the engagement literally fulfilled. As a boy, no less than since, Abraham Lincoln had an honorable conscientiousness, integrity, industry, and an ardent love of knowledge.

———:o:———

Little Lincoln Firing at Big Game Through the Cracks of His Cabin Home.

While yet a little boy, one day when Lincoln was in his cabin home, in what was then a wilderness in Indiana, he chanced to look through a crack in the log walls of the humble residence and espied a flock of wild turkeys feeding within range of his father's trusty rifle. He at once took in the possibilities of the situation and ventured to take down the old gun, and putting the long barrel through the opening, with a hasty aim, fired into the flock. When the smoke had cleared away, it was observed that one of the turkeys lay dead on the field. This is said to have been the largest game on which Lincoln ever pulled a trigger, his brilliant success in this instance having no power to excite in him the passion for hunting.

———:o:———

An Incident of Lincoln's Early Hardships and Narrow Escape from Death.

A little incident occurred while young Lincoln lived in Indiana, which illustrates the early hardships and surroundings to which he was subjected. On one occasion he was obliged to take his grist upon the back of his father's horse, and go fifty miles to get it ground. The mill itself was very rude, and driven by horse-power, The customers were obliged to wait their "turn," without reference to their distance from home, and then use their own horse to propel the machinery. On this occasion, Abraham, having arrived at his turn, fastened his mare to the lever, and was following her closely upon her rounds, when, urging her with a switch, and "clucking" to her in the usual way, he received a kick from her which prostrated him, and made him insensible. With the first instant of returning consciousness, he finished the cluck, which he had commenced when he received the kick (a fact for the psychologist), and with the next he probably thought about getting home, where he arrived at last, battered, but ready for further service.

———:o:———

Young Lincoln's Kindness of Heart—He Carries Home and Nurses a Drunkard.

An instance of young Lincoln's practical humanity at

an early period of his life is recorded, as follows: One evening, while returning from a "raising" in his wide neighborhood, with a number of companions, he discovered a straying horse, with saddle and bridle upon him. The horse was recognized as belonging to a man who was accustomed to excess in drink, and it was suspected at once that the owner was not far off. A short search only was necessary to confirm the suspicions of the young men.

The poor drunkard was found in a perfectly helpless condition, upon the chilly ground. Abraham's companions urged the cowardly policy of leaving him to his fate, but young Lincoln would not hear to the proposition. At his request, the miserable sot was lifted on his shoulders, and he actually carried him eighty rods to the nearest house. Sending word to his father that he should not be back that night, with the reason for his absence, he attended and nursed the man until the morning, and had the pleasure of believing that he had saved his life

———:o:———

Young Lincoln and His Books—Their Influence on His Mind.

The books which Abraham had the early privilege of reading were the Bible, much of which he could repeat, Æsop's Fables, all of which he could repeat, Pilgrim's Progress, Weems' Life of Washington, and a Life of Henry Clay, which his mother had managed to purchase for him. Subsequently he read the Life of Franklin and Ramsey's Life of Washington. In these books, read and re-read, he found meat for his hungry mind. The Holy

Bible, Æsop and John Bunyan—could three better books have been chosen for him from the richest library?

For those who have witnessed the dissipating effects of many books upon the minds of modern children it is not hard to believe that Abraham's poverty of books was the wealth of his life. These three books did much to perfect that which his mother's teachings had begun, and to form a character which, for quaint simplicity, earnestness, truthfulness and purity has never been surpassed among the historic personages of the world. The Life of Washington, while it gave him a lofty example of patriotism, incidentally conveyed to his mind a general knowledge of American history; and the Life of Henry Clay spoke to him of a living man who had risen to political and professional eminence from circumstances almost as humble as his own.

The latter book undoubtedly did much to excite his taste for politics, to kindle his ambition, and to make him a warm admirer and partisan of Henry Clay. Abraham must have been very young when he read Weems' Life of Washington, and we catch a glimpse of his precocity in the thoughts which it excited, as revealed by himself in a speech made to the New Jersey Senate, while on his way to Washington to assume the duties of the Presidency.

Alluding to his early reading of this book, he says: "I remember all the accounts there given of the battle fields and struggles for the liberties of the country, and none fixed themselves upon my imagination so deeply as the struggle here at Trenton, New Jersey. * * * *I recollect thinking then, a boy even though I was, that there must have been something more than common that those* *men struggled for."* Even at this age, he was not only an interested reader of the story, but a student of motives.

―――:o:―――

Lincoln and His Gentle Annie—A Touching Incident.

The following interesting particulars connected with the early life of Abraham Linclon, are from the Virginia (Ill.) *Enquirer*, of date March 1, 1879:

John McNamer was buried last Sunday, near Petersburg, Menard County. A long while ago he was Assessor and Treasurer of the county for several successive terms. Mr. McNamer was an early settler in that section, and before the Town of Petersburg was laid out was in business at Old Salem, a village that existed many years ago two miles south of the present site of Petersburg. Abe Lincoln was then postmaster of the place, and sold whisky to its inhabitants. There are old-timers yet living in Menard who bought many a jug of corn-juice from Old Abe, when he lived at Salem. It was here that Annie Rutlege dwelt, and in whose grave Lincoln wrote that his heart was burried. As the story runs, the fair and gentle Annie was originally John McNamer's sweetheart, but Abe took a "shine" to the young lady, and succeeded in heading off McNamer, and won her affections. But Annie Rutlege died, and Lincoln went to Springfield, where he some time afterwards married.

It is related that during the war a lady belonging to a prominent Kentucky family visited Washington to beg for her sons pardon, who was then in prison under sentence of death for belonging to a band of guerrillas who had committed many murders and outrages. With the mother

was her daughter, a beautiful young lady, who was an accomplished musician. Mr. Lincoln received the visitors in his usual kind manner, and the mother made known the object of her visit, accompanying her plea with tears and sobs and all the customary dramatic incidents.

There were probably extenuating circumstances in favor of the young rebel prisoner, and while the President seemed to be deeply pondering, the young lady moved to a piano near by, and taking a seat commenced to sing "Gentle Annie," a very sweet and pathetic ballad, which, before the war, was a familiar song in almost every household in the Union, and is not yet entirely forgotten, for that matter. It is to be presumed that the young lady sang the song with more plaintiveness and effect than Old Abe had ever heard it in Springfield. During its rendition, he arose from his seat, crossed the room to a window in the westward, through which he gazed for several minutes with that "sad, far-away look," which has so often been noted as one of his peculiarities. His memory, no doubt, went back to the days of his humble life on the banks of the Sangamon, and with visions of Old Salem and its rustic people, who once gathered in his primitive store, came a picture of the "Gentle Annie" of his youth, whose ashes had rested for many long years under the wild flowers and brambles of the old rural burying-ground, but whose spirit then, perhaps, guided him to the side of mercy. Be that as it may, Mr. Lincoln drew a large red silk handkerchief from his coat-pocket, with which he wiped his face vigorously. Then he turned, advanced quickly to his desk, wrote a brief note, which he handed to the lady, and informed her that it was the pardon she sought. The scene was no doubt touching in a great degree, and proves that a nice song, well sung, has often a powerful influence in recalling tender recollections. It proves, also, that Abraham Lincoln was a man of fine feelings, and that, if the occurrence was a put-up job on the lady's part, it accomplished its purpose all the same.

―.――:o:――

Incidents Illustrating Lincoln's Honesty.

Lincoln could not rest for an instant under the consciousness that he had, even unwittingly, defrauded anybody. On one occasion, while clerking in Offutt's store, at New Salem, Ill., he sold a woman a little bill of goods, amounting in value by the reckoning, to two dollars six and a quarter cents. He received the money, and the woman went away. On adding the items of the bill again, to make himself sure of correctness, he found that he had taken six and a quarter cents too much. It was night, and, closing and locking the store, he started out on foot, a distance of two or three miles, for the house of his defrauded customer, and, delivering over to her the sum whose possession had so much troubled him, went home satisfied.

On another occasion, just as he was closing the store for the night, a woman entered, and asked for a half pound of tea. The tea was weighed out and paid for, and the store was left for the night. The next morning Lincoln entered to begin the duties of the day, when he discovered a four-ounce weight on the scales. He saw at once that he had made a mistake, and, shutting the store, he took a long walk before breakfast to deliver the remainder of the tea. These are very humble incidents, but they illustrate the man's perfect conscientiousness— his sensitive honesty—better, perhaps, than they would if they were of greater moment.

―――:o:―――

How Lincoln Helped to Build a Boat, and How He Loaded the Live Stock.

While a laboring man, Lincoln, Hanks & Johnston on one occasion contracted to build a boat on Sangamon River, at Sangamon Town, about seven miles northwest of Springfield. For this work they were to receive twelve dollars a month each. When the boat was finished (and every plank of it was sawed by hand with a whip-saw), it was launched on the Sangamon, and floated to a point below New Salem, in Menard (then Sangamon) County, where a drove of hogs was to be taken on board. At this time, the hogs of the region ran wild, as they do now in portions of the border states. Some of them were savage, and all after the manner of swine, were difficult to manage. They had, however, been gathered and penned, but not an inch could they be made to move toward the boat. All the ordinary resources were exhausted in the attempts to get them on board. There was but one alternative, and this Abraham adopted. He actually carried them on board, one by one. His long arms and great strength enabled him to grasp them as in a vise, and to transfer them rapidly from the shore to the boat. They then took the boat to New Orleans, according to contract.

How Lincoln Resented an Insult.

While showing goods to two or three women in Offutt's store one day, a bully came in and began to talk in an offensive manner, using much profanity, and evidently wishing to provoke a quarrel. Lincoln leaned over the counter and begged him, as ladies were present, not to indulge in such talk. The bully retorted that the opportunity had come for which he had long sought, and he would like to see the man who could hinder him from saying anything he might choose to say. Lincoln, still cool, told him that if he would wait until the ladies retired he would hear what he had to say, and give him any satisfaction he desired.

As soon as the women were gone, the man became furious. Lincoln heard his boasts and his abuse for a time, and finding that he was not to be put off without a fight, said: "Well, if you must be whipped, I suppose I may as well whip you as any other man." This was just what the bully had been seeking, he said, so out of doors they went, and Lincoln made short work with him. He threw him upon the ground, held him there as if he had been a child, and gathering some "smart-weed" which grew upon the spot, rubbed it into his face and eyes, until the fellow bellowed with pain. Lincoln did all this without a particle of anger, and when the job was finished, went immediately for water, washed his victim's face, and did everything he could to alleviate his distress. The upshot of the matter was that the man became his fast and life-long friend, and was a better man from that day. It was impossible then, and it always remained for Lincoln to cherish resentment or revenge.

What Some Men Say About Lincoln—His First Meeting With Richard Yates.

Lincoln was a marked and peculiar young man. People talked about him. His studious habits, his greed for information, his thorough mastery of the difficulties of every new position in which he was placed, his intelligence touching all matters of public concern, his unwearying good nature, his skill in telling a story, his great athletic power, his quaint, odd ways, his uncouth appearance, all tending to bring him in sharp contrast with the dull mediocrity by which he was surrounded. Denton Offutt, his old employer in the store, said, after having a conversation with Lincoln, that the young man "had talent enough in him to make a President." In every circle in which he found himself, whether refined or coarse, he was always the center of attraction.

William G. Greene says that when he (Greene) was a member of the Illinois College, he brought home with him, on a vacation, Richard Yates, afterwards Governor of the State, and some other boys, and; in order to entertain them, took them all up to see Lincoln. He found him in his usual position and at his usual occupation. He was flat on his back, on a cellar door, reading a newspaper. That was the manner in which a President of the United States and a Governor of Illinois became acquainted with one another. Mr. Greene says that Lincoln then repeated the whole of Burns, and was a devoted student of Shakspeare. So the rough backwoodsman, self-educated, entertained the college boys, and was invited to dine with them on bread and milk. How he managed to upset his bowl of milk is not a mat-

EARLY HOME OF THE LINCOLNS IN ILLINOIS.

Located in Macon County, in the Sangamon Valley, about ten miles from Decatur. It was here, during the first year, that Abraham Lincoln and John Hanks split several thousand rails. Lincoln was about twenty years of age at this time.

ter of history, but the fact that he did so, as is the further fact that Greene's mother, who loved Lincoln, tried to smooth over the accident and relieve the young man's embarassment.

---:o:---

A Pig Story—Lincoln's Kindness to the Brute Creation.

An amusing incident occurred in connection with "riding the circuit," which gives a pleasant glimpse into the good lawyer's heart. He was riding by a deep slough, in which, to his exceeding pain, he saw a pig struggling, and with such faint efforts that it was evident that he could not extricate himself from the mud. Mr. Lincoln looked at the pig and the mud which enveloped him, and then looked at some new clothes with which he had but a short time before enveloped himself. Deciding against the claims of the pig, he rode on, but he could not get rid of the vision of the poor brute, and, at last, after riding two miles, he turned back, determined to rescue the animal at the expense of his new clothes. Arrived at the spot, he tied his horse, and cooly went to work to build of old rails a passage to the bottom of the hole. Descending on these rails, he seized the pig and dragged him out, but not without serious damage to the clothes he wore. Washing his hands in the nearest brook, and wiping them on the grass, he mounted his gig and rode along. He then fell to examining the motive that sent him back to the release of the pig, At the first thought it seemed to be pure benevolence, but, at length, he came to the conclusion that it was selfishness, for he certainly went to the pig's relief in order (as he

EARLY LIFE. 33

said to the friend to whom he related the incident,) "to take a pain out of his own mind." This is certainly a new view of the nature of sympathy; and one which it will be well for the casuist to examine.

———:o:———

A Hard Tussle With Seven Negroes—Life on a Mississippi Flat-Boat.

At the age of nineteen, Abraham made his second essay in navigation, and this time caught something more than a glimpse of the great world in which he was destined to play so important a part. A trading neighbor applied to him to take charge of a flat-boat and its cargo, and, in company with his own son, to take it to the sugar plantations near New Orleans. The entire business of the trip was placed in Abraham's hands. The fact tells its own story touching the young man's reputation for capacity and integrity. He had never made the trip, knew nothing of the journey, was unaccustomed to business transactions, had never been much upon the river; but his tact, ability and honesty were so trusted that the trader was willing to risk his cargo and his son in Lincoln's care.

The incidents of a trip like this were not likely to be exciting, but there were many social chats with settlers and hunters along the banks of the Ohio and Mississippi. and there was much hailing of similar craft afloat. Arriving at a sugar plantation somewhere between Natchez and New Orleans, the boat was pulled in, and tied to the shore for purposes of trade; and here an incident occurred which was sufficiently exciting, and one which, in the memory of recent events, reads somewhat strangely.

Here seven negroes attempted the life of the future liberator of the race, and it is not improbable that some of them have lived to be emancipated by his proclamation. Night had fallen, and the two tired voyagers had lain down on their hard bed for sleep. Hearing a noise on shore, Abraham shouted:

"Who's there?"

The noise continuing, and no voice replying, he sprang to his feet, and saw seven negroes, evidently bent on plunder.

Abraham guessed the errand at once, and seizing a hand-spike, rushed towards them, and knocked one into the water the moment he touched the boat. The second, third and fourth who leaped on board were served in the same rough way. Seeing that they were not likely to make headway in their thieving enterprise, the remainder turned to flee. Abraham and his companion growing excited and warm with their work, leaped on shore, and followed them. Both were too swift on foot for the negroes, and all of them received a severe pounding. They returned to their boat just as the others escaped from the water, but the latter fled into the darkness as fast as their legs could carry them. Abraham and his fellow in the fight were both injured, but not disabled. Not being armed, and unwilling to wait until the negroes had received reinforcements, they cut adrift, and floated down a mile or two, tied up to the bank again, and watched and waited for the morning.

The trip was brought at length to a successful end. The cargo, or 'load," as they called it, was all disposed of for money, the boat itself sold for lumber, and the

EARLY LIFE. 35

young men retraced the passage, partly, at least, on shore and on foot, occupying several weeks in the difficult and tedious journey.

———:o:———

Lincoln Splits Several Hundred Rails for a Pair of Pants—How He Looked, as Described by a Companion.

A gentleman by the name of George Cluse, who used to work with Abraham Lincoln during his first years in Illinois, says that at that time he was the roughest looking person he ever saw. He was tall, angular and ungainly, wore trousers made of flax and tow, cut tight at the ankle and out at both knees. He was known to be very poor, but he was a welcome guest in every house in the neighborhoood. Mr. Cluse speaks of splitting rails with Abraham, and reveals some very interesting facts concerning wages. Money was a commodity never reckoned upon. Lincoln split rails to get clothing, and he made a bargain with Mrs. Nancy Miller to split four hundred rails for every yard of brown jeans, dyed with white walnut bark, that would be necessary to make him a pair of trousers, In these days Lincoln used to walk five, six and seven miles to work.

———:o:———

Lincoln's Story of a Girl in New Salem.

Among the numerous delegations which thronged Washington during the early part of the war, was one from New York, which urged very strenuously the sending of a fleet to the Southern cities—Charleston, Mobile and Savannah—with the object of drawing off the rebel army from Washington. Mr. Lincoln said the object reminded him of the case of a girl in New Salem, who was greatly troubled with a "singing" in her head. Various remedies were suggested by the neighbors, but nothing tried afforded any relief. At last a man came along —"a common sense sort of a man," inclining his head toward the gentlemen complimentarily—"who was asked to prescribe for the difficulty. After due inquiry and examination, he said the cure was very simple.

'What is it?' was the question.

'Make a plaster of *psalm-tunes*, and apply to her feet, and draw the "singing" *down*," was the rejoinder."

———:o:———

Mrs. Brown's Story of Young Abe—How a Man Slept With the President of the United States.

Rev. A. Hale, of Springfield, Ill., is responsible for the following interesting story:

Mr. Hale, in May, 1861, (after Lincoln's election to the Presidency) went out about seven miles from his home to visit a sick lady, and found there a Mrs. Brown who had come in as a neighbor. Mr. Lincoln's name having been mentioned, Mrs. Brown said:

"Well, I remember Mr. Linken. He worked with my old man thirty-four year ago, and made a crap. We lived on the same farm where we live now, and the next winter they hauled the crap all the way to Galena, and sold it for two dollars and a half a bushel. At that time there were no public houses, and travelers were obliged to stay at any house along the road that could take them in. One evening a right smart looking man rode up to the fence, and asked my old man if he could get to stay over night·

" 'Well,' said Mr. Brown, "we can feed your crittur, and give you something to eat, but we can't lodge you unless you can sleep on the same bed with the hired man.'

"The man hesitated, and asked:

" 'Where is he?'

" 'Well,' said Mr. Brown, 'you can come and see him.'

"So the man got down from his crittur, and Mr. Brown took him around to where, in the shade of the house, Mr. Linken lay his full length on the ground, with an open book before him.

" 'There,' said Mr. Brown, pointing at him, 'he is.'

"The stranger looked at him a minute, and said:

" 'Well, I think he'll do.' and he staid and slept with the President of the United States."

———:o:———

When and Where Lincoln Obtained the Name of "Honest Abe."

During the year that Lincoln was in Denton Offcutt's store, that gentleman, whose business was somewhat widely and unwisely spread about the country, ceased to prosper in his finances, and finally failed. The store was shut up, the mill was closed, and Abraham Lincoln was out of business. The year had been one of great advance, in many respects. He had made new and valuable acquaintances, read many books, mastered the grammar of his own tongue, won multitudes of friends,

WHITE PIGEON CHURCH.
The unpretentious edifice where Abraham Lincoln attended Divine Service in early life.

and became ready for a step still further in advance. Those who could appreciate brains respected him, and those whose ideas of a man related to his muscles were devoted to him. It was while he was performing the work of the store that he acquired the soubriquet " Honest Abe."—a characterization that he never dishonored, and an abbreviation that he never outgrew. He was judge, arbitrator, referee, umpire, authority, in all disputes, games and matches of man-flesh and horse-flesh; a pacificator in all quarrels; everybody's friend; the best natured, the most sensible, the best informed, the most modest and unassuming, the kindest, gentlest, roughest, strongest, best young fellow in all New Salem and the region round about.

———:o:———

Lincoln's Mechanical Ingenuity.

That he had enough mechanical genius to make him a good mechanic, there is no doubt. With such rude tools as were at his command he had made cabins and flat-boats; and after his mind had become absorbed in public and professional affairs he often recurred to his mechanical dreams for amusement. One of his dreams took form, and he endeavored to make a practical matter of it. He had had experience in the early navigation of the Western rivers. One of the most serious hindrances to this navigation was low water, and the lodgment of the various craft on the shifting shoals and bars with which these rivers abound. He undertook to contrive an apparatus which, folded to the hull of the boat like a bellows, might be inflated on occasion, and, by its levity, lift it over any obstruction upon which it might rest. On this contrivance, illustrated by a model whittled out by himself. and now preserved in the Patent Office at Washington, he secured letters patent; but it is certain that the navigation of the Western rivers was not revolutionized by it.

———:o:———

A Remarkable Story—"Honest Abe" as Post-master.

Mr. Lincoln was appointed Postmaster by President Jackson. The office was too insignificant to be considered politically, and it was given to the young man because everybody liked him, and because he was the only man willing to take it who could make out the returns. He was exceedingly pleased with the appointment, because it gave him a chance to read every newspaper that was taken in the vicinity. He had never been able to get half the newspapers he wanted before, and the office gave him the prospect of a constant feast. Not wishing to be tied to the office, as it yielded him no revenue that would reward him for the confinement, he made a Post-office of his hat. Whenever he went out the letters were placed in his hat. When an anxious looker for a letter found the Postmaster, he had found his office; and the public officer, taking off his hat, looked over his mail wherever the public might find him. He kept the office until it was discontinued, or removed to Petersburg.

One of the most beautiful exhibitions of Mr. Lincoln's rigid honesty occurred in connection with the settlement of his accounts with the Post-office Department, several **years afterward.**

It was after he had become a lawyer, and had been a legislator. He had passed through a period of great poverty, had acquired his education in the law in the midst of many perplexities, inconviencies, and hardships, and had met with temptations, such as few men could resist, to make a temporary use of any money he might have in his hands. One day, seated in the law office of his partner, the agent of the Post-office Department entered, and inquired if Abraham Lincoln was within. Mr. Lincoln responded to his name, and was informed that the agent had called to collect a balance due the Department since the discontinuance of the New Salem office. A shade of perplexity passed over Mr. Lincoln's face, which did not escape the notice of friends present. One of them said at once:

"Lincoln if you are in want of money, let us help you."

He made no reply, but suddenly rose, and pulled out from a pile of books a little old trunk, and, returning to the table, asked the agent how much the amount of his debt was. The sum was named, and then Mr. Lincoln opened the trunk, pulled out a little package of coin wrapped in a cotton rag, and *counted out the exact sum*, amounting to something more than seventeen dollars. After the agent had left the room, he remarked quietly that he had never used any man's money but his own. Although this sum had been in his hands during all these years, he had never regarded it as available, even for any temporary use of his own.

———:o:———

How Lincoln Piloted a Flat-Boat Over a Mill-Dam.

Governor Yates, of Illinois, in a speech at Springfield, quoted one of Mr. Lincoln's early friends—W. T. Greene—as having said that the first time he ever saw Mr. Lincoln, he was in the Sangamon River with his trousers rolled up five feet, more or less, trying to pilot a flat-boat over a mill-dam. The boat was so full of water that it was hard to manage. Lincoln got the prow over, and then, instead of waiting to bail the water out, bored a hole through the projecting part and let it run out; affording a forcible illustration of the ready ingenuity of the future President in the quick invention of moral expedients.

———:o:———

Splitting Rails and Studying Mathemetics-Simmons, Lincoln & Company.

In the year 1855 or '56, George B. Lincoln, Esq., of Brooklyn, was traveling through the West in connection with a large New York dry-goods establishment. He found himself one night in a town on the Illinois River, by the name of Naples. The only tavern of the place had evidently been constructed with reference to business on a small scale. Poor as the prospect seemed, Mr. Lincoln had no alternative but to put up at the place.

The supper-room was also used as a lodging-room. Mr. L. told his host that he thought he would "go to bed."

"Bed!" echoed the landlord; "there is no bed for you in this house, unless you sleep with that man yonder. He has the only one we have to spare."

EARLY LIFE. 43

"Well," returned Mr. Lincoln, "the gentleman has possession, and perhaps would not like a bedfellow."

Upon this a grizzly head appeared out of the pillows, and said:

"What is your name?"

"They call me Lincoln at home," was the reply.

"Lincoln!" repeated the stranger; "any connection of our Illinois Abraham?"

"No," replied Mr. L., "I fear not."

"Well," said the old gentleman, "I will let any man by the name of 'Lincoln' sleep with me, just for the sake of the name. You have heard of Abe?" he inquired.

"Oh, yes, very often," replied Mr. Lincoln. "No man could travel far in this State without hearing of *him*, and I would be very glad to claim connection, if I could do so honestly."

"Well," said the old gentleman, "my name is Simmons. 'Abe' and I used to live and work together when we were young men. Many a job of wood-cutting and rail-splitting have I done up with him. Abe Lincoln was the *likeliest* boy in God's world. He would work all day as hard as any of us—and study by fire-light in the log house half the night; and in this way he made himself a thorough, practical surveyor. Once, during those days, I was in the upper part of the State, and I met General Ewing, whom President Jackson had sent to the Northwest to make surveys. I told him about Abe Lincoln, what a student he was, and that I wanted he should give him a job. He looked over his memorandum, and, pulling out a paper, said:

" 'There is ―――― county must be surveyed; if your friend can do the work properly, I shall be glad to have him undertake it—the compensation will be six hundred dollars.'

"Pleased as I could be, I hastened to Abe, after I got home, with an account of what I had secured for him. He was sitting before the fire in the log cabin when I told him; and what do you think was his answer? When I finished, he looked up very quietly, and said:

" 'Mr. Simmons, I thank you very sincerely for your kindness, but I don't think I will undertake the job.'

" 'In the name of wonder,' said I, 'why? Six hundred dollars does not grow upon every bush out here in Illinois.'

" 'I know that,' said Abe, 'and I need the money bad enough, Simmons, as you know; but I have never been under obligation to a Democratic administration, and I never intend to be so long as I can get my living another way. General Ewing must find another man to do his work.' "

Mr. Carpenter related this story to the President one day, and asked him if it were true.

"Pollard Simmons!" said Lincoln, "well do I remember him. It is correct about our working together, but the old man must have stretched the facts somewhat about the survey of the county. I think I should have been very glad of the job at that time, no matter what administration was in power."

Notwithstanding this, however, Mr. Carpenter was inclined to believe Mr. Simmons was not far out of the way and thought this seemed very characteristic of what Abraham Lincoln may be supposed to have been at twenty-three or twenty-five years of age.

———:o:———

How Lincoln Became a Captain.

In the threatening aspect of affairs at the time of the Black Hawk War, Governor Reynolds issued a call for volunteers. and among the companies that immediately responded was one from Menard County, Illinois. Many of the volunteers were from New Salem and Clarey's Grove, and Lincoln, being out of business, was first to enlist. The company being full, they held a meeting at Richland for the election of officers. Lincoln had won many hearts and they told him that he must be their captain. It was an office that he did not aspire to, and one for which he felt that he had no special fitness; but he consented to be a candidate. There was but one other candidate for the office (a Mr. Kirkpatrick), and he was one of the most influential men in the county. Previously, Kirkpatrick had been an employer of Lincoln, and was so overbearing in his treatment of the young man that the latter left him.

The simple mode of electing their captain, adopted by the company, was by placing the candidates apart, and telling the men to go and stand with the one they preferred. Lincoln and his competitor took their positions, and then the word was given. At least three out of every four went to Lincoln at once. When it was seen by those who had ranged themselves with the other candidate that Lincoln was the choice of the majority of the company, they left their places, one by one, and came over to the successful side, until Lincoln's opponent in the friendly strife was left standing almost alone.

"I felt badly to see him cut so," says a witness of the scene.

Here was an opportunity for revenge. The humble laborer was his employer's captain, but the opportunity was never improved. Mr. Lincoln frequently confessed that no subsequent success of his life had given him half the satisfaction that this election did. He had acheived public recognition; and to one so humbly bred, the distinction was inexpressibly delightful.

———:o:———

A Humorous Speech — Lincoln in the Black Hawk War.

The friends of General Cass, when that gentleman was a candidate for the Presidency, endeavored to endow him with a military reputation. Mr. Lincoln, at that time a representative in Congress, delivered a speech before the House, which in its allusions to Mr. Cass, was exquisitely sarcastic and irresistably humorous:

"By the way, Mr. Speaker," said Mr. Lincoln, "do you know I am a military hero? "Yes, sir, in the days of the Black Hawh War, I fought, bled and came away. Speaking of General Cass' career reminds me of my own. I was not at Stillman's Defeat, but I was about as near it as Cass to Hull's surrender; and like him I saw the place very soon afterward. It is quite certain I did not break my sword, for I had none to break, but I bent my musket pretty badly on one occasion. * * * * If General Cass went in advance of me in picking whortleberries, I guess I surpassed him in charges upon the wild onion. If he saw any live; fighting Indians, it is more than I did, but I had a good many bloody strugles with the musquitoes, and although I never fainted from loss of blood, I can truly say I was often very hungry."

Mr. Lincoln concluded by saying that if he ever turned Democrat and should run for the Presidency, he hoped they would not make fun of him by attempting to make him a military hero!

———:o:———

Elected to the Legislature.

In 1834, Lincoln was a candidate for the legislature, and was elected by the highest vote cast for any candidate. Major John T. Stuart, an officer in the Black Hawk War, and whose acquaintance Lincoln made at Beardstown, was also elected. Major Stuart had already conceived the highest opinion of the young man, and seeing much of him during the canvass for the election, privately advised him to study law. Stuart was himself engaged in a large and lucrative practice at Springfield.

Lincoln said he was poor—that he had no money to buy books, or to live where books might be borrowed or used. Major Stuart offered to lend him all he needed, and he decided to take the kind lawyer's advice, and accept his offer. At the close of the canvass which resulted in his election, he walked to Springfield, borrowed "a load" of books of Stuart, and took them home with him to New Salem.

Here he began the study of law in good earnest, though with no preceptor. He studied while he had bread, and then started out on a surveying tour to win the money that would buy more.

One who remembers his habits during this period says that he went, day after day, for weeks, and sat under an oak tree near New Salem and read, moving around

THE OLD CAPITOL BUILDING AT SPRINGFIELD, ILL.

EARLY LIFE. 49

to keep in the shade as the sun moved. He was so much absorbed that some people thought and said that he was crazy.

Not unfrequently he met and passed his best friends without noticing them. The truth was that he had found the pursuit of his life, and had become very much in earnest.

During Lincoln's campaign he possessed and rode a horse, to procure which he had quite likely sold his compass and chain, for, as soon as the canvass had closed, he sold the horse and bought these instruments indispensable to him in the only pursuit by which he could make his living.

When the time for the assembling of the legislature had arrived Lincoln dropped his law books, shouldered his pack, and, on foot, trudged to Vandalia, then the capital of the State, about a hundred miles, to make his entrance into public life.

————.o:————

"The Long Nine."

The Sangamon County delegation to the Illinois Legislature, in 1834, of which Lincoln was a member, consisting of nine representatives, was so remarkable for the physical altitude of its members that they were known as "The Long Nine." Not a member of the number was less than six feet high, and Lincoln was the tallest of the nine, as he was the leading man intellectually in and out of the House.

Among those who composed the House were General John A. McClernand, afterwards a member of Congress; Jesse K. DuBois, afterwards Auditor of the State; Jas.

50 LINCOLN'S STORIES AND SPEECHES.

Semple, afterwards twice the Speaker of the House of Representatives, and subsequently United States Senator; Robert Smith, afterwards member of Congress; John Hogan, afterwards a member of Congress from St. Louis; General James Shields, afterwards United States Senator (who died recently); John Dement, who has since been Treasurer of the State; Stephen A. Douglas, whose subsequent career is familiar to all; Newton Cloud, President of the convention which framed the present State Constitution of Illinois; John J. Hardin, who fell at Buena Vista; John Moore, afterwards Lieutenant Governor of the State; William A. Richardson, subsequently United States Senator, and William McMurtry, who has since been Lieutenant Governor of the State.

This list does not embrace all who had then, or who have since been distinguished, but it is large enough to show that Lincoln was, during the term of this legislature, thrown into association, and often into antagonism, with the brightest men of the new State.

———:o:———

A Joke on Lincoln's Big Feet.

He had walked his hundred miles to Vandalia; in 1836, as he did in 1834, and when the session closed he walked home again. A gentleman in Menard County remembers meeting him and a detachment of "The Long Nine" on their way home. They were all mounted except Lincoln, who had thus far kept up with them on foot.

If he had money he was hoarding it for more important purposes than that of saving leg-weariness and leather. The weather was raw, and Lincoln's clothing was none of the warmest.

Complaining of being cold to one of his companions, this irreverent member of "The Long Nine" told his future President that it was no wonder he was cold—"there was so much of him on the ground." None of the party appreciated this homely joke at the expense of his feet (they were doubtless able to bear it) more thoroughly than Lincoln himself.

We can imagine the cross-fires of wit and humor by which the way was enlivened during this cold and tedious journey. The scene was certainly a rude one, and seems more like a dream than a reality, when we remember that it occurred not very many years ago, in a State which contains hardly less than three millions of people and seven thousand and six hundred miles of railway.

―――:o:―――

Lincoln's Marriage—Interesting Letters.

In 1842, in his thirty-third year, Mr. Lincoln married Miss Mary Todd, a daughter of Hon. Robert S. Todd, of Lexington, Kentucky. The marriage took place in Springfield, where the lady had for several years resided, on the fourth of November of the year mentioned. It is probable that he married as early as the circumstances of his life permitted, for he had always loved the society of women, and possessed a nature that took profound delight in intimate female companionship.

A letter written on the eighteenth of May following his marriage, to J. F. Speed, Esq., of Louisville, Kentucky, an early and a life-long personal friend, gives a pleasant glimpse of his domestic arrangements at this time. "We are not keeping house," Mr. Lincoln says in this letter, "but boarding at the Globe Tavern, which is very well kept by a widow lady of the name of Beck. Our rooms are the same Dr. Wallace occupied there, and boarding only costs four dollars a week. * * * I most heartily wish you and your Fanny will not fail to come. Just let us know the time, a week in advance, and we will have a room prepared for you, and we'll all be merry together for awhile."

He seems to have been in excellent spirits, and to have been very hearty in the enjoyment of his new relation. The private letters of Mr. Lincoln were charmingly natural and sincere. His personal friendships were the sweetest sources of his happiness.

To a particular friend, he wrote February 25, 1842: "Yours of the 16th, announcing that Miss —— and you 'are no longer twain, but one flesh,' reached me this morning. I have no way of telling you how much happiness I wish you both, though I believe you both can conceive it. I feel somewhat jealous of both of you now, for you will be so exclusively concerned for one another that I shall be forgotten entirely. My acquaintance with Miss —— (I call her thus lest you should think I am speaking of your mother), was too short for me to reasonably hope to long be remembered by her; and still I am sure I shall not forget her soon. Try if you cannot remind her of that debt she owes me, and be sure you do not interfere to prevent her paying it.

"I regret to learn that you have resolved not to return to Illinois. I shall be very lonesome without you. How miserably things seem to be arranged in this world! If

ABRAHAM LINCOLN'S RESIDENCE AT SPRINGFIELD, ILL.

we have no friends we have no pleasure; and if we have them, we are sure to lose them, and be doubly pained by the loss.

"I did hope she and you would make your home here, yet I own I have no right to insist. You owe obligations to her ten thousand times more sacred than any you can owe to others, and in that light let them be respected and observed. It is natural that she should desire to remain with her relations and friends. As to friends, *she* should not need them anywhere—she would have them in abundance here. Give my kind regards to Mr. —— and his family, particularly to Miss E. Also to your mother, brothers and sisters. Ask little E. D—— if she will ride to town with me if I come there again. And, finally, give —— a double reciprocation of all the love she sent me. Write me often, and believe me, yours forever, LINCOLN.

———:o:———

Lincoln's Mother—How He Loved Her.

"A great man," says J. G. Holland, "never drew his infant life from a purer or more womanly bosom than her own; and Mr. Lincoln always looked back to her with unspeakable affection. Long after her sensitive heart and weary hands had crumbled into dust, and had climbed to life again in forest flowers, he said to a friend, with tears in his eyes: 'All that I am, or hope to be, I owe to my angel mother—blessings on her memory!'" She was five feet, five inches high, a slender, pale, sad and sensitive woman, with much in her nature that was truly heroic, and much that shrank from the rude life around her.

Her death occurred in 1818, scarely two years after her removal from Kentucky to Indiana, and when Abraham was in his tenth year. They laid her to rest under the trees near their cabin home, and, sitting on her grave, the little boy wept his irreparable loss.

———:o:———

Gen. Linder's Early Recollections—Amusing Stories.

I did not travel, says Gen. Linder, on the circuit in 1835, on account of my health and the health of my wife, but attended court at Charleston that fall, held by Judge Grant, who had exchanged circuits with our judge, Justin Harlan.

It was here I first met Abraham Lincoln, of Springfield, at that time a very retiring and modest young man, dressed in a plain suit of mixed jeans. He did not make any marked impression upon me, or any other member of the bar. He was on a visit to his relations in Coles, where his father and stepmother lived, and some of her children.

Lincoln put up at the hotel, and here was where I saw him. Whether he was reading law at this time I cannot say. Certain it is, he had been admitted to the bar, although he had some celebrity, having been a captain in the Blackhawk campaign, and served a term in the Illinois Legislature; but if he won any fame at that season I have never heard of it. He had been one of the representatives from Sangamon.

If Lincoln at this time felt the divine afflatus of greatness stir within him I have never heard of it. It was rather common with us then in the West to suppose that there was no Presidential timber growing in the Northwest, yet, he doubtless had at that time the stuff out of which to make half a dozen Presidents.

I had known his relatives in Kentucky, and he asked me about them. His uncle, Mordecai Lincoln, I had known from my boyhood, and he was naturally a man of considerable genius; he was a man of great drollery, and it would almost make you laugh to look at him. I never saw but one other man whose quiet, droll look excited in me the same disposition to laugh, and that was Artemus Ward.

He was quite a story-teller, and in this Abe resembled his Uncle Mord, as we called him. He was an honest man, as tender-hearted as a woman, and to the last degree charitable and benevolent.

No one ever took offense at Uncle Mord's stories—not even the ladies. I heard him once tell a bevy of fashionable girls that he knew a very large woman who had a husband so small that in the night she often mistook him for the baby, and that upon one occasion she took him up and was singing to him a soothing lullaby, when he awoke and told her that she was mistaken, that the baby was on the other side of the bed.

Lincoln had a very high opinion of his uncle, and on one occasion he said to me: "Linder, I have often said that Uncle Mord run off with the talents of the family."

Old Mord, as we sometimes called him, had been in his younger days a very stout man, and was quite fond of playing a game of fisticuffs with any one who was noted as a champion.

He told a parcel of us once of a pitched battle that he

had fought on the side of a hill or ridge; that at the bottom there was a rut or canal, which had been cut out by the freshets. He said they soon clinched, and he threw his man and fell on top of him.

He said he always thought he had the best eyes in the world for measuring distances, and having measured the distance to the bottom of the hill, he concluded that by rolling over and over till they came to the bottom his antagonist's body would fill it, and he would be wedged in so tight that he could whip him at his leisure. So he let the fellow turn him, and over and over they went, when about the twentieth revolution brought Uncle Mord's back in contact with the rut, "and," said he, "before fire could scorch a feather, I cried out in stentorian voice: 'Take him off!'"

———:o:———

"Clary's Grove Boys"—A Wrestling Match.

There lived at the time young Lincoln resided at New Salem, Illinois, in and around the village, a band of rollicking fellows, or more properly, roystering rowdies, known as the "Clary's Grove Boys." The special tie that united them was physical courage and prowess. These fellows, although they embraced in their number many men who have since become respectable and influential, were wild and rough beyond toleration in any community not made up like that which produced them. They pretended to be "regulators," and were the terror of all who did not acknowledge their rule; and their mode of securing allegiance was by flogging every man who failed to acknowledge it.

They took it upon themselves to try the mettle of every new comer, and to learn the sort of stuff he was made of.

Some of their number was appointed to fight, wrestle, or run a foot-race with each incoming stranger. Of course Abraham Lincoln was obliged to pass the ordeal.

Perceiving that he was a man who would not easily be floored; they selected their champion, Jack Armstrong, and imposed upon him the task of laying Lincoln upon his back.

There is no evidence that Lincoln was an unwilling party to the sport, for it was what he had always been accustomed to. The bout was entered upon, but Armstrong soon discovered that he had met more than his match.

The boys were looking on, and seeing that their champion was likely to get the worst of it, did after the manner of such irresponsible bands. They gathered around Lincoln, struck and disabled him, and then Armstrong, by "legging" him, got him down.

Most men would have been indignant, not to say furiously angry, under such foul treatment as this; but if Lincoln was either, he did not show it. Getting up in perfect good humor, he fell to laughing over his discomfiture, and joking about it. They had all calculated upon making him angry, and they intended, with the amiable spirit which characterized the "Clary's Grove Boys," to give him a terrible drubbing. They were disappointed, and, in their admiration of him, immediately invited him to become one of the company.

———:o.———

Reminiscences—The Turning Point.

It was while young Lincoln was engaged in the duties of Offutt's store that the turning point in his life occurred. Here he commenced the study of English grammar. There was not a text-book to be obtained in the neighborhood, but, hearing that there was a copy of Kirkham's Grammar in the possession of a person seven or eight miles distant, he walked to his house and succeeded in borrowing it.

L. M. Green, a lawyer in Petersburg, Menard County, says that every time he visited New Salem, at this period, Lincoln took him out upon a hill and *asked him to explain some point* in Kirkham that had given him trouble. After having mastered the book, he remarked to a friend that if that was what they called a science, he thought he could "*subdue another.*"

Mr. Green says that Mr. Lincoln's talk at this time showed that he was beginning to think of a great life and a great destiny. Lincoln said to him, on one occasion, that all his family seemed to have good sense, but, somehow, none had ever become distinguished. He thought that perhaps he might become so. He had talked, he said, with men who had the reputation of being great men, but he could not see that they *differed much from others!*

During this year he was also much engaged with debating clubs, often walking six or seven miles to attend them. One of these clubs held its meetings at an old storehouse in New Salem, and the first speech young Lincoln ever made was made there.

He used to call the exercise "practicing polemics."

As these clubs were composed principally of men of no education whatever, some of their "polemics" are remembered as the most laughable of farces.

His favorite newspaper, at this time, was the Louisville *Journal,* a paper which he received regularly by mail, and paid for during a number of years when he had not money enough to dress decently He liked its politics, and was particularly delighted with its wit and humor, of which he had the keenest appreciation. When out of the store, he was always busy in the pursuit of knowledge.

One gentlemen who met him during this period says that the first time he saw him he was lying on a trundle-bed covered with books and papers, and *rocking a cradle with his foot.*

The whole scene, however, was entirely characteristic —Lincoln reading and studying, and at the same time helping his landlady by quieting her child.

"My early history," said Mr. Lincoln to J. L. Scripps, "is perfectly characterized by a single line of Gray's Elegy:

"The short and simple annals of the poor.' "

A gentleman who knew Mr. Lincoln well in early manhood says: "Lincoln at this period had nothing but *plenty of friends.*"

Says J. G. Holland: "No man ever lived, probably, who was more a self-made man than Abraham Lincoln. Not a circumstance of life favored the development which he had reached."

After the customary handshaking on one occasion at Washington, several gentlemen came forward and asked the President for his autograph. One of them gave his name as "Cruikshank." "That reminds me," said Mr. Lincoln, "of what I used to be called when a young man —'*Long-shanks!*'"

Mr. Holland says: "Lincoln was a religious man. The fact may be stated without any reservation—with only an explanation. He believed in God, and in His personal supervision of the affairs of men. He believed himself to be under His control and guidance. He believed in the power and ultimate triumph of the right, through his belief in God."

Governor Yates, in a speech at Springfield, before a meeting at which William G. Greene presided, quoted Mr. Greene as having said that the first time he ever saw Lincoln he was "in the Sangamon River, with his trowsers rolled up five feet, more or less, trying to pilot a flatboat over a mill-dam. The boat was so full of water that it was hard to manage. Lincoln got the prow over, and then, instead of waiting to bail the water out, bored a hole through the projecting part, and let it run out."

A prominent writer says: "Lincoln was a childlike man. No public man of modern days has been fortunate enough to carry into his manhood so much of the directness, truthfulness and simplicity of childhood as distinguished him. He was exactly what he seemed."

Mr. Lincoln and Douglas met for the first time when the latter was only 23 years of age. Lincoln, in speaking of the fact, subsequently said that Douglas was then "the least man he ever saw." He was not only very short, but very slender.

Lincoln's mother died in 1818, scarcely two years after her removal to Indiana from Kentucky, and when Abraham was in his tenth year. They laid her to rest under the trees near the cabin, and, sitting on her grave, the little boy wept his irreparable loss.

The Blackhawk war was not a very remarkable affair. It made no military reputations, but it was noteworthy in the single fact that the two simplest, homliest and truest men engaged in it afterwards became Presidents of the United States, viz: General (then Colonel) Zachary Taylor, and then Abraham Lincoln. Mr. Lincoln never spoke of it as anything more than an interesting episode in his life, except upon one occasion when he used it as an instrument for turning the military pretensions of another into ridicule.

———:o:———

How Lincoln Treated His Early Friend, Dennis Hanks, in Washington.

Dennis Hanks was once asked to visit Washington to secure the pardon of certain persons in jail for participation in copperheadism. Dennis went and arrived in Washington, and instead of going, as he said, to a "tavern," he went to the White House. There was a porter on guard, and he asked:

"Is Abe in?"

"Do you mean Mr. Lincoln," asked the porter.

"Yes: is he in there?" and brushing the porter aside he strode into the room and said: "Hello, Abe, how are you?"

"And Abe said: "Well, well," and just gathered him up in his arms and talked of the days gone by.

O, the days gone by! They talked of their boyhood days, and by and by Lincoln said:

What brings you here all the way from Illinois?"

And then Dennis told him his mission and Lincoln replied:

"I will grant it, Dennis, for old times' sake. I will send for Mr. Stanton. It is his business."

Stanton came into the room and strode up and down and said the men ought to be punished more than they were. Mr. Lincoln sat quietly in his chair and awaited for the tempest to subside and then quietly said to Stanton he would like to have the papers the next day.

When he had gone Dennis said:

"Abe, if I was as big and ugly as you are I would take him over my knee and spank him."

Lincoln replied: "No, Stanton is an able and valuable man to this nation, and I am glad to bear his anger for the service he can give this nation.

———:o:———

Judge Ewing's Story.

Judge Ewing, at a Lincoln banquet in Chicago, February, 1894, speaking on the "Reminiscences of Lincoln," said his first acquaintance with the war President was very early in his own life.

"It was in McLean County, Illinois;" he said, "about 1840. My father was then a candidate for the State Senate, on the Democratic ticket. Mr. Lincoln was stumping the State as an elector for William Henry Harrison. One day he stopped at my father's house and, after a friendly discussion of antagonistic party principles, said, by way of a partial compromise: 'You have got a lot of fine-looking boys here, Mr. Ewing, can't you give me one of them to raise up for a good Whig?'

"'Well, there is my youngest son,' said my father, pointing to me. 'He is about the no-accountest chap of the lot, you can take him.'

Mr. Lincoln patted me on the chin with a smile of acceptance, and from that day until I was grown the neighborhood boys called me 'Whig Ewing."'

———:o:———

Judge Moses' Early Recollections of Lincoln.

Judge John Moses, President of the Chicago Historical Society, at a Lincoln celebration in Chicago, February 12, 1894, gave the following interesting account of the early life of the war President.

"Besides myself there are at present living in Chicago only two men who knew Lincoln as well as I. Mr. Lincoln began his public career nearly half a century ago. The first time I saw him was at the great convention at Peoria, in June, 1844, during the Clay-Polk campaign. Great crowds were gathered at the city, and among them were all the leaders of the old Whig party. At that time I was only a boy.

I can well remember the tall, slim, sallow-complexioned man, with long, bushy hair, addressing the crowd from one of the many platforms. The man was Abraham Lincoln, and he was discussing the tariff question.

He was then 35 years old, married, and had one son, Robert T. Lincoln.

In 1836, Lincoln, who was living on a farm in West Salem, borrowed a horse and rode to Springfield. He secured a room of Mr. Steel, and in partnership with John

EARLY LIFE.

T. Stuart started a law office. The business was only partially successful, and in a short time Lincoln returned home and rented a room at the home of old 'Aunt Susan' Johnson. There he stayed for ten weeks and studied hard. He then returned to Springfield, and previous to the Peoria convention was an elector and canvassed the State.

Two years afterwards, in 1846, he was elected to Congress and took a prominent part in the election of 1848, when General Taylor was elected President. During Taylor's administration Lincoln was a candidate for land commissioner at Washington, but failed to get the office. He then retired from politics for a time and studied and continued to practice law

Lincoln's really active political life began in 1854, after the repeal of the Missouri compromise. He went to Winchester, Ill., where he made his first speech on the Missouri compromise. At that time it was generally conceded that Lincoln ought to be a nominee for Senator, and he was afterward indorsed as such, but on account of the refusal of three Democrats to support him he lost the ballot.

After the campaign came the presidential election of 1856. The Republican party was then formed in the State by a conference of editors at Decatur. A large convention was called at Bloomington, and Lincoln was the most conspicuous person there and seemed to dominate the convention.

Among the speakers were O. H. Browning, Owen Lovejoy and Colonel Bissell. Lincoln was the first to speak, and at the convention made a platform against slavery. During this great speech the audience became so excited that it rose to its feet in a body, and Lincoln with both hands raised said: 'We will not dissolve the Union, and they shall not."

———:o:———

Senator Cullum's Interesting Reminiscences of Lincoln.

At the third annual banquet of the Lincoln Association of Philadelphia, given February 12, 1894, Senator Cullum of Illinois, among other good things, gave the following reminisceoces:

It was my fortune to know Mr. Lincoln well. My knowledge of him dates baek in my own life to the time I was ten or twelve years old, and even before this time I can remember that men would come twenty or thirty miles to see my father in those pioneer days to learn whom to employ as a lawyer when they were likely to have cases in court. He would say to them: "If Judge Stephen T. Logan is there employ him; if he is not; there is a young man by the name of Lincoln who will do just about as well."

In my boyhood days I was permitted to attend the sessions of the Circuit Court one week, twice a year. The first time I enjoyed the privilege I saw Mr. Lincoln and the gallant Col. E. D. Baker engaged in defence of a man charged with the crime of murder, That great trial, espceially the defence hy those great lawyers, made an impression on my mind which will never be effaced.

Late in 1846, when Mr. Lincoln became the Whig candidate for Congress, I heard him deliver a political speech. The county in which my father and family resided was a

EARLY LIFE. 67

part of his Congressional district. When Mr, Lincoln came to the county my father met him with his carriage and took him to all his appointments. I went to the meeting nearest my home; it was an open-air meeting in a grove· On being introduced Mr. Lincoln began his speech as follows:

"Fellow-citizens: Ever since I have been in Tazewell county my old friend Major Cullum has taken me around; he has heard all my speeches, and the only way I can fool the old Major and make him believe I am making a new speech is by turning it end for end once in awhile.

"I knew him at the bar, both when I was a boy and afterwards when I came to the practice of the law in the capital of Illinois, his home then, mine now. I knew him in the private walks of life, in the law office, in the court room, in the political campaigns of the time, and to the close of his great career. I knew him as the leader of the great Republican party, when, as now, it was full of enthusiasm for liberty and equal rights, when the platform was, in substance the declaration of independence, and he was its champion.

"He believed in 'preserving the jewel of liberty in the family of freedom.' Aye, he believed in making the American people one great family of freedom.

"I heard much of the great debate between him and Douglas, the greatest political debate which ever took place in America. I heard him utter the memorable words in the Republican Convention of my State, in 1858.

"A house divided against itself cannot stand. I believe this Government cannot permanently endure half slave and half free. I do not expect the Union to be dissolved—I do not expect the house to fall, but I do expect it will cease to be divided. It will become all one thing or all the other

"What words of wisdom! He could look through the veil between him and the future and see the end. It is said that before this great speech was delivered he read it to friends, and all of them but one advised against its delivery. With a self-reliance born of earnest conviction he said the time had come when these sentiments should be uttered, and that, if he should go down because of their utterances by him, then he would go down linked with the truth.

"It lifts up and ennobles mankind to hear and study brave words of truth uttered by great men. 'Let me die in the advocacy of what is just and right,' he said again.

"In these days of apparent shallow convictions on many subjects; days of greed for wealth, of rushing for the mighty dollar, is it not well to pause and think over the lives of great men of our own country and the world? We are now in the very shadow of the death of a great and good man—George W. Childs—just passed away. A man who lived to do good; to make the pathway of his fellows smoother and easier; a great hearted philanthropist whose fame is world-wide, and will endure as long as sympathy and generosity are found in the human heart.

"Mr. Lincoln was a great debater, as was Douglas. They often met in debate. On one occasion Douglas

EARLY LIFE. 69

charged that there was an alliance between Lincoln and the Federal office holders, and that he would deal with them as the Russians did with the allies in the Crimean War, not stopping to inquire whether an Englishman, Frenchman or Turk was hit. Lincoln replied, denying the alliance, but mildly suggested to Douglas that the allies took Sebastapol.

"Lincoln was a man of faith in the right when the great contest between him and Douglas ended and the election was over. Lincoln had carried the popular vote of the State, but Douglas secured a majority of the Legislature.

"When it was settled that Douglas had triumphed in securing a majority of the Legislature, I happened to meet him in the street and said to Mr. Lincoln, is it true that Douglas has a majority of the Legislature?

"He said 'yes.'

"I felt greatly disappointed, and so expressed myself, when he said:

"'Never mind, my boy, it will come all right,' and in two years from that day the country was ablaze with bonfires all over the land celebrating its first national Republican victory in his election as President of the United States.

"It has been said Mr. Lincoln never went to school. He never did very much, but in the broad sense he was an educated man. He was a student—a thinker—he educated himself, and mastered any question which claimed his attention.

"In my belief there has been no man in this country possessing greater power of analyzation than he did. Webster and Lincoln, while unlike in intellect, were two of the greatest men intellectually this country has produced.

"Mr. Lincoln was said to be slow and timid when, as President he walked along the danger path before him. He learned the truth of an observation by Cicero, 'that whoever enters upon public life should take care that the question how far the measure is virtuous be not the sole consideration, but also how far he may have the means of carrying it into execution.' So in the great struggle for national life he sought to go on no faster than he could induce the loyal people to go with him.

"As we look back over the period of agitation of slavery and of the great Civil War, we see Lincoln towering above all as the savior of his country and as the liberator of three millions of slaves. Lincoln was a shrewd and crafty man. After, as you remember, Vallandigham, of Ohio, was sent South, through the Rebel lines, he got round on the Canada border and finally returned home without leave. People thought his return would cause trouble.

"It is said that Fernando Wood called on the President and cautiously inquired if he had been informed that Vallandigham had got home. Lincoln knew that by sending him South he had broken his power for evil, and in reply to Mr. Wood he said:

"'No, sir; I have received no official information of that act, and what is more, sir, don't intend to.'"

"Another illustration of his great good nature and shrewdness is told. As the war approached its close, Mr. Lincoln and General Sherman were in consultation at City point. One of the questions considered was what should be done with Jeff Davis when captured.

General Sherman inquired if he should let him escape. Mr. Lincoln told him the story of the temperance lecturer who was plentifully supplied with lemonade. The host in a modest way inquired if the least bit of something stronger to brace him up would be agreeable. The lecturer answered he could not think of it—he was opposed to it on principal; but, glancing at the black bottle near by, he added:

" 'If you could manage to put in a little drop unbeknown to me, it wouldn't hurt me much.'

" 'Now, General,' said Mr. Lincoln, 'I am bound to oppose the escape of Jeff Davis, but if you can manage to let him slip out unbeknown'st like, I guess it won't hurt me much.'

"Mr. Lincoln was never disturbed by little things. Mr. Chase was President Lincoln's Secretary of the Treasury. As the time approached the Presidential nomination, Mr. Lincoln was understood to be a candidate, and Mr. Chase was a candidate, retaining his place in the Cabinet. Being in Washington for a time, I had a conversation with Mr. Lincoln about Mr. Chase's candidacy, and I advised Mr. Lincoln to turn him out. He replied:

" 'No, let him alone; he can do me no more harm in office than out.'

"When the President was considering Mr. Chase in connection with the high office of Chief Justice of the United States, a deputation of great men from Ohio— Ohio always had and has yet many—came to Washington to protest against Mr. Chase's appointment, and presented some letters at some time written by Mr.

Chase,. criticising Mr. Lincoln. He read them, and with his usual good nature, remarked:

" 'If Mr. Chase has said some hard things about me, I in turn have said some hard things about him, which, I guess, squares the account.'

"Mr. Chase was appointed.

"He was an American in the highest sense. He stood for America, for liberty, for the Declaration of Independence, for equality of rights, and he journeyed from his home to the National Capital to obey the call of the people and guide the ship of state through the portending storm, he came to his own historic city and in old Independence Hall he declared 'that if the Government could not be saved without giving up the Declaration of Independence, he would rather be assassinated on the spot than surrender it.'

"He was a Republican, as we are; he not only believed in union, liberty and equality, but under his guidance the policy of the Government was established, which has been maintained for more than thirty years and never seriously interfered with until now, and which has given the people unexampled prosperity.

"Mr. President and gentlemen, his life and public utterances speak to us now in this period of peril to business and commerce. Yes, to sustain the honor of our nation as a Republic, to stand fast by our colors, save the people from poverty and distress, the nation from financial wreck, and its flag in this and other lands from dishonor."

———:o:———

Baby Foot Prints.

The Rev. Robert McIntyre in a Lincoln Eulogy at the Auditorium, Chicago, among other good things, said:

One day at the cabin in which Mr. Lincoln spent his early years I was told this story: Sometime before he was elected President Mr. Lincoln visited some of his people there and he stood in the doorway watching a summer shower hunted by a pack of sunbeams, which laid the rain in puddles gleaming in the yard.

They say that Mr. Lincoln, taking up a little girl who was kin to him, carried her out into the yard and dipped her baby feet in the mud-puddle.

Then, carrying her into the cabin he lifted her and marked the ceiling with her feet, leaving marks that remained there for many years. We are told that something of that kind happened to him, by a power greater than himself that lifted him up among the heights and leaving those footprints that will shine forever in the annals of human endeavor. I do not like this theory because it takes away hope from our youth.

Lincoln was like other men. He was not a miraculous man in any sense of the word. He had indeed less of the supernatural about him than any man in history and more of the natural, and it was this that made him so great and lovable in the eyes of the people.

Washington has been idealized until we have forgotten his real character. I confess he is a nebulous character to me.

Now they are going to refine and sandpaper and veneer Lincoln until nothing of the simple, loving, commonplace soul is left to us. We don't want this. We want him just as he is.

ABRAHAM LINCOLN, WHEN A YOUNG LAWYER.

PROFESSIONAL LIFE STORIES.

How Lincoln and Judge B. Swapped Horses.

When Abraham Lincoln was a lawyer in Illinois, he and a certain Judge once got to bantering one another about trading horses; and it was agreed that the next morning at 9 o'clock they should make a trade, the horses to be unseen up to that hour, and no backing out, under a forfeiture of $25.

At the hour appointed the Judge came up, leading the sorriest looking specimen of a horse ever seen in those parts. In a few minutes Mr. Lincoln was seen approaching with a wooden saw-horse upon his shoulders. Great were the shouts and the laughter of the crowd, and both were greatly increased when Mr. Lincoln, on surveying the Judge's animal, set down his saw-horse, and exclaimed: "Well, Judge, this is the first time I ever got the worst of it in a horse trade."

―――:o:―――

A Remarkable Law Suit About a Colt.

The controversy was about a colt, in which thirty-four witnesses swore that they had known the colt from its falling, and it was the property of the plaintiff, while thirty swore that they had known the colt from its falling, and that it was the property of the defendant. It may be stated, at starting, that these witnesses were all honest, and that the mistake grew out of the exact resemblances which the two colts bore to each other.

One circumstance was proven by all the witnesses, or nearly all of them, viz: that the two claimants of the colt agreed to meet on a certain day with the two mares which were respectively claimed to be the dams of the colt, and permit the colt to decide which of the two he belonged to.

The meeting occurred according to agreement, and, as it was a singular case and excited a good deal of popular interest, there were probably a hundred men assembled on their horses and mares from far and near.

Now, the colt really belonged to the defendant in the case. It had strayed away and fallen into company with the plaintiff's horses. The plaintiff's colt had, at the same time, strayed away and had not retutned, and was not to be found. The moment the two mares were brought upon the ground, the defendant's mare and the colt gave signs of recogoition. The colt went to its dam and would not leave her. They fondled each other; and although the plaintiff brought his mare between them, and tried in various ways to divert the colt's attention, the colt would not be separated from the dam. It then followed her home, a distance of eight or ten miles, and when within a mile or two of the stables, took a short cut to them in advance of its dam. The plaintiff had sued to recover the colt thus gone back to his owner.

In the presentation of this case to the jury, there were thirty-four witnesses on the side of the plaintiff, while the defendant had, on his side, only thirty witnesses; but he had on his side the colt itself and its dam—thirty-four men against thirty men and two brutes.

Here was a case that was to be decided by the preponderance of evidence. All the witnesses were equally positive, and equally credible. Mr. Lincoln was on the side of the defendant, and contended that the voice of nature in the mare and colt ought to outweigh the testimony of a hundred men. The jury were all farmers, and all illiterate men, and he took great pains to make them understand what was meant by the "preponderance of evidence." He said that in a civil suit, absolute certainty, or such certainty as would be required to convict a man of crime, wos not essential. They must decide the case according to the impression which the evidence had produced upon their minds, and, if they felt puzzled at all, he would give them a test by which they could bring themselves to a just conclusion.

"Now," said he. "it you were going to bet on this case, on which side would you be willing to risk a picayune? That side on which you would be willing to bet a picaynue is the side on which rests the preponderance of evideuce in your minds. It is possible that you may not be right, but that is not the question. The question is as to where the preponderance of evidence lies, and you can judge exactly where it lies in your minds by deciding as to which side you would be willing to bet on."

The jury understood this. There was no mystification about it. They had got hold of a test by which they could render an intelligent verdict. Mr. Lincoln saw into their minds, aud knew exactly what they needed;

and the moment they received it he knew his case was safe, as a quick verdict for the defendant proved it to be. In nothing connected with this case was the ingenuity of Mr. Lincoln more evident, perhaps, than in the insignificance of the sum which he placed in risk by the hypothetical wager. It was not a hundred dollars, or a thousand dollars, or even a dollar, but the smallest silver coin, to show to them that the verdict should go with the preponderance of evidence, even if the preponderance should be only a hair's weight.

———:o:———

A Famous Story.

It is said that Mr. Lincoln was always ready to join in a laugh at the expense of his person, concerning which he was indifferent. Many of his friends will recognize the following story—the incident actually occurred—which he always told with great glee:

"In the days when I used to be 'on the circuit,'" said Lincoln, "I was accosted in the cars by a stranger, who said:

"Excuse me, sir, but I have an article in my possession which belongs to you."

"How is that?" I asked, considerably astonished.

The stranger took a jack-knife from his pocket. "This knife," said he, "was placed in my hands some years ago, with the injunction that I was to keep it until I found a man uglier than myself. I have carried it from that time to this. Allow me now to say, sir, that I think you are fairly entitled to the property."

GEN. JAMES A. GARFIELD.

Lincoln's Story of a Young Lawyer as he told it to General Garfield.

General Garfield, of Ohio, received from the President the account of the capture of Norfolk with the following preface:

"By the way, Garfield," said Mr. Lincoln, "you never

heard, did you, that Chase, Stanton and I had a campaign of our own? We went down to Fortress Monroe in Chase's revenue cutter and consulted with Admiral Goldsborough as to the feasibility of taking Norfolk by landing on the north shore and making a march of eight miles. The admiral said, very positlvely, there was no landing on that shore, and we should have to double the cape and approach the place from the sonth side, which would be a long and difficult journey. I thereupon asked him if he had ever tried to find a landing, and he replied that he had not.

"Now," said I, "Admiral, that reminds me of a chap out West who had studied law, but had never tried a case. Being sued, and not having confidence in his ability to manage his own case, he employed a fellow-lawyer to manage it for him. He had only a confused idea of the meaning of law terms, but was anxious to make a display of learning, and on the trial constantly made suggestions to his lawyer, who paid no attention to him. At last, fearing that his lawyer was not handling the opposiog counsel very well, he lost all patience, and springing to his feet, cried out: 'Why don't you go at him with a *capias*, or a *surre-butter*, or something. and not stand there like a confounded old *nunum-prctum?*'"

Lincoln and His SteprMother.

Soon after Mr. Lincoln entered upon his profession at Springfield, he was engaged in a criminal case in which it was thought there was little chance of success. Throwing all his powers into it he came off victorious, and promptly received for his services five hundred dollars.

PROFSSIONAL LIFE. 81

A legal friend calling upon him the next morning found him sitting before a table, upon which his money was spread out, counting it over and over.

"Look here, Judge," said he; "See what a heap of

MRS. SARAH BUSH LINCOLN; LINCOLN'S STEPMOTHER.

money I've got from the —— case. Did you ever see anything like it? Why, I never had so much money in my life before, put it all together?" Then crossing his arms upon the table, his manner sobering down, he added, "I have got just five hundred dollars; if it were only seven hundred and fifty, I would go directly and purchase a quarter section of land, and settle it upon my old stepmother."

His friend said that if the deficiency was all he needed he would loan him the amount, taking his note, to which Mr. Lincoln instantly acceded.

His friend then said:

"Lincoln I would not do just what you have indicated. Your step-mother is getting old, and will not probably live many years. I would settle the property upon her for her use during her lifetime, to revert to you upon her death."

With much feeling Mr. Lincoln replied:

"I shall do no such thing. It is a poor return at best for all the good woman's devotion and fidelity to me, and there is not going to be any half-way business about it;" and so saying, he gathered up his money and proceeded forthwith to carry his long-cherished purpose into execution.

A Letter to His Beloved Stepmother.

Lincoln's love for his second mother was most filial and affectionate. In a letter of Nov. 4, 1851, just after the death of his father, he writes to her as follows:

"DEAR MOTHER:

Chapman tells me he wants you to go and live with him. If I were you I would try it awhile. If you get tired of it (as I think you will not) you can return to your own home. Chapman feels very kindly to you, and I have no doubt he will make your situation very pleasant.

Sincerely, your son,

A. LINCOLN.

The Lincoln-Shields Duel.

The late Gen. Shields was Auditor of the State of Illinois in 1839. While he occupied this important office he was involved in an "affair of honor" with a Springfield lawyer—no less a personage than Abraham Lincoln. At this time "James Shields, Auditor," was the pride of the young Democracy, and was considered a dashing fellow by all, the ladies included.

In the summer of 1842 the Springfield Journal contained some letters from the "Lost Township," by a contributor whose non de plume was "Aunt Becca," which held up the gallant young Auditor as "a ballroom dandy, floatin' about on the earth without heft or substance, just like a lot of cat-fur where cats had been fightin'."

These letters caused intense excitement in the town. Nobody knew or guessed their authorship. Shields swore it would be coffee and pistols for two if he should find out who had been lampooning him so unmercifully. Thereupon "Aunt Becca" wrote another letter, which made the furnace of his wrath seven times hotter than before, in which she made a very humble apology and offered to let him squeeze her hand for satisfaction, adding:

"If this should not answer, there is one thing more I would rather do than to get a lickin'. I have all along expected to die a widow; but, as Mr. Shields is rather good-looking than otherwise, I must say I don't care if we compromise the matter by—really, Mr. Printer, I can't help blushin'—but I—must come out—I—but widowed modesty—well, if I must, I must—wouldn't he—maybe sorter let the old grudge drap if I was to consent to be—be—his wife. I know he is a fightin' man, and would rather fight than eat; but isn't marryin, better than fightin', though it does sometimes run into it? And I don't think, upon the whole, I'd be sich a bad match, neither; I'm not over sixty, and am just four feet three in my bare feet, and not much more round the gerth; and for color, I wouldn't turn my back to nary a girl in the Lost Townships. But, after all, maybe I'm countin' my chickens before they're hatched, and dreamin' of matrimonial bliss when the only alternative reserved for me maybe a lickin'. Jeff tells me the way these fire-eaters do is to give the challenged party the choice of weapons, which, being the case, I tell you in confidence, I never fight with anything but broomsticks or hot water, or a shovelful of coals or some such thing; the former of which, being somewhat like a shillelah, may not be so very objectionable to him. I will give him a choice, however, in one thing, and that is whether, when we fight, I shall wear breeches or he petticoats, for I presume this change is sufficient to place us on an equality.'

Of course some one had to shoulder the responsibility of these letters after such a shot. The real author was none other than Miss Mary Todd, afterward the wife of Abraham Lincoln, to whom she was engaged, and who was in honor bound to assume, for belligerent purposes, the responsibility of her sharp pen-thrusts. Mr. Lincoln accepted the situation. Not long after the two men, with their seconds, were on their way to the field of of honor. But the affair was fixed up without any fighting, and thus ended in a fizzle the Lincoln-Shields duel of the Lost Township.

———:o:———

An Amusing Story Concerning Thompson Campbell.

Among the numerous visitors on one of the President's reception days were a party of Congressmen, among whom was the Hon. Thomas Shannon of California. Soon after the customary greeting, Mr. Shannon said:

"Mr. President, I met an old friend of yours in California last summer, Thompson Campbell, who had a good deal to say of your Springfield life."

"Ah!" returned Mr. Lincoln, "I am glad to hear of him. Campbell used to be a dry fellow," he continued. "For a time he was Secretary of State. One day, during the legislative vacation, a meek, cadaverous-looking man, with a white neck-cloth, introduced himself to him at his office, and stating that he had been informed that Mr. C. had the letting of the Assembly Chamber, said that he wished to secure it, if possible, for a course to lecture he desired to deliver in Springfield.

"May I ask," said the Secretary, "what is to be the subject of your lectures?"

"Certainly," was the reply, with a very solemn expression of countenance. "The course I wish to deliver is on the second coming of our Lord."

"It is no use," said Mr. C. "If you will take my advice you will not waste your time in this city. It is my private opinion that if the Lord has been in Springfield once, He will not come the second time!"

Lincoln's Story of Joe Wilson and His "Spotted Animals."

Although the friendly relations which existed between the President and Secretary Cameron were not interrupted by the retirement of the latter from the War Office, so important a change in the Administration could not of course take place without the irrepressible "story" from Mr. Lincoln. Shortly after this event some gentlemen called upon the President, and expressing much satisfaction at the change, intimated that in their judgment the interests of the country required an entire reconstruction of the Cabinet.

Mr. Lincoln heard them through, and then shaking his head dubiously, replied, with his peculiar smile: "Gentlemen, when I was a young man I used to know very well one Joe Wilson, who built himself a log-cabin not far from where I lived. Joe was very fond of eggs and chickens, and he took a good deal of pains in fitting up a poultry shed. Having at length got together a choice lot of young fowls—of which he was very proud —he began to be much annoyed by the depredations of those little black and white spotted animals, which it is not necessary to name. One night Joe was awakened by an unusual cackling and fluttering among his chickens. Getting up, he crept out to see what was going on.

"It was a moonlight night, and he soon caught sight of half a dozen of the little pests, which, with their dam, were running in and out of the shadow of the shed. Very wrathy, Joe put a double charge into his old musket, and thought he would 'clean' out the whole tribe at one shot. Somehow he only killed *one*, and the balance scampered off across the field. In telling the story, Joe would always pause here, and hold his nose.

" 'Why didn't you follow them up, and kill the rest?' inquired the neighbors.

" 'Blast it," said Joe, 'why, it was eleven weeks before I got over killin' *one*. If you want any more skirmishing in that line you can just do it yourselves!'"

———:o:———

An Incident Related by One of Lincoln's Clients.

It was not possible for Mr. Lincoln to regard his clients simply in the light of business. An unfortunate man was a subject of his sympathy, a Mr. Cogdal, who related the incident to Mr. Holland, met with a financial wreck in 1843. He employed Mr. Lincoln as his lawyer, and at the close of the business, gave him a note to cover the regular lawyer's fees. He was soon afterwards blown up by an accidental discharge of powder, and lost his hand. Meeting Mr. Lincoln some time after the accident, on the steps of the State House, the kind lawyer asked him how he was getting along.

"Badly enough," replied Mr. Cogdal, "I am both broken up in business and crippled." Then he added, "I have been thinking about that note of yours."

Mr. Lincoln, who had probably known all about Mr. Cogdal's troubles, and had prepared himself for the meeting, took out his pocket-book, and saying, with a laugh, "well, you needn't think any more about it," handed him the note.

Mr. Cogdal protesting, Mr. Lincoln said, "if you had the money, I would not take it," and hurried away.

At this same date he was frankly writing about his poverty to his friends, as a reason for not making them a visit, and probably found it no easy task to take care of his family, even when board at the Globe Tavern was "only four dollars a week."

———:o:———

Lincoln Defends Col. Baker.

On one occasion when Col. Baker was speaking in a court-house, which had been a store-house, and, on making some remarks that were offensive to certain political rowdies in the crowd, they cried: "Take him off the stand." Immediate confusion ensued, and there was an attempt to carry the demand into execution. Directly over the speaker's head was an old scuttle, at which it appeared Mr. Lincoln had been listening to the speech. In an instant, Mr. Lincoln's feet came through the scuttle, followed by his tall and sinewy frame, and he was standing by Col. Baker's side. He raised his hand, and the assembly subsided immediately into silence.

"Gentlemen," said Mr, Lincoln, "let us not disgrace the age and country in which we live. This is a land where freedom of speech is guaranteed. Mr. Baker has a right to speak, and ought to be permitted to do so. I am here to protect him, and no man shall take him from this stand if I can prevent it."

The suddenness of his appearance, his perfect calmness and fairness, and the knowledge that he would do what he had promised to do, quieted all disturbance, and the speaker concluded his remarks without difficulty.

———:o———

The Judge and the Drunken Coachman.

Attorney-General Bates was once remonstrating with the President against the appointment to a judicial position of considerable importance of a western man, who, though on the "bench," was of indifferent reputation as a lawyer.

"Well now, Judge," returned Mr. Lincoln, "I think you are rather too hard on ——. Besides that, I must tell you, he did me a good turn long ago. When I took to the law, I was walking to court one morning, with some ten or twelve miles of bad road before me, when —— overtook me in his wagon.

"'Hallo, Lincoln!' said he; 'going to the court-house? Come in and I will give you a seat.'

"Well, I got in, and —— went on reading his papers. Presently the wagon struck a stump on one side of the road: then it hopped off to the other. I looked out and saw the driver was jerking from side to side in his seat; so said I, 'Judge; I think your coachman has been taking a drop too much this morning.'

"'Well, I declare, Lincoln,' said he, 'I should not much wonder if you are right, for he has nearly upset me half-a-dozen times since starting.' So, putting his head out of the window, he shouted, 'Why, you infernal scoundrel you are drunk!'

"Upon which pulling up his horses and turning round with great gravity, the coachman said. 'Be dad! but that's the first rightful decision your honor has given for the last twelve months!'"

———:o:———

Honest Abe and His Lady Client.

About the time Mr. Lincoln began to be known as a successful lawyer, he was waited upon by a lady, who held a real-estate claim which she desired to have him prosecute, putting into his hands, with the necessary papers, a check for two hundred and fifty dollars, as a retaining fee. Mr. Lincoln said he would look the case over, and asked her to call again the next day. Upon presenting herself, Mr. Lincoln told her that he had gone through the papers very carefully, and must tell her frankly that there was not a "peg" to hang her claim

upon, and he could not conscientiously advise her to bring an action. The lady was satisfied, and, thanking him, rose to go.

"Wait," said Mr, Lincoln, fumbling in his vest pocket; "here is the check you left with me."

"But, Mr. Lincoln," returned the lady, "I think you earned *that*."

"No, no," he responded, handing it back to her; "that would not be right. I can't take *pay* for doing my duty."

―――:o:―――

Attention Shown to Relatives.

One of the most beautiful traits of Mr. Lincoln was his considerate regard for the poor and obscure relatives he had left, plodding along in their humble ways of life. Wherever upon his circuit he found them, he always went to their dwellings, ate with them, and, when convenient, made their houses his home. He never assumed in their presence the slightest superiority to them, in the facts and conditions of his life. He gave them money when they needed and he possessed it. Countless times he was known to leave his companions at the village hotel, after a hard day's work in the court room, and spend the evening with these old friends and campanions of his humbler days. On one occasion, when urged not to go, he replied, "Why, aunt's heart would be broken if I should leave town without calling upon her;" yet he was obliged to walk several miles to make the call.

―――:o:―――

How Lincoln Kept His Business Accounts.

A little fact in Lincoln's work will illustrate his ever present desire to deal honestly and justly with men. He had always a partner in his professional life, and, when he went out upon the circuit, this partner was usually at home. When out he frequently took up and disposed of cases that were never entered at the office. In these cases, after receiving his fees, he divided the money in his pocket-book, labeling each sum (wrapped in a piece of paper), that belonged to his partner, stating his name, and the case on which it was received. He could not be content to keep an account. He divided the money, so that if he, by any casualty should fail of an opportunity to pay it over, there could be no dispute as to the exact amount that was his partner's due. This may seem trivial, nay, boyish, but it was like Mr. Lincoln.

———:o:———

Lincoln in Court.

Senator McDonald states that he saw a jury trial in Illinois, at which Lincoln defended an old man charged with assault and battery. No blood had been spilled, but there was malice in the prosecution, and the chief witness was eager to make the most of it. On cross-examination, Lincoln gave him rope and drew him out; asked him how long the fight lasted, and how much ground it covered. The witness thought the fight must have lasted half an hour, and covered an acre of ground. Lincoln called his attention to the fact that nobody was hurt, and then, with an inimitable air, asked him if he didn't think it was "a mighty small crop for an acre of ground." The jury rejected the case with contempt as beneath the dignity of twelve brave, good men and true.

In another cause the son of his old friend, who had employed him and loaned him books, was charged with a murder committed in a riot at a camp-meeting. Lincoln volunteered for the defense. A witness swore that he saw the prisoner strike the fatal blow. It was night, but be swore that the full moon was shining clear, and he saw everything distinctly. The case seemed hopeless, but

Lincoln produced an almanac, and showed that at the hour there was no moon. Then he depicted the crime of perjury with such eloquence that the false witness fled the Court House. One who heard the trial says: "It was near night when he concluded, saying: 'If justice was done, before the sun set it would shine upon his client a free man.'"

The Court charged the jury; they retired, and presently returned a verdict—"Not guilty." The prisoner fell into his weeping mother's arms, and then turned to thank Mr. Linclon, who, looking out at the sun, said: "It is not yet sundown, and you are free."

———:o:———

One of Lincoln's "Hardest Hits."

In Abbott's "History of the Civil War," the following story is told of one of Lincoln's "hardest hits:" "I once knew," said Lincoln, "a sound churchman by the name of Brown, who was a member of a very sober and pious committee having in charge the erection of a bridge over a dangerous and rapid river. Several architects failed, and at last Brown said he had a friend named Jones, who had built several bridges and undoubtedly could build that one. So Mr. Jones was called in.

" 'Can you build this bridge ?' inquired the committee.

" 'Yes,' replied Jones, or any other. I could build a bridge to the infernal regions, if necessary !'

The committee were shocked, and Brown felt called upon to defend his friend. 'I know Jones so well,' said he, 'and he is so honest a man and so good an architect that if he states soberly and positively that he can build a bridge to—to——, why, I believe it; but I feel bound to say that I have my doubts about the abutment on the infernal side.'

"So," said Mr. Lincoln, "when politicians told me that the northern and southern wings of the Democracy could be harmonized, why, I believed them, of course; but I always had my doubts about the 'abutment' on the *other* side."

———:o:———

A Good Temperance Man.

Immediately after Mr. Lincoln's nomination for President at the Chicago Convention, a committee, of which

Governor Morgan, of New York, was Chairman, visited him in Springfield, Ill., where he was officially informed of his nomination.

After this ceremony had passed, Mr. Lincoln remarked to the company that as an appropriate conclusion to an interview so important and interesting as that which had just transpired, he supposed good manners would require that he should treat the committee with something to drink; and opening a door that led into a room in the rear, he called out, "Mary! Mary!" A girl responded to the call, to whom Mr. Lincoln spoke a few words in an under-tone, and, closing the door, returned again to converse with his guests. In a few minutes the maiden entered, bearing a large waiter, containing several glass tumblers, and a large pitcher in the midst, and placed it upon the center-table. Mr. Lincoln arose, and gravely addressing the company, said: "Gentlemen, we must pledge our mutual healths in the most healthy beverage which God has given to man—it is the only beverage I have ever used or allowed in my family, and I cannot conscientiously depart from it on the present occasion—it is pure Adam's ale from the spring;" and, taking a tumbler, he touched it to his lips, and pledged them his highest respects in a cup of *cold water*. Of course, all his guests were constrained to admire his consistency, and to join in his example.

———;o;———

Gen. Linder's Account of the Lincoln-Shields Duel.

When the famous challenge was sent by General Shields to Mr. Lincoln, it was at once accepted, and by the advice of his especial friend and second, Dr. Merriman, he chose broadswords as the weapons with which to fight. Dr. Merriman being a splendid swordsman trained him in the use of that instrument, which made it almost certain that Shields would be killed or discomfited, for he was a small, short-armed man, while Lincoln was a tall, sinewy, long-armed man, and as stout as Hercules.

They went to Alton, and were to fight on the neck of land between the Missouri and Mississippi Rivers, near their confluence. John J. Hardin, hearing of the contemplated duel, determined to prevent it, and hastened to Alton, with all imaginable celerity, where he fell in with the belligerent parties, and aided by some other friends of both Lincoln and Shields, succeeded in effecting a reconciliation.

After this affair between Lincoln and Shields, I met Lincoln at the Danville court, and in a walk we took together, seeing him make passes with a stick, such as are made in the broadsword exercise, I was induced to ask him why he had selected that weapon with which to fight Shields. He promptly answered in that sharp, ear-splitting voice of his:

"To tell you the truth, Linder, I did not want to kill Shields, and felt sure I could disarm him, having had about a month to learn the broadsword exercise; and furthermore, I didn't want the darned fellow to kill me, which I rather think he would have done if we had selected pistols."

———:o:———

Lincoln Defends the Son of An Old Friend Indicted for Murder.

Jack Armstrong, the leader of the "Clarey Grove Boys," with whom Lincoln in early life had a scuffle which "Jack" agreed to call "a drawn battle," in consequence of his own foul play, afterwards became a lifelong, warm friend of Mr. Lincoln. Later in life the rising lawyer would stop at Jack's cabin home, and here Mrs. Armstrong, a most womanly person, learned to respect Mr. Lincoln. There was no service to which she did not make her guest abundantly welcome, and he never ceased to feel the tenderest gratitude for her kindness.

At length her husband died, and she became dependent upon her sons. The oldest of these, while in attendance upon a camp-meeting; found himself involved in a melee, which resulted in the death of a young man, and young Armstrong was charged by one of his associates with striking the fatal blow. He was examined, and imprisoned to await his trial. The public mind was in a blaze of excitement, and interested parties fed the flame.

Mr. Lincoln knew nothing of the merits of this case, that is certain. He only knew that his old friend Mrs. Armstrong was in sore trouble; and he sat down at once, and volunteered by letter to defend her son. His first act was to procure the postponement and a change of the place of trial. There was too much fever in the minds of the immediate public to permit of fair treatment. When the trial came on, the case looked very hopeless to all but Mr. Lincoln, who had assured himself that the young man was not guilty. The evidence on behalf of the State being all in, and looking like a solid and consistent mass of testimony against the prisoner, Mr. Lincoln undertook the task of analyzing and destroying it, which he did in a manner that surprised every one. The principal witness testified that "by the aid of the brightly shining moon, he saw the prisoner inflict the death-blow with a slung shot." Mr. Lincoln proved by the almanac that there was no moon shining at the time. The mass of testimony against the prisoner melted away, until "not guilty" was the verdict of every man present in the crowded court-room.

There is, of course, no record of the plea made on this occasion, but it is remembered as one in which Mr. Lincoln made an appeal to the sympathies of the jury, which quite surpassed his usual efforts of the kind, and melted all to tears. The jury were out but half an hour, when they returned with their verdict of "not guilty." The widow fainted in the arms of her son, who divided his attention between his services to her and his thanks to his deliverer. And thus the kind woman who cared for the poor young man, and showed herself a mother to him in his need, received the life of a son, saved from a cruel conspiracy, as her reward, from the hand of her grateful beneficiary.

———:o:———

Some of Lincoln's "Cases" and How He Treated Them.

A sheep-grower on a certain occasion sold a number of sheep at a stipulated average price. When he delivered the animals, he delivered many lambs, or sheep too young to come fairly within the terms of the contract. He was sued for damages by the injured party, and Mr. Lincoln was his attorney. At the trial, the facts as to the character of the sheep were proved, and several witnesses testified as to the usage by which all under a certain age were regarded as lambs, and of inferior value. Mr. Lincoln, on comprehending the facts, at once changed his line of effort, and confined himself to ascertaining the real number of inferior sheep delivered. On addressing the jury, he said that from the facts proved, they must give a verdict against his client, and he only asked their scrutiny as to the actual damage suffered.

In another case, Mr. Lincoln was conducting a suit against a railroad company. Judgment having been given in his favor, and the court being about to allow the amount claimed by him, deducting an approved and allowed offset, he rose and stated that his opponents had not proved all that was justly due them in an offset; and proceeded to state and allow a further sum against his client, which the court allowed in its judgment. His desire for the establishment of exact justice overcame his own selfish love of victory, as well as his partiality for his clients' feelings and interests.

———:o:———

Lincoln's Pungent Retort.

A little incident occurred during a political campaign that illustrated Mr. Lincoln's readiness in turning a political point. He was making a speech at Charleston, Coles County, Illinois, when a voice called out:

"Mr. Lincoln, is it true that you entered this State barefoot, driving a yoke of oxen?"

Mr. Lincoln paused for full half a minute, as if considering whether he should notice such cruel impertinence, and then said that he thought he could prove the fact by at least a dozen men in the crowd, any one of whom was more respectable than his questioner. But the question seemed to inspire him, and he went on to show what free institutions had done for himself, and to exhibit the evils of slavery to the white man wherever it existed, and asked if it was not natural that he should hate slavery and agitate against it.

"Yes," said he, "we will speak for freedom and against slavery, as long as the Constitution of our country guarantees free speech, until everywhere on this wide land the sun shall shine, and the rain shall fall, and the wind shall blow upon no man who goes forth to unrequitted toil."

A Revolutionary Pensioner Defended by Lincoln.

An old woman of seventy-five years, the widow of a revolutionary pensioner, came tottering into his law office one day, and, taking a seat, told him that a certain pension agent had charged her the exhorbitant fee of two hundred dollars for collecting her claim. Mr. Lincoln was satisfied by her representations that she had been swindled, and finding that she was not a resident of the town, and that she was poor, gave her money, and set about the work of procuring restitution. He immediately entered suit against the agent to recover a portion of his ill-gotten money. The suit was entirely successful, and Mr. Lincoln's address to the jury before which the case was tried is remembered to have been peculiarly touching in its allusions to the poverty of the widow, and the patriotism of the husband she had sacrificed to secure the Nation's independence. He had the gratification of paying back to her a hundred dollars, and sending her home rejoicing.

———:o:———

Lincoln Threatens a Twenty Years' Agitation in Illinois.

One afternoon an old negro woman came into the office of Lincoln & Herndon, in Springfield, and told the story of her trouble, to which both lawyers listened. It appeared that she and her offspring had been born slaves in Kentucky, and that her owner, one Hinkle, had brought the whole family into Illinois, and given them them their freedom. Her son had gone down the Mississippi as a waiter or deck hand, on a steamboat. Arriving at New Orleans, he had imprudently gone ashore, and had been snatched up by the police, in accordance with the law then in force concerning free negroes from other States, and thrown into confinement. Subsequently, he was brought out and tried. Of course he was fined, and, the boat having left, he was sold, or was in

W. H. HERNDON, LINCOLN'S LAW PARTNER.

immediate danger of being sold, to pay his fine and expenses. Mr. Lincoln was very much moved, and requested Mr. Herndon to go over to the State House, and inquire of Governor Bissel if there was not something he could do to obtain possession of the negro. Mr. Herndon made the inquiry, and returned with the report that the Governor regretted to say that he had no legal or constitutional right to do anything in the premises. Mr. Lincoln rose to his feet in great excitement and exclaimed:

"By the Almighty, I'll have that negro back here, or I'll have a twenty years' agitation in Illinois, until the Governor does have a legal and constitutional right to do something in the premises."

He was saved from the latter alternative—at least in the direct form which he proposed. The lawyers sent money to a New Orleans correspondent—money of their own—who procured the negro, and returned him to his mother.

———:o:———

How Lincoln Always Turned a Story to His Advantage.

One of his modes of getting rid of troublesome friends, as well as troublesome enemies, was by telling a story. He began these tactics early in life; and he grew wonderfully adept in them. If a man broached a subject which he did not wish to discuss, he told a story which changed the direction of the conversation. If he was called upon to answer a question, he answered it by telling a story. He had a story for everything—something had occurred at some place where he used to live, that illustrated every possible phase of every possible subject with which he might have connection. His faculty of making or finding a story to match every event in his history, and every event to which he bore any relation, was really marvelous.

That he made, or adapted, some of his stories, there is no question, It is beyond belief that those which entered his mind left it no richer than they came. It is not to be supposed that he spent any time in elaborating them, but by some law of association every event that occurred suggested some story, and, almost by an involuntary process, his mind harmonized their discordant points, and the story was pronounced "pat," because it was made so before it was uttered. Every truth, or combination of truths, seemed immediately to clothe itself in a form of life, where he kept it for reference. His mind was full of stories; and the great facts of his life and history on entering his mind seemed to take up their abode in these stories, and if the garment did not fit it was so modified that it did.

A good instance of the execution which he sometimes effected with a story, occurred in the legislature. There was a troublesome member from Wabash County, who gloried particularly in being a "strict constructionist." He found something "unconstitutional" in every measure that was brought forward for discussion. He was a member of the Judiciary Committee. No amount of sober argument could floor the member from Wabash. At last he came to be considered a man to be silenced, and Mr. Lincoln was resorted to for an expedient by which this object might be accomplished. He soon honored the draft thus made upon him.

A measure was brought forward in which Mr. Lincoln's constiuents were interested, when the member from Wabash arose and discharged all his batteries upon its unconstitutional points. Mr. Lincoln then took the floor, and, with the quizzical expression of features which he could assume at will, and a mirthful twinkle in his gray eyes, said:

"Mr. Speaker, the attack of the member from Wabash upon the constitutionality of this measure, reminds me of an old friend of mine. He's a peculiar looking old fellow, with shaggy, overhanging eyebrows, and a pair of spectacles under them. (Everybody turned to the member from Wabash, and recognized a personal description.) One morning just after the old man got up, he imagined, on looking out of his door, that he saw rather a lively squirrel on a tree near his house, So he took down his rifle and fired at the squirrel, but the squirrel paid no attention to the shot. He loaded and fired again, and again, until, at the thirteenth shot, he set down his gun impatiently, and said to his boy, who was looking on:

" 'Boy, there's something wrong about this rifle.'

" 'Rifle's all right, I know 'tis,' responded the boy, 'but where's your squirrel?'

" 'Don't you see him, humped up about half way up the tree?" inquired the old man, peering over his spectacles, and getting mystified.

" 'No I don't,' responded the boy; and then turning and looking into his father's face he exclaimed, 'I see your squirrel! You've been firing at a louse on your eyebrow!'

The story needed neither application nor explanation. The House was in convulsions of laughter; for Mr. Lincoln's skill in telling a story was not inferior to his appreciation of its points and his power of adapting them to the case in hand. It killed off the member from Wabash, who was very careful afterwards not to provoke any allusion to his "eyebrows."

Hon. Newton Bateman's Thrilling Story of Mr. Lincoln—The Great Man Looking to See How the Springfield Preachers Voted.

At the time of Lincoln's nomination, at Chicago, Mr. Newton Bateman, Superintendent of Public Instruction for the State of Illinois, occupied a room adjoining and opening into the Executive Chamber at Springfield. Frequently this door was open during Mr. Lincoln's receptions, and throughout the seven months or more of his occupation, he saw him nearly every day. Often when Mr. Lincoln was tired, he closed the door against all intruders, and called Mr. Bateman into his room for a quiet talk. On one of these occasions, Mr. Lincoln took up a book containing a careful canvass of the city of Springfield, in which he lived, showing the candidate for whom each citizen had declared it his intention to vote in the approaching election. Mr. Lincoln's friends had, doubtless at his own request, placed the result of the canvass in his hands. This was towards the close of October, and only a few days before election. Calling Mr. Bateman to a seat by his side, having previously locked all the doors, he said:

'Let us look over this book; I wish particularly to see how the ministers of Springfield are going to vote.'

The leaves were turned, one by one, and as the names were examined Mr. Lincoln frequently asked if this one and that were not a minister, or an elder, or a member of such or such church, and sadly expressed his surprise on receiving an affirmative answer. In that manner they went through the book, and then he closed it and

THE REPUBLICAN WIGWAM AT CHICAGO, WHERE LINCOLN WAS NOMINATED.

[107]

sat silently for some minutes regarding a memorandum in pencil which lay before him. At length, he turned to Mr. Bateman, with a face full of sadness, and said:

"Here are twenty-three ministers of different denominations, and all of them are against me but three, and here are a great many prominent members of churches, a very large majority are against me. Mr. Bateman, I am not a Christian,—God knows I would be one,—but I have carefully read the Bible and I do not so understand this book,' and he drew forth a pocket New Testament. 'These men will know,' he continued, 'that I am for freedom in the Territories, freedom everywhere as free as the Constitution and the laws will permit, and that my opponents are for slavery. They know this, and yet, with this book in their hands, in the light of which human bondage cannot live a moment, they are going to vote against me; I do not understand it at all.'

"Here Mr. Lincoln paused—paused for long minutes, his features surcharged with emotion. Then he rose and walked up and down the reception-room in the effort to retain or regain his self-possession. Stopping at last he said, with a trembling voice and cheeks wet with tears:"

" 'I know there is a God, and that he hates injustice and slavery. I see the storm coming, and I know that His hand is in it. If He has a place and work for me, and I think He has, I believe I am ready. I am nothing, but Truth is everything: I know I am right, because I know that liberty is right, for Christ teaches it, and Christ is God. I have told them that a house divided against itself can not stand; and Christ and Reason say the same; and they will find it so.'

" 'Douglas don't care whether slavery is voted up or

down, but God cares, and humanity cares, and I care; and with God's help I shall not fail. I may not see the end; but it will come, and I shall be vindicated; and these men will find they have not read their Bible right.

"Much of this was uttered as if he were speaking to himself, and with a sad, earnest solemnity of manner impossible to be described. After a pause, he resumed:

" 'Dosen't it seem strange that men can ignore the moral aspect of this contest? No revelation could make it plainer to me that slavery or the Government must be destroyed. The future would be something awful, as I look at it, but for this rock on which I stand,' (alluding to the Testament which he still held in his hand,) 'especially with the knowledge of how these ministers are going to vote. It seems as if God had borne with this thing (slavery) until the very teachers of religion had come to defend it from the Bible, and to claim for it a divine character and sanction; and now the cup of iniquity is full, and the vials of wrath will be poured out.'

"Everything he said was of a peculiarly deep, tender, and religious tone, and all was tinged with a touching melancholy. He repeatedly referred to his conviction that the day of wrath was at hand, and that he was to be an actor in the terrible struggle which would issue on the overthrow of slavery, although he might not live to see the end.

"After further reference to a belief in the Divine Providence, and the fact of God in history, the conversation turned upon prayer. He freely stated his belief in the duty, privilege, and efficacy of prayer, and intimated, in no unmistakable terms, that he had sought in that way the Divine guidance and favor. The effect of this conversation upon the mind of Mr. Bateman, a Christian gentleman whom Mr. Lincoln profoundly respected, was to convince him that Mr. Lincoln had, in a quiet way, found a path to the Christian standpoint— that he had found God, and rested on the eternal truth of God. As the two men were about to separate, Mr. Bateman remarked:

" 'I have not supposed that you were accustomed to think so much upon this class of subjects; cetainly your friends generally are ignorant of the sentiments you have expressed to me.'

"He replied quickly: 'I know they are, but I think more on these subjects than upon all others, and I have done so for years; and I am willing you should know it.'"

When his clients had practiced gross deception upon him, Mr. Lincoln forsook their cases in mid-passage; and he always refused to accept fees of those whom he advised not to prosecute. On one occasion, while engaged upon an important case, he discovered that he was on the wrong side. His associate in the case was immediately informed that he (Lincoln) would not make the plea. The associate made it, and the case, much to the surprise of Lincoln, was decided for his client. Perfectly convinced that his client was wrong, he would not receive one cent of the fee of nine hundred dollars which he paid. It is not wonderful that one who knew him well spoke of him as "perversely honest.

Lincolns Visit to Kansas.

Captain J. R. Fitch, of Evanston, Ill., in a contribution to the N. W. Christion Advocate, gives a very interesting account of Mr. Lincoln's visit to Kansas, which is as follows:

In the winter of 1859, shortly after the memorable contest between Abraham Lincoln and Stephen A. Douglas for the United States Senate, in which, although Illinois had given a Republican majority of 4,000 votes, the Democrats secured a majority of the Legislature on joint ballot, thereby securing the election of the minority candidate, an invitation was extended to Mr. Lincoln to pay a visit to the then Territory of Kansas.

Mr. Lincoln graciously accepted the invitation, and appointed a time convenient for him to come. A committee was appointed to meet him at the nearest railroad station, which was in Missouri between St. Joseph and Neston.

If my memory serves me, the committee consisted of Mark W. Delahay, afterwards United States District Judge; D. J. Brewer, now one of the Associate Justices of the Supreme Court; Hon. Henry J. Adams, Uncle George Keller, Josiah H. Kellogg, and myself. On the appointed day we met Mr. Lincoln at the station with carriages and drove down to Leavenworth city.

In the evening a meeting was held in Stockton's hall. The hall was crowded to its utmost capacity, and when Mr. Lincoln rose to speak he seemed to unwind himself, and, as he straightened himself up, he reminded me of a telescope being opened out, joint by joint. He stood there at first like a whipped boy at school, the most awkward specimen of humanity it had ever been my pleasure to look upon.

When he began his address, however, the impression was instantaneous that an orator was talking—a man who thoroughly believed every word he was saying. The audience was spellbound as he told of the crimes committed for the perpetuation of slavery.

The pro-slavery Democrats had secured seats for themselves in one part of the hall. Among them was a Presbyterian minister from Kentucky, a fine looking but very vain man.

After Mr. Lincoln had poured his hot shot into the pro-slavery party as long as the minister, whose name was Pitzer, could stand it, he rose and called out in a loud voice:

"How about amalgamation?"

Mr. Lincoln, turning toward him, said:

"I'll attend to you in a minute, young man," then went on and finished his sentence. Then, turning to where Mr. Pitzer had been standing, said:

"Where is the young man who asked me about amalgamation?"

Mr. Pitzer rose in all dignity, and in a tone of voice that seemed to say: "Watch me squelch him," replied, "I am the gentleman."

Mr. Lincoln, pointing his long, bony finger at him, and swinging his arm up and down, replied:

"I never knew but one decent, respectable white man to marry a colored woman, and that was an ex-Democratic Vice-president from the State of Kentucky."

Mr. Pitzer turned, and with the exclamation of, "I never heard Colonel Richard M. Johnson so insulted before," made his way out of the hall amid the jeers and gibes of the crowd.

Whether Mr. Lincoln knew that Mr. Pitzer was from Kentucky or not I never knew, but all Democrats and Republicans alike felt that the rebuke was well merited.

After the meeting was over, Mr. Lincoln and friends were invited to the home of Judge Delahay, where Mr. Lincoln was entertained. We had refreshments, including wine, of which almost everyone, except Mr. Lincoln, partook.

The next day we escorted him back to the train, and to my dying day I shall never forget our parting. I was only twenty-two years old.

Mr. Lincoln bade each one good-bye, and gave each a hearty grasp of the hand. He bade me good-bye last, and as he took my hand in both of his, and stood there towering above me, he looked down into my eyes with that sad, kindly look of his, and said:

"My young friend, do not put an enemy in your mouth to steal away your brains."

At that moment I thought I never should again.

And, oh, how that look haunted me in after years before I knew the better way, when in my moments of weakness I was tempted to put the intoxicating cup to my lips.

And though those loving eyes are closed in death, yet that look is never very far from me. It is with me now while I pen these lines; it is photographed on my heart, a blessed memory of our martyred President.

———:o:———

Lincoln and the Little Chicago Girls.

Mr. Lincoln made a hurried trip to Chicago on business, and was received with great enthusiasm by Democrats as well as Republicans. At the house of a friend he beholds a group of little girls. One of them gazes at him wistfully.

"What is it you would like, dear?"

"I would like, if you please, to have you write your name for me."

"But here are several of your mates, quite a number of them, and they will feel badly if I write my name for you and not for them also. How many are there, all told?"

"Eight of us."

"Oh, very well; then give me eight slips of paper and pen and ink, and I will see what I can do."

Eeach of the little misses, when she went home that evening carried his autograph.

———:o:———

Why Mr. Lincoln Let His Whiskers Grow.

If we had been in the village of Westfield, on the shore of Lake Erie, Chautauqua County, N. Y., on an October evening, we might have seen little Grace Bedell looking at a portrait of Mr. Lincoln and a picture of the log cabin which he helped build for his father in 1830.

"Mother," said Grace, "I think that Mr. Lincoln would look better if he wore whiskers, and I mean to write and tell him so."

"Well, you may, if you want to," the mother answered.

Grace's father was a Republican and was going to vote for Mr. Lincoln. Two older brothers were Democrats, but she was a Republican.

Among the letters going West the next day was one with this inscription:

"Hon. Abraham Lincoln, Esq., Springfield, Illinois."

It was Grace's letter, telling him how old she was, where she lived, that she was a Republican, that she thought he would make a good President, but would look better if he would let his whiskers grow. If he would she would try to coax her brothers to vote for him. She thought the rail fence around the cabin very pretty.

"If you have not time to answer my letter, will you allow your little girl to reply for you?" wrote Grace at the end.

Mr. Lincoln was sitting in his room at the State house with a great pile of letters before him from the leading Republicans all over the Northern States in regard to the progress of the campaign; letters from men who would want an office after his inauguration; letters abusive and indecent, which were tossed into the waste basket. He came to one from Westfield, N. Y. It was not from anyone who wanted an office, but from a little girl who wanted him to let his whiskers grow. That was a letter which he must answer.

A day or two later Grace Bedell comes out of the Westfield postoffice with a letter in her hand postmarked Springfield, Ill. Her pulse beat as never before. It is a cold morning—the wind blowing bleak and chill across the tossing waves of the lake. Snowflakes are falling. She cannot wait till she reaches home, but tears open the letter. The melting flakes blur the writing, but this is what she reads:

"SPRINGFIELD, ILL., Oct. 19, 1860.
MISS GRACE BEDELL:

My Dear Little Miss—Your very agreeable letter of the 15th is received. I regret the necessity of saying I have no daughter. I have three sons, one seventeen, one nine, and one seven years of age. They, with their mother, constitute my whole family. As to the whiskers, having never worn any, do you not think people would call it a piece of silly affection (affectation) if I should begin it now?

Your very sincere well-wisher,
A. LINCOLN."

It was natural that the people should desire to see the man who had been elected President, and the route to Washington was arranged to take in a number of the large cities—Indianapolis, Cincinnati, Columbus, Pittsburg, Cleveland and Buffalo. In each of these he spent a night and addressed great crowds of people. When the train left Cleveland, Mr. Patterson, of Westfield, was invited into Mr. Lincoln's car.

"Did I understand that your home is in Westfield?" Mr. Lincoln asked.

"Yes, sir, that is my home."

"Oh, by the way, do you know of anyone living there by the name of Bedell?"

"Yes, sir, I know the family very well."

"I have a corresdondent in that family. Mr. Bedell's little girl, Grace, wrote me a very interesting letter advising me to wear whiskers, as she thought it would improve my looks. You see that I have followed her suggestion. Her letter was so unlike many that I have received—some that threatened assassination in case I was elected—that it was really a relief to receive it and a pleasure to answer it."

The train reached Westfield, and Mr. Lincoln stood upon the platform of the car to say a few words to the people.

"I have a little correspondent here, Grace Bedell, and if the little miss is present I would like to see her."

Grace was far down the platform, and the crowd prevented her seeing or hearing him.

"Grace, Grace, the President is calling for you!" they shouted.

A friend made his way with her through the crowd.

"Here she is."

Mr. Lincoln stepped down from the car, took her by the hand, and gave her a kiss.

"You see, Grace, I have let my whiskers grow for you."

The kindly smile was upon his face. The train whirled on. His heart was lighter. For one brief moment he had forgotten the burdens that were pressing on him.

JOHN HANKS, LINCOLN'S RAIL-SPLITTING COMPANION.

Lincoln's Simplicity.

It was during the dark days of 1863, says Schuyler Colfax, on the evening of a public reception given at the White House. The foreign legations were there gathered about the President.

A young English nobleman was just being presented to the President. Inside the door, evidently overawed by the splendid assemblage, was an honest-faced old farmer, who shrank from the passing crowd until he and the plain-faced old lady clinging to his arm were pressed back to the wall.

The President, tall and, in a measure, stately in his personal presence, looking over the heads of the assembly, said to the English nobleman: "Excuse me, my Lord, there's an old friend of mine."

Passing backward to the door, Mr. Lincoln said, as he grasped the old farmer's hand:

"Why, John, I'm glad to see you. I haven't seen you since you and I made rails for old Mrs. —— in Sangamon county, in 1837. How are you?"

The old man turned to his wife with quivering lip, and without replying to the President's salutation, said:

"Mother, he's just the same old Abe!"

"Mr. Lincoln," he said finally, "you know we had three boys; they all enlisted in the same company; John was killed in the 'seven days' fight;' Sam was taken prisoner and starved to death, and Henry is in the hospital. We had a little money, an' I said: 'Mother, we'll go to Washington an' see him. An' while we were here I said we'll go up and see the President."

Mr. Lincoln's eyes grew dim, and across his rugged, homely, tender face swept the wave of sadness his friends had learned to know, and he said: "John, we all hope this miserable war will soon be over.

I must see all these folks here for an hour or so and I want to talk with you." The old lady and her husband were hustled into a private room in spite of their protests.

[UNITED STATES CAPITOL.]

WHITE HOUSE INCIDENTS.

Trying the "Greens" on Jake.

A deputation of bankers were one day introduced to the President by the Secretary of the Treasury. One of the party, Mr. P—— of Chelsea. Mass., took occasion to refer to the severity of the tax laid by Congress upon State Banks.

"Now," said Mr. Lincoln, "that reminds me of a circumstance that took place in a neighborhood where I lived when I was a boy. In the spring of the year the farmers were very fond of a dish which they called greens, though the fashionable name for it now-a-days is spinach, I believe. One day after dinner, a large family were taken very ill. The doctor was called in, who attributed it to the greens, of which all had frequently partaken. Living in the family was a half-witted boy named Jake. On a subsequent occasion, when greens had been gathered for dinner, the head of the house said:

" 'Now, boys, before running any further risk in this thing, we will first try them on Jake, If he stands it, we are all right.'

"And just so, I suppose," said Mr. Lincoln, "Congress thought it would try this tax on State Banks!"

A Story Which Lincoln Told the Preachers.

A year or more before Mr. Lincoln's death, a delegation of clergymen waited upon him in reference to the appointment of the army chaplains The delegation consisted of a Presbyterian, a Baptist, and an Episcopal clergyman. They stated that the character of many of the chaplains was notoriously bad, and they had come to urge upon the President the necessity of more discretion in these appointments.

"But, gentlemen," said the President, that is a matter which the Government has nothing to do with; the chaplains are chosen by the regiments."

Not satisfied with this, the clergymen pressed, in turn, a change in the system. Mr. Lincoln heard them through without remark, and then said, "Without any disrespect, gentlemen, I will tell you a 'little story.'

"Once, in Springfield, I was going off on a short journey, and reached the depot a little ahead of time. Leaning against the fence just outside the depot was a little darkey boy, whom I knew, named 'Dick,' busily digging with his toe in a mud-puddle. As I came up, I said, 'Dick, what are you about?'

" 'Making a church,' said he.

" 'A church,' said I; 'what do you mean?'

" 'Why, yes,' said Dick, pointing with his toe, 'don't you see there is the shape of it; there's the steps and front door—here the pews, where the folks set—and there's the pulpit.'

" Yes, I see,' said I; 'but why don't you make a minister?'

" 'Laws,' answered Dick, with a grin, 'I hain't got mud enough.' "

———:o:———

How Lincoln Stood Up for the Word "Sugar-Coated."

Mr. Defrees, the Government printer, states, that, when one of the President's message was being printed, he was a good deal disturbed by the use of the term ''sugar-coated," and finally went to Mr. Lincoln about it. Their relations to each other being of the most intimate character, he told the President frankly, that he ought to remember that a message to Congress was a different affair from a speech at a mass meeting in Illinois; that the messages became a part of history, and should be written accordingly.

"What is the matter now?" inquired the President.

"Why," said Mr. Defrees, "you have used an undignified expression in the message;" and then, reading the paragraph aloud, he added, "I would alter the structure of that if I were you."

"Defrees," replied Mr. Lincoln, "that word expresses exactly my idea, and I am not going to change it. The time will never come in this country when the people won't know exactly what 'sugar-coated' means.'

On a subsequent occasion, Mr. Defrees states that a certain sentence of another message was very awkwardly constructed. Calling the President's attention to it in the proof-copy, the latter acknowledged the force of the objection raised, and said, "Go home, Defrees, and see if you can better it."

The next day Mr, Dufrees took into him his amendment. Mr. Lincoln met him by saying:

"Seward found the same fault that you did, and he has been rewriting the paragraph, also." Then, reading Mr. Defrees' version, he said, "I believe you have beaten Seward; but, 'I jings,' I think I can beat you both." Then, taking up his pen, he wrote the sentence as it was finally printed.

———:o:———

Lincoln's Advice to a Prominent Bachelor.

Upon the bethrothal of the Prince of Wales to the Princess Alexandra, Queen Victoria sent a letter to each of the European sovereigns, and also to President Lincoln, announcing the fact. Lord Lyons, her ambassador at Washington,—a "bachelor," by the way,—requested an audience of Mr. Lincoln, that he might present this important document in person. At the time appointed he was received at the White House, in company with Mr. Seward.

"May it please your Excellency," said Lord Lyons, "I hold in my hand an autograph letter from my royal mistress, Queen Victoria, which I have been commanded to present to your Excellency. In it she informs your Excellency that her son, his Royal Highness the Prince of Wales, is about to contract a matrimonial alliance with her Royal Highness the Princess Alexander of Denmark."

After continuing in this strain for a few minutes, Lord Lyons tendered the letter to the President and awaited his reply. It was short, simple, expressive, and consisted simply of the words:

"Lord Lyons, go thou and do likewise."

It is doubtful if an English embassador was ever addressed in this manner before, and it would be interesting to learn what success he met with in putting the reply in diplomatic language when he reported it to her Majesty.

———:o:———

Mr. Lincoln and the Bashful Boys.

The President and a friend were standing upon the threshold of the door under the portico of the White

House, awaiting the coachman, when a letter was put into his hand. While he was reading this, people were passing, as is customary, up and down the promenade, which leads through the grounds of the War Department, crossing, of course, the portico. Attention was attracted to an approaching party. apparently a countryman, plainly dressed, with his wife and two little boys, who had evidently been straying about, looking at the places of public interest in the city. As they reached the portico the father, who was in advance, caught sight of the tall figure of Mr. Lincoln, absorbed in his letter. His wife and the little boys were ascending the steps.

The man stopped suddenly, put out his hand with a "hush" to his family, and, after a moment's gaze, he bent down and whispered to them, "There is the President!" Then leaving them, he slowly made a circuit around Mr. Lincoln, watching him intently all the while.

At this point, having finished his letter, the President turned and said: "Well, we will not wait any longer for the carriage; it won't hurt you and me to walk down."

The countryman here approached very diffidently, and asked if he might be allowed to take the President by the hand; after which, "Would he extend the same privilege to his wife and little boys?"

Mr. Lincoln, good-naturedly, approached the latter, who had remained where they were stopped, and, reaching down, said a kind word to the bashful little fellows, who shrank close up to their mother, and did not reply. This simple act filled the father's cup full.

"The Lord is with you, Mr. President," he said, reverently; and then, hesitating a moment, he added, with strong emphasis, "and the people, too, sir; and the people, too!"

A few moments later Mr. Lincoln remarked to his friend: "Great men have various estimates. When Daniel Webster made his tour throgh the West years ago, he visited Springfield among other places, where great preparations had been made to receive him. As the procession was going through the town, a barefooted little darkey boy pulled the sleeve of a man named T., and asked:

'What the folks were all doing down the street?'

'Why, Jack,' was the reply, 'the biggest man in the world is coming.'

"Now, there lived in Springfield a man by the name of G——, a very corpulent man. Jack darted off down the street, but presently returned, with a very disappointed air.

'Well, did you see him?' inquired T.

'Yees,' returned Jack; 'but laws he ain't half as big as old G.','

———:o:———

An Irish Soldier Who Wanted Something Stronger Than Soda Water.

Upon Mr. Lincoln's return to Washington, after the capture of Richmond, a member of the Cabinet asked him if it would be proper to permit Jacob Thompson to slip through Maine in disguise, and embark from Portland. The President, as usual, was disposed to be merciful, and to permit the arch-rebel to pass unmolested, but the Secretary urged that he should be arrested as a traitor. "By permitting him to escape the penalties of treason," persistently remarked the Secretary, "you sanction it." "Well," replied Mr. Liucoln, "let me tell you a story."

"There was an Irish soldier here last summer, who wanted something to drink stronger than water, and stopped at a drug-shop, where he espied a soda-fountain.

"'Mr. Doctor' said he, 'give me, plase, a glass of soda wather, an' if yees can put in a few drops of whisky unbeknown to any one, I'll be obleeged.'

"Now," said Mr. Lincoln, if Jake Thompson is permitted to go through Maine unbeknown to any one, what's the harm? So don't have him arrested."

Looking Out for Breakers.

In a time of despondency, some visitors were telling the President of the "breakers" so often seen ahead— "this time surely coming." "That," said he, "suggests the story of the school-boy, who never could pronounce the names 'Shadrach,' 'Meshach,' and 'Abednego.' He had been repeatedly whipped for it without effect. Sometimes afterwards he saw the names of the regular lesson for the day. Putting his finger upon the place, he turned to his next neighbor, an older boy, and whispered, 'Here comes those "tormented Hebrews" again!"

A Story About Jack Chase.

A farmer from one of the border counties went to the President on a certain occasion with the complaint that the Union soldiers in passing his farm had helped themselves not only to hay but to his horse; and he hoped the proper officer would be required to consider his claim immediately.

"Why, my good sir," replied Mr. Lincoln, "if I should attempt to consider every such individual case, I should find work enough for twenty Presidents!

"In my early days I knew one Jack Chase who was a lumberman on the Illinois, and when steady and sober the best raftsman on the river. It was quite a trick twenty-five years ago to take the logs over the rapids, but he was skillful with a raft, and always kept her straight in the channel. Finally a steamer was put on, and Jack—he's dead now, poor fellow!—was made captain of her. He always used to take the wheel going through the rapids. One day when the boat was plunging and wallowing along the boiling current, and Jack's utmost vigilance was being exercised to keep her in the narrow channel, a boy pulled his coat-tail and hailed him with: 'Say, Mister Captain! I wish you would just stop your boat a minute—I've lost an apple overboard!'

———:o:———

Stories Illustrating Lnicoln's Memory.

Mr. Lincoln's memory was very remarkable. At one of the afternoon receptions at the White House a stranger shook hands with him, and as he did so remarked, casually, that he was elected to Congress about the time Mr. Lincon's term as representative expired, which happened many years before.

"Yes, ' said the President, "you are from ——," mentioning the state. "I remember reading of your election in a newspaper one morning on a steamboat going down to Mount Vernon."

At another time a gentleman addressed him, saying, "I presume, Mr. President, you have forgotten me?"

"No," was the prompt reply; "your name is Flood. I saw you last, twelve years ago at ——," naming the place and the occasion. "I am glad to see," he continued, "that the Flood flows on,"

Subsequent to his re-election a deputation of bankers

from various sections were introduced one day by the Secretary of the Treasury. After a few moments of general conversation, Mr. Lincoln turned to one of them and said: "Your district did not give me so strong a vote at the last election as it did in 1860."

":I think, sir, that you must be mistaken," replied the banker. "I have the impression that your majority was considerably increased at the last election,"

"No," rejoined the President. "you fell off about six hundred votes." Then taking down from the bookcase the official canvass of 1860 and 1864 he referred to the vote or the district named and proved to be quite right in his assertion.

———:o:———

Philosophy of Canes.

A gentleman calling at the White House one evening carried a cane which in the course of conversation attracted the President's attention. Taking it in his hand he said: "I always used a cane when I was a boy. It was a freak of mine. My favorite one was a knotted beech stick, and I carved the head myself. There's a mighty amount of character in sticks. Don't you think so? You have seen these fishing-polls that fit into a cane? Well, that was an old idea of mine. Dogwood clubs were favorite ones with the boys. I suppose they use them yet. Hickory is too heavy. unless you get it from a young sapling. Have you ever noticed how a stick in one's hand will change his appearance? Old women and witches wouldn't look so without sticks. Meg Merrilies understands that."

Common Sense.

The Hon. Mr. Hubbard, of Connecticut, once called upon the President in reference to a newly invented gun, concerning which a committee had been appointed to make a report.

The "report" was sent for, and when it came in was found to be of the most voluminous description. Mr. Lincoln glanced at it and said: "I should want a new lease of life to read this through!" Throwing it down upon the table he added: "Why can't a committee of this kind occasionally exhibit a grain of common sense? If I send a man to buy a horse for me, I expect him to tell me his points—not how many hairs there are in his tail."

———:o:———

Lincoln's Confab with a Committee on "Grant's Whisky."

Just previous to the fall of Vicksburg a self-constituted committee, solicitous for the *morale* of our armies, took it upon themselves to visit the President and urge the removal of General Grant.

In some surprise Mr. Lincoln inquired, "For what reason?"

"Why," replied the spokesman, "he drinks too much whisky."

"Ah!" rejoined Mr. Lincoln, dropping his lower lip. "By the way, gentlemen, can either of you tell me where General Grant procures his whisky? because, if I can find out, I will send every general in the field a barrel of it!"

A "Pretty Tolerable Respectable Sort of a Clergyman."

Some one was discussing in the presence of Mr. Lincoln the character of a time-serving Washington clergyman Said Mr. Lincoln to his visitor:

"I think you are rather hard upon Mr. ——. He reminds me of a man in Illinois, who was tried for passing a counterfeit bill. It was in evidence that before passing it he had taken it to the cashier of a bank and asked his opinion of the bill, and he received a very prompt reply that it was a counterfeit. His lawyer, who had heard the evidence to be brought against his client, asked him just before going into court, 'Did you take the bill to the cashier of the bank and ask him if it was good?'

" 'I did,' was the reply,

" 'Well, what was the reply of the cashier?'

"The rascal was in a corner, but he got out of it in this fashion: 'He said it was a pretty tolerable, respectable sort of a bill.'" Mr. Lincoln thought the clergyman was "a pretty talerable, respectable sort of a clergyman."

Opened His Eyes.

Mr. Lincoln sometimes had a very effective way of dealing with men who troubled him with questions. A visitor once asked him how many men the Rebels had in the field.

The President replied, very seriously, "*Twelve hundred thousand, according to the best authority.*"

The interrogator blanched in the face, and ejaculated. "*Good Heavens!*"

"Yes, sir, twelve hundred thousand—no doubt of it.

You see, all of our generals, when they get whipped, say the enemy outnumbers them from three or five to one, and I must believe them. We have four hundred thousand men in the field, and three times four makes twelve. Don't you see it?"

―――:o:―――

Minnehaha and Minneboohoo!

Some gentlemen fresh from a Western tour, during a call at the White House, referred in the course of conversation to a body of water in Nebraska, which bore an Indian name signifying "weeping water." Mr. Lincoln instantly responded: "As 'laughing water,' according to Mr. Longfellow, is 'Minnehaha," this evidently should be 'Minneboohoo.'"

―――:o:―――

Lincoln and the Artist.

F. B. Carpenter, the celebrated artist and author of the well-known painting of Lincoln and his Cabinet issuing the Emancipation Proclamation, describes his first meeting with the President, as follows:

"Two o'clock found me one of the throng pressing toward the center of attraction, the 'blue' room. From the threshold of the 'crimson' parlor as I passed, I had a glimpse of the gaunt figure of Mr. Lincoln in the distance, haggard-looking, dressed in black, relieved only by the prescribed white gloves; standing, it seemed to me, solitary and alone, though surrounded by the crowd, bending low now and then in the process of hand-shaking, and responding half abstractedly to the well-meant greetings of the miscellaneous assemblage.

"Never shall I forget the electric thrill which went through my whole being at this instant. I seemed to see lines radiating from every part of the globe, converging to a focus where that plain, awkward-looking man stood, and to hear in spirit a million prayers, 'as the sound of many waters,' ascending in his behalf.

"Mingled with supplication I could discern a clear symphony of triumph and blessing, swelled with an ever-increasing volume. It was the voice of those who had been bondmen and bondwomen, and the grand diapason swept up from the coming ages.

"It was soon my privilege in the regular succession, to take that honored hand. Accompanying the act, my name and profession were announced to him in a low tone by one of the assistant secretaries, who stood by his side.

"Retaining my hand, he looked at me inquiringly for an instant, and said, 'Oh, yes; I know; this is the painter.' Then straightening himself to his full height, with a twinkle of the eye, he added, playfully, 'Do you think, Mr. C——, that you could make a hadsome picture of *me?*' emphasizing strongly the last word.

"Somewhat confused at this point-blank shot, uttered in a voice so loud as to attract the attention of those in immediate proximity, I made a random reply, and took the occasion to ask if I could see him in his study at the close of the reception.

"To this he replied in the peculiar vernacular of the West, 'I reckon,' resuming meanwhile the mechanical and traditional exercise of the hand which no President has ever yet been able to avoid, and which, severe as is the ordeal, is likely to attach to the position so long as the Republic endures."

An Apt Illustration.

At the White House one day some gentlemen were present from the West, excited and troubled about the comissions or omissions of the Admistration. The President heard them patiently, and then replied: "Gentlemen, suppose all the property you have were in gold, and you had put it in the hands of Blondin to carry across the Niagara River on a rope, would you shake the cable, or keep shouting out to him, 'Blondin, stand up a little straighter—Blondin, stoop a little more—go a little faster—lean a little more to the north—lean a little more to the south?' No! you would hold your breath as well as your tongue, and keep your hands off until he was safe over. The Government is carrying an immense weight. Untold treasures are in her hands. They are doing the very best they can. Don't badger them. Keep silence, and we'll get you safe across."

———:o:———

More Light and Less Noise.

An editorial in a New York journal opposing Lincoln's re-nomination, is said to have called out from him the following story:

A traveler on the frontier found himself out of his reckoning one night in a most inhospitable region. A terrific thunder storm came up to add to his trouble. He floundered along until his horse at length gave out. The lightning afforded him the only clew to his way, but the peals of thunder were frightful. One bolt, which seemed to crash the earth beneath him, brought him to his knees.

By no means a praying man, his petition was short and to the point—"O, Lord, if it is all the same to you, give us a little *more light and a little less noise!*"

"Browsed Around."

A party of gentlemen, among whom was a doctor of divinity of much dignity of manner, calling at the White House one day, was informed by the porter that the President was at dinner, but that he would present their cards.

The doctor demurred at this, saying that he would call again. "Edward" assured them that he thought it would make no difference, and went in with the cards. In a few minutes the President walked into the room, with a kindly salutation, and a request that the friends would take seats. The doctor expressed regret that their visit was so ill-timed, and that his Excellency was disturbed while at dinner.

"Oh! no consequence at all," said Mr. Lincoln, good-naturedly. "Mrs. Lincoln is absent at present, and when she is away I generally '*browse*' around."

Cutting Red Tape.

Upon entering the President's office one afternoon, says a Washington correspondent, I found the President busily counting greenbacks.

"This, sir," said he, "is something out of my usual line; but a President of the United States has a multiplicity of duties not specified in the Constitution or acts of Congress. This is one of them. This money belongs to a poor negro who is a porter in the Treasary Department, at present very bad with the small-pox. He is now in the hospital, and could not draw his pay because he could not sign his name.

"I have been at considerable trouble to over comethe difficulty and get it for him, and have at length succeeded in *cutting red tape*, as you newspaper men say. I am now dividing the money and putting by a portion labeled, in an envelope, with my own hands, according to his wish;" and he proceeded to indorse the package very carefully.

No one witnessing the transaction could fail to appreciate the goodness of heart which prompted the President of the United States to turn aside for a time from his weighty cares to succor one of the humblest of his fellow-creatures in sickness and sorrow.

———:o:———

One of Lincoln's Drolleries.

Concerning a drollery of President Lincoln, this story is told:

During the rebellion an Austrian Count applied to President Lincoln for a position in the army. Being introduced by the Austrian Minister, he needed, of course, no further recommendation; but, as if fearing that his importance might not be duly appreciated, he proceeded to explain that he was a Count, that his family were ancient and highly respectable, when Lincoln, with a merry twinkle in his eye, tapping the aristiocratic lover of titles on the shoulder, in a fatherly way, as if the man had confessed to some wrong, interrupted in a soothing tone:

"Never mind; you shall be treated with just as much consideration for all that.

———:o:———

How Lincoln and Stanton Dismissed Applicants for Office.

A gentleman states in a Chicago journal:

In the winter of 1864, after serving three years in the Union army, and being honorably discharged, I made application for the post sutlership at Point Lookout. My father being interested, we made application to Mr. Stanton, then Secretary of War.

We obtained an audience, and was ushered into the presence of the most pompous man I ever met. As I entered he waved his hand for me to stop at a given distance from him, and then put these questions, viz:

" Did you serve three years in the army?"

" I did, sir."

" Were you honorably discharged?"

" I was, sir."

" Let me see your discharge."

I gave it to him. He looked it over, and then said:

" Were you ever wounded?"

I told him yes, at the battle of Williamsburg, May 5, 1861

He then said:

"I think we can give this position to a soldier who has lost an arm or leg, he being more deserving;" and he then said that I looked hearty and healthy enough to serve three years more. He would not give me a chance to argue my case.

The audience was at an end. He waved his hand to me. I was then dismissed from the august presence of the Honorable Secretary of War.

My father was waiting for me in the hallway, who saw by my countenance that I was not successful. I said to my father:

"Let us go over to Mr. Lincoln; he may give us more satisfaction."

He said it would do no good, but we went over. Mr. Lincoln's reception room was full of ladies and gentlemen when we entered, and the scene was one I shall never forget.

On her knees was a woman in the agonies of despair, with tears rolling down her cheeks, imploring for the life of her son, who had deserted and had been condemned to be shot. I heard Mr. Lincoln say:

"Madam, do not act this way, it is agony to me; I would pardon your son if it was in my power, but there must be an example made or I will have no army."

At this speech the woman fainted. Lincoln motioned to his attendant, who picked the woman up and carried her out. All in the room were in tears.

But, now changing the scene from the sublime to the ridiculous, the next applicant for favor was a big, buxom Irish woman, who stood before the President with arms akimbo, saying:

"Mr. Lincoln, can't I sell apples on the railroad?"

Lincoln said: "Certainly, madam, you can sell all you wish."

But she said: "You must give me a pass, or the soldiers will not let me."

Lincoln then wrote a few lines and gave it to her, who said:

"Thank you, sir; God bless you."

This shows how quick and clear were all this man's decisions.

I stood and watched him for two hours, and he dismissed each case as quickly as the above, with satisfaction to all.

My turn soon came. Lincoln turned to my father and said:

"Now, gentlemen, be pleased to be as quick as possible with your business, as it is growing late."

My father then stepped up to Lincoln and introduced me to him. Lincoln then said:

"Take a seat, gentlemen, and state your business as quick as possible."

There was but one chair by Lincoln, so he motioned my father to sit, while I stood. My father stated the business to him as stated above. He then said:

"Have you seen Mr. Stanton?"

We told him yes, that he had refused. He (Mr. Lincoln) then said:

"Gentlemen, this is Mr. Stanton's business; I cannot interfere with him; he attends to all these matters, and I am sorry I can not help you."

He saw that we were disappointed, and did his best to revive our spirits. He succeeded well with my father, who was a Lincoln man, and who was a staunch Republican.

Mr. Lincoln then said:

"Now, gentlemen, I will tell you what it is; I have thousands of applications like this every day, but we can not satisfy all for this reason, that these positions are like office seekers—there are too many pigs for the tits."

The ladies who were listening to the conversation placed their handkerchiefs to their faces and turned away. But the joke of Old Abe put us all in a good humor. We then left the presence of the greatest and most just man who ever lived to fill the Presidential chair.

―――:o:―――

Where the President's Mind Wandered.

An amusing, yet touching instance, of the President's pre-occupation of mind, occurred at one of his levees when he was shaking hands with a host of visitors passing him in a continuous stream. An intimate acquaintance received the usual conventional hand-shake and salutation, but perceiving that he was not recognized, kept his ground instead of moving on, and spoke again; when the President, roused to a dim consciousness that something unusual had happened, perceived who stood before him, and seizing his friend's hand, shook it again heartily, saying:

"How do you do? How do you do? Excuse me for not noticing you. I was thinking of a man down South."

He afterwards privately acknowledged that the "man down South" was Sherman, then on his march to the sea.

―――:o:―――

Lincoln and the Preacher.

An officer of the Government called one day at the White House and introduced a clerical friend. "Mr. President," said he, "allow me to present to you my friend, the Rev. Mr F., of——. He has expressed a desire to see you and have some conversation with you, and I am happy to be the means of introducing him."

The President shook hands with Mr. F., and desiring him to be seated took a seat himself. Then his countenance, having assumed an air of patient waiting, he said:

"I am now ready to hear what you have to say."

"Oh, bless you, sir," said Mr. F., "I have nothing special to say; I merely called to pay my respects to you, and, as one of the million, to assure you of my hearty sympathy and support."

"My dear sir," said the President, rising promptly, his face showing instant relief, and with both hands grasping that of his visitor, "I am very glad to see you, indeed. I thought you had come to preach to me!"

———:o:———

Lincoln and Little "Tad."

The day after the review of Burnside's division some photographers, says Mr. Carpenter, came up to the White House to make some stereoscopic studies for me of the President's office. They requested a dark closet in which to develop the pictures, and without a thought that I was infringing upon anybody's rights, I took them to an unoccupied room of which little "Tad" had taken possession a few days before, and with the aid of a couple of the servants had fitted up a miniature theatre, with stage, curtains, orchestra, stalls, parquette and all. Knowing that the use required would interfere with none of his arrangements, I led the way to this apartment.

Everything went on well, and one or two pictures had been taken, when suddenly there was an uproar. The operator came back to the office and said that "Tad" had taken great offense at the occupation of his room without his consent, and had locked the door, refusing all admission.

The chemicals had been taken inside, and there was no way of getting at them, he having carried off the key. In the midst of this conversation "Tad" burst in, in a fearful passion. He laid all the blame upon me—said that I had no right to use his room, and the men should not go in even to get their things. He had locked the door and they should not go there again—"they had no business in his room!"

Mr. Lincoln was sitting for a photograph, and was still in the chair. He said, very mildly, "Tad, go and unlock the door." Tad went off muttering into his mother's room, refusing to obey. I followed him into the passage, but no coaxing would pacify him. Upon my return to the President I found him still patiently in the chair, from which he had not risen. He said: "Has not the boy opened the door?" I replied that we could do nothing with him —he had gone off in a great pet. Mr. Lincoln's lips came together firmly, and then, suddenly rising, he strode across the passage with the air of one bent on punishment, and disappeared in the domestic apartments. Directly he returned with the key to the theatre, which he unlocked himself.

"Tad," said he, half apologetically, " is a peculiar

child. He was violently excited when I went to him. I said, 'Tad, do you know that you are making your father a great deal of trouble?' He burst into tears, instantly giving me up the key."

———:o:———

A Touching Incident.

After the funeral of his son, William Wallace Lincoln, in February, 1862, the President resumed his official duties, but mechanically, and with a terrible weight at his heart. The following Thursday he gave way to his feelings, and shut himself from all society. The second Thursday it was the same; he would see no one, and seemed a prey to the deepest melancholy. About this time the Rev. Francis Vinton, of Trinity, Church, New York, had occasion to spend a few days in Washington. An acquaintance of Mrs. Lincoln and of her sister, Mrs. Edwards, of Springfield, he was requested by them to come up and see the President.

The setting apart of Thursday for the indulgence of his grief had gone on for several weeks, and Mrs. Lincoln began to be seriously alarmed for the health of her husband, of which fact Dr. Vinton was apprised.

Mr. Lincoln received him in the parlor, and an opportunity was soon embraced by the clergyman to chide him for showing so rebellious a disposition to the decree of Providence. He told him plainly that the indulgence of such feelings, though natural, was sinful. It was unworthy one who believed in the Christian religion. He had duties to the living greater than those of any other man, as the chosen father, and leader of the people, and he was unfitting himself for his responsibilities by thus giving way to his grief. To mourn the departed as lost belonged to heathenism—not to Christianity. "Your son," said Dr. Vinton, "is alive in Paradise. Do you remember that passage in the Gospels: 'God is not the God of the dead but of the living, for all live unto Him?'"

The President had listened as one in a stupor, until his ear caught the words: "Your son is alive." Starting from the sofa, he exclaimed, "Alive! alive! Surely you mock me."

"No, sir, believe me," replied Dr. Vinton, "it is a most comfortiog doctrine of the church, founded upon the words of Christ Himself."

Mr. Lincoln looked at him a moment, and then stepping forward, he threw his arm around the clergyman's neck, and, laying his head upon his breast, sobbed aloud, "Alive? alive?" he repeated.

"My dear sir," said Dr. Vinton, greatly moved, as he twined his own arm around the weeping father, "believe this, for it is God's most precious truth. Seek not your son among the dead; he is not there; he lives to-day in Paradise!

Think of the full import of the words I have quoted. The Sadducees. when they questioned Jesus, had no other conception than that Abraham, Isaac and Jacob were dead and buried. Mark the reply: "Now that the dead are raised, even Moses showed at the bush when he called the Lord the God of Abraham, the God of Isaac, and the God of Jacob. For He is not the God of the dead, but of the living, for all live unto Him! Did not the aged patriarch mourn his sons as dead? 'Jo-

LINCOLN'S FAMILY AT HOME IN THE WHITE HOUSE.

seph is not, and Simeon is not, and ye will take Benjamin, also.' But Joseph and Simeon were both living though he believed it not. Indeed, Joseph being taken from him, was the eventual means of the preservation of the whole family. And so God has called your son into His upper kingdom—a kingdom and an existence as real, more real, than your own. It may be that he, too. like Joseph, has gone, in God's good providence, to be the salvation of his father's household. It is a part of the Lord's plan for the ultimate happiness of you and yours. Doubt it not. I have a sermon," continued Dr. Vinton, "upon this subject, which I think might interest you."

Mr. Lincoln begged him to send it at an early day— thanking him repeatedly for his cheering and hopeful words. The sermon was sent, and read over and over by the President, who caused a copy to be made for his own private use before it was returned.

———:o:———

Lincoln Wipes the Tears from His Eyes and Tells a Story.

A. W. Clark, member of Congress from Watertown, New York, relates the following interesting story:

During the war a constituent came to me and stated that one of his sons was killed in a battle, and another died at Andersonville, while the third and only remaining son was sick at Harper's Ferry.

These disasters had such effect on his wife that she had become insane. He wanted to get this last and sick son discharged and take him home, hoping it would restore his wife to reason. I went with him to President Lincoln and related the facts as well as I could, the father sitting by and weeping. The President, much affected, asked for the papers and wrote across them, "Discharge this man."

Then, wiping the tear from his cheek, he turned to the man at the door, and said, "Bring in that man," rather as if he felt bored, which caused me to ask why it was so.

He replied that it was a writing-master who had spent a long time in copying his Emancipation Proclamation, had ornamented it with flourishes, and which made him think of an Irishman who said it took him an hour to catch his old horse, and when he had caught him he was not worth a darn!

———:o:———

Comments of Mr. Lincoln on the Emancipation Proclamation.

The final proclamation was signed on New Year's day, 1863. The President remarked to Mr. Colfax, the same evening, that the signature appeared somewhat tremulous and uneven. "Not," said he, "because of any uncertainty or hesitation on my part; but it was just after the public reception, and three hours' hand-shaking is not calculated to improve a man's chirography." Then changing his tone, he added: "The South had fair warning, that if they did not return to their duty, I should strike at this pillar of their strength. The promise must now be kept, and I shall never recall one word."

Lincoln Arguing against the Emancipation Proclamation that he may learn all About it.

When Lincoln's judgment, which acted slowly, but which was almost as immovable as the eternal hills when settled, was grasping some subject of importance, the arguments against his own desires seemed uppermost in his mind, and, in conversing upon it, he would present those arguments to see if they could be rebutted.

This is illustrated by the interview between himself and the Chicago delegation of clergymen, appointed to urge upon him the issue of a Proclamation of Emancipation, which occurred September 13, 1862, more than a month after he had declared to the Cabinet his established purpose to take this step.

He said to this committee:

"I do not want to issue a document that the whole world will see must necessarily be inoperative, like the Pope's bull against the comet!"

After drawing out their views upon the subject, he concluded the interview with these memorable words:

"Do not misunderstand me, because I have mentioned these objections. They indicate the difficulties which have thus far prevented my action in some such way as you desire. I have not decided against a proclamation of liberty to the slaves, but hold the matter under advisement. And I can assure you that the subject is on my mind, by day and night, more than any other. Whatever shall appear to be God's will, I will do! I trust that, in the freedom with which I have canvassed your views, I have not in any respect injured your feelings."

Mr. Lincoln's Laugh.

Mr. Lincoln's "laugh" stood by itself. The neigh of a wild horse on his native prairie is not more undisguised and hearty. A group of gentlemen, among whom was his old Springfield friend and associate, Hon. Isaac N. Arnold, were one day conversing in the passage near his office, while awaiting admission. A congressional delegation had proceded them, and presently an unmistakable voice was heard through the partition, in a burst of mirth. Mr. Arnold remarked, as the sound died away: "That laugh has been the President's life-preserver!"

―――:o:―――

Lincoln and the Newspapers.

On a certain occasion, the President was induced by a committee of gentlemen to examine a newly-invented "repeating" gun, the peculiarity of which was, that it prevented the escape of gas. After due inspection, he said: "Well, I believe this really does what it is represented to do. Now, have any of you heard of any machine or invention for preventing the escape of 'gas' from newspaper establishments?"

―――:o;―――

Lincoln's Bull-frog Story.

Violent criticism, attacks and denunciations, coming either from radicals or conservatives, rarely ruffled the President, if they reached his ears. It must have been in connection with something of this kind, that he once told a friend this story:

"Some years ago," said he, "a couple of emigrants, fresh from the Emerald Isle, seeking labor, were making their way toward the West. Coming suddenly one evening upon a pond of water, they were greeted with a grand chorus of frogs—a kind of music they had never before heard. 'B-a-u-m! B-a-u-m!'

"Overcome with terror, they clutched their 'shillcluhs,' and crept cautiously forward, straining their eyes in every direction to catch a glimpse of the enemy; but he was not to be found!

"At last a happy idea seized the foremost one—he sprang to his companion and exclaimed, 'And sure, Jamie! it is my opinion it is nothing but a noise!'"

———:o:———

Lincoln's Story of a Poodle Dog.

A friend who was walking over from the White House to the War Department with Mr. Lincoln, repeated to him the story of a "contraband" who had fallen into the hands of some good, pious people, and was being taught by them to read and pray.

Going off by himself one day, he was overheard to commence a prayer by the introduction of himself as "Jim Williams—a berry good nigga' to wash windows; 'spec's you know me now?"

After a hearty laugh at what he called this "direct way of putting the case," Mr. Lincoln said:

'The story that suggests to me, has no resemblance to it, save in the 'washing windows' part. A lady in Philadelphia had a pet poodle dog, which mysteriously disappeared. Rewards were offered for him, and a great ado made without effect. Some weeks passed, and all hope of the favorite's return had been given up, when a servant brought him in one day in the filthiest condition imaginable. The lady was overjoyed to see her pet again, but horriffed at his appearance.

"Where did you find him!" she exclaimed.

"Oh," replied the man, very unconcernedly, "a negro down the street had him tied to the end of a pole, swabbing windows."

———:o:———

Lincoln's Speech to the Union League.

The day following the adjournment at Baltimore, various political organizations call to pay their respects to the President. First came the convention committee, embracing one from each state represented—appointed to announce to him, formally, the nomination. Next came the Ohio delegation, with Mentor's band, of Cincinnati. Following these were the representatives of the National Union League, to whom he said, in concluding his brief response:

"I do not allow myself to suppose that either the convention or the League have concluded to decide that I am either the greatest or the best man in America; but, rather they have concluded that it is not best to swap horses while crossing the river, and have further concluded that I am not so poor a horse, but that they might make a botch of it in trying to swap!"

Ejecting a Cashiered Officer from the White House.

Among the callers at the White House one day was an officer who had been cashiered from the service. He had prepared an elaborate defence of himself, which he consumed much time in reading to the President. When he had finished, Mr. Lincoln replied, that even upon his own statement of the case. the facts would not warrant executive interference. Disappointed and considerably crestfallen, the man withdrew.

A few days afterwards he made a second attempt to alter the President's convictions, going over substantially the same ground, and occupying about the same space of time, but without accomplishing his end.

The third time he succeeded in forcing himself into Mr. Lincoln's presence, who with great forbearance listened to another repetition of the case to its conclusion, but made no reply. Waiting for a moment, the man gathered from the expression of his countenance that his mind was unconvinced. Turning very abruptly, he said:

"Well, Mr. President, I see you are fully determined not to do me justice."

This was too aggravating, even for Mr. Lincoln. Manifesting, however, no more feeling than that indicated by a slight compression of the lips, he very quietly arose, laid down a package of papers he held in his hand, and then suddenly seizing the defunct officer by the coat-collar, he marched him forcibly to the door, saying, as he ejected him into the passage:

"Sir, I give you fair warning never to show yourself in this room again. I can bear censure, but not insult!"

In a whining tone the man begged for his papers, which he had dropped.

"Begone, sir," said the President, "your papers will be sent to you. I never wish to see your face again!"

Lincoln and the Wall Street Gold Gamblers.

Mr. Carpenter, the artist, is responsible for the following:

The bill empowering the Secretary of the Treasury to sell the surplus gold had recently passed, and Mr. Chase was then in New York giving his attention personally to the experiment. Governor Curtin referred to this, saying to the President:

"I see by the quotations that Chase's movement has already knocked gold down several per cent."

This gave occasion for the strongest expression I ever heard fall from the lips of Mr. Lincoln. Knotting his face in the intensity of his feeling, he said:

"Curtin, what do you think of those fellows in Wall Street who are gambling in gold at such a time as this?"

"They are a set of sharks," returned Curtin.

"For my part," continued the President, bringing his clinched hand down upon the table, "I wish every one of them had his devilish head shot off!"

How the Negroes Regarded "Massa Lincoln."

In 1863, Colonel McKaye of New York, with Robert Dale Owen and one or two other gentlemen, were associated as a committee to investigate the condition of the freedmen on the coast of North Carolina. Upon their return from Hilton Head they reported to the President, and in the course of the interview Col. McKaye related the following incident:

He had been speaking of the ideas of power entertained by these people. He said they had an idea of God, as the Almighty, and they had realized in their former condition the power of their masters. Up to the time of the arrival among them of the Union forces, they had no knowledge of any other power. Their masters fled upon the approach of our soldiers, and this gave the slaves a conception of a power greater than that exercised by them. This power they called "Massa Linkum."

Colonel McKaye said that their place of worship was a large building which they called "the praise house;" and the leader of the meeting, a venerable black man, was known as "the praise man." On a certain day, when there was quite a large gathering of the people, considerable confusion was created by different persons attempting to tell who and what "Massa Linkum" was. In the midst of the excitement the white-headed leader commanded silence.

"Brederin," said he, "you don't know nosen' what you'se talkin' 'bout. Now, you just listen to me. Massa Linkum, he eberywhar. He know eberyting." Then, solemnly looking up, he added,—"He walk de earf like de Lord!"

Colonel McKaye said that Mr. Lincoln seemed much affected by this account. He did not smile, as another man might have done, but got up from his chair and walked in silence two or three times across the floor. As he resumed his seat, he said very impressively:

"It is a momentous thing to be the instrument, under Providence, of the liberation of a race."

———:o:———

One of Lincoln's Last Stories.

One of the last stories heard from Mr. Lincoln wass concerning John Tyler, for whom it was to be expected, as an old Henry Clay Whig, he would entertain no great respect. "A year or two after Tyler's accession to the Presidency," said he, "contemplating an excursion in some direction. his son went to order a special train of cars. It so happened that the railroad superintendent was a very strong Whig. On Bob's making known his errand, that official bluntly informed him that his road did not run any special trains for the President.

"What!" said Bob, "did you not furnish a special train for the funeral of General Harrison?"

"Yes," said the superintendent, stroking his whiskers; "and if you will only bring your father here in that shape you shall have the best train on the road!"

Lincoln's Habits in the White House.

Mr. Lincoln's habits at the White House were as simple as they were at his old home in Illinois. He never alluded to himself as "Presideut," or as occupying "the Presidency. His office he always designated as "the place." Call me Lincoln," said he to a friend; "Mr. President" had become so very tiresome to him. "If you see a newsboy down the street send him up this way," said he to a passenger, as he stood waiting for the morning news at his gate. Friends cautioned him against exposing himself so openly in the midst of enemies; but he never heeded them, He frequently walked the streets at night, entirely unprotected; and felt any check upon his free movements a great annoyance. He delighted to see his familiar Western friends; and he gave them always a cordial welcome. He met them on the old footing, and fell at once into the accustomed habits of talk and story-telling.

An old acquaintance, with his wife, visited Washington. Mr. and Mrs. Lincoln proposed to these friends a ride in the Presidential carriage. It should be stated in advance that the two men had probably never seen each other with gloves on in their lives, unless when they were used as protection from the cold.

The question of each—Mr. Lincoln at the White House and his friend at the hotel—was, whether he should wear gloves. Of course the ladies urged gloves; but Mr. Lincoln only put his in his pocket, to be used or not, according to circumstances.

When the Presidential party arrived at the hotel, to take in their friends, they found the gentleman, overcome by his wife's persuasions, very handsomely gloved. The moment he took his seat he began to draw off the clinging kids, while Mr. Lincoln began to draw his on!

"No! no! no!" protested his friend, tugging at his gloves. "It is none of my doings; put up your gloves, Mr. Lincoln."

So the two old friends were on even and easy terms, and had their ride after their old fashion.

———:o:———

MRS. GEN. JOHN A LOGAN.

Lincoln's High Compliment to the Women of America.

A Fair for the benefit of the soldiers, held at the Patent Office, in Washington, called out Mr. Lincoln as an interested visitor; and he was not permitted to retire without giving a word to those in attendance. "In this extraordinary war," said he, "extraordinary developments have manifested themselves, such as have not been seen in former wars; and among these manifestations nothing has been more remarkable than these fairs for the relief of suffering soldiers and their families, And the chief agents in these fairs are the women of America. I am not accustomed to the use of language of eulogy; I have never studied the art of paying compliments to women; but I must say that if all that has been said by orators and poets since the creation of the world, in praise of women, were applied to the women of America, it would not do them justice for their conduct during the war. I will close by saying, God bless the women of America!"

———:o:———

Lincoln in the Hour of Great Sorrow.

In February, 1862, Mr. Lincoln was visited by a severe affliction in the death of his beautiful son, Willie, and the extreme illness of his son Thomas, familiarly called "Tad." This was a new burden, and the visitation which, in his firm faith in Providence, he regarded as providential, was also inexplicable. A Christian lady from Massachusetts, who was officiating as nurse in one of the hospitals at the time, came to attend the sick children. She reports that Mr. Lincoln watched with her about the bedside of the sick ones, and that he often walked the room, saying sadly:

"This is the hardest trial of my life; why is it? Why is it?"

In the course of conversations with her, he questioned

her concerning his situation. She told him that she was a widow, and that her husbad and two children were in heaven; and added that she saw the hand of God in it all, and that she had never loved Him so much before as she had since her affliction.

"How is that brought about?" inquired Mr. Lincoln.

"Simply by trusting in God, and feeling that He does all things well," she replied.

"Did you submit fully under the first loss?" he asked,

"No," she answered, "not wholly; but, as blow came upon blow, and all were taken, I could and did submit, and was very happy."

He responded: "I am glad to hear you say that. Your experience will help me to bear my affliction."

On being assured that many Christians were praying for him on the morning of the funeral, he wiped away the tears that sprang in his eyes, and said:

"I am glad to hear that. I want them to pray for me. I need their prayers."

As he was going out to the burial, the good lady expressed her sympathy with him. He thanked her gently, and said:

"I will try to go to God with my sorrows."

A few days afterward she asked him if he could trust God. He replied:

"I think I can, and will try. I wish I had that child-like faith you speak of, and I trust He will give it to me." And then he spoke of his mother, whom so many years before he had committed to the dust among the wilds of Indiana. In this hour of his great trial the memory of her who had held him upon her bosom, and soothed his childish griefs, came back to him with tenderest recollections. "I remember her prayers," said he, "and they have always followed me. They have clung to me all my life."

———:c:———

A Praying President.

After the second defeat of Bull Run, Mr. Lincoln appeared very much distressed about the number of killed and wounded, and said to a lady friend: "I have done the best I could. I have asked God to guide me, and now I must leave the event with him."

On another occasion, having been made acquainted with the fact that a great battle was in progress at a distant but important point, he came into the room where this lady was engaged in nursing a member of the family, looking worn and haggard, and saying that he was so anxious that he could eat nothing. The possibility of defeat depressed him greatly; but the lady told him he must trust, and that he could at least pray.

"Yes," said he, and taking up a Bible, he started for his room.

Could all the people of the nation have overheard the earnest petition that went up from that inner chamber as it reached the ears of the nurse, they would have fallen upon their knees with tearful and reverential sympathy.

At one o'clock in the afternoon, a telegram reached him announcing a Union victory; and then he came directly to the room, his face beaming with joy, saying:

"Good news! Good news! The victory is ours, and God is good."

"Nothing like prayer," suggested the pious lady, who traced a direct connection between the event and the prayer which preceded it.

"Yes, there is," he replied—"praise—prayer and praise."

The good lady who communicates these incidents, closes them with the words: "I do believe he was a true Christian, though he had very little confidence in himself.

———:o:———

Telling a Story and Pardoning a Soldier.

General Fisk, attending the reception at the White House on one occasion saw, waiting in the ante-room, a poor old man from Tennessee. Sitting down beside him, he inquired his errand, and learned that he had been waiting three or four days to get an audience, and that on his seeing Mr. Lincoln probably depended the life of his son, who was under sentence of death for some military offense.

General Fisk wrote his case in outline on a card, and sent it in, with a special request that the President would see the man. In a moment the order came; and past senators, governors and generals, waiting impatiently, the old man went into the President's presence.

He showed Mr. Lincoln his papers, and he, on taking them, said he would look into the case and give him the result on the following day.

The old man, in an agony of apprehension, looked up into the President's sympathetic face, and actually cried out:

"To-morrow may be too late! My son is under sentence of death! The decision ought to be made now!" and the streaming tears told how much he was moved.

"Come," said Mr. Lincoln, "wait a bit, and I'll tell you a story;" and then he told the old man General Fisk's story about the swearing driver, as follows:

The General had begun his military life as a Colonel, and, when he raised his regiment in Missouri, he proposed to his men that he should do all the swearing of the regiment. They assented; and for months no instance was known of the violation of the promise. The Colonel had a teamster named John Todd, who, as roads were not always the best, had some difficulty in commanding his temper and his tongue. John happened to be driving a mule team through a series of mud-holes a little worse than usual, when, unable to restrain himself any longer, he burst forth into a volley of energetic oaths. The Colonel took notice of the offense, and brought John to an account.

"John," said he, "didn't you promise to let me do all the swearing of the regiment?"

"Yes, I did, Colonel," he replied, "but the fact was the swearing had to be done then or not at all, and you weren't there to do it."

As he told the story, the old man forgot his boy, and both the President and his listener had a hearty laugh together at its conclusion. Then he wrote a few words which the old man read, and in which he found new occasion for tears; but the tears were tears of joy, for the words saved the life of his son.

———:o:———

Bishop Turner's Reminiseences.

Bishop H. M. Turner, of the African M E. Church, in the Northwestern Advocate, says:

I well remember President Lincoln. My recollections of his form, size, visage, walk, the easy swing of his body, stern but pleasant countenan,c, eyeflash and rapid wink, the forward bend of his person, when speaking, the genial smile which lit up his face occasionally, removing the impression that he was a man of sad and forlorn disposition, the prominent forehead somewhat receding toward the top, and visibly wrinkled just above the eyebrows, the projecting nose, and disheveled hair— are vivid and distinct. There was nothing about him that was repulsive or frigorific, yet there was a dignity and genial majesty that would make anyone feel when brought in contact with him that he was in the presence of no ordinary man. A little child might be wooed by the magic touch of his friendship, gentleness and the tenderness of his nature; while a king or an emperor might feel that a peer was in his presence. He had none of the qualities of the dude, the assumptions of a cavalier, the display of the knight, nor the pretensions of an aristocrat. If he ever had a suit of clothes that fitted him I never saw it. Yet I have seen him scores of times— walking the streets, riding in his carriage, speaking from the platform, delivering his inaugural on the east side of the capitol, in the executive mansion, inspecting the army in front of Petersburg with General Grant, and in the department of war exchanging words with that lordly, stern, and inflexible man of iron nerve, Edwin M. Stanton, his great Secretary of war.

Late in the fall of 1862 a portly but venerable-looking colored gentleman from Poughkeepsie, N. Y., came to Washington and assuming to represent a large body of colored men who were anxious to enlist as soldiers in the army to defend their country and its flag, he delivered a most eloquent speech to a crowded house in my church, and requested me to accompany him in waiting upon the President and presenting the readiness of his constituents to bleed and die for the country. After some delay we succeeded in reaching the President, and he delivered one of the most eloquent addresses to President Lincoln in the space of ten minutes I have ever heard since or before. At the conclusion of his grandiloquent speech the President responded in a few words, thanking him for his visit, for his patriotic sentiments, and requested him to return home and get the names, streets, and numbers of this army of would-be colored soldiers and bring them to him, and he would call for them at his earliest convenience. We left the White House together; he was a little chagrined and crestfallen, and disappeared from the city to return no more. The truth is, he represented nobody but himself. He thought that Mr. Lincoln would commission him a lieutenant or captain to drum up colored soldiers; but when the President failed to do so he had no further use for him.

The first colored regiment which was raised and organized under the direct auspices of the general government (I do not refer to those enlisted by General Butler in New Orleans or Governor Andrews in Massachusetts)

was raised in Washington, D. C. The first two companies were enlisted in the basement of Israel Church; but the regiment was completed on Mason's Island, just across the Potomac from Washington City. All the commissioned officers, being white, were appointed from the colonel down, and a white chaplain had been assigned to duty in the same regiment temporarily by the colonel in command. This writer, however, was the choice of the colored members of the regiment for the position of chaplain, and, at their solicitation, I applied for the same.

Hon. Edwin M. Stanton, Secretary of War, and Hon. Salmon P. Chase, Secretary of the Treasury, and afterward Chief Justice of the United States Supreme Court, were favorable; but the other cabinet officers were either unfavorable or in doubt as to the advisability of making a colored man a commissioned officer in any form; at least, I was so informed by Secretary Chase. When the question came up in the cabinet for final decision before Mr. Lincoln, Mr. Stanton and Mr. Chase held that the colored soldiers should have their own spiritual director and guide, and that my labors in the organization of the regiment entitled me to the position. Messrs. Seward, Blair, Welles, and others of the cabinet thought it rather too early to risk public sentiment in commissioning a colored man to any position whatever. Mr. Lincoln sat with great patience and heard the discussion, but finally put a quietus to the question at issue by saying, "Well, we have far graver matters for consideration than this," and, turning to the secretary of war, simply said, "Stanton, issue his commission as chaplain. Now, gentlemen, let us proceed to business-" Mr. Chase sent for me the same afternoon to come to his residence, and, after congratulating me upon being a United States chaplain, and the first one of my race to receive a commission, gave a detailed narrative of the whole transaction, but pledged me to secresy. I do not think I am violating the contract in relating it at this remote period.

———:o:———

Seward and Chase.

The antagonism between the conservatives represented in the cabinet by Seward and the radicals, represented by Chase, was a source of much embarrassment to Mr. Lincoln. Finally the radicals appointed a committee to demand the dismissal of Seward. Before the committee arrived Mr. Seward, in order to relieve the President of embarrassment, tendered his resignation. In the course of the discussion with the committee Mr. Chase found his position so embarrassing and equivocal that he thought it wise to tender his resignation the next day. Mr. Lincoln refused to accept either, stating that "the public interest does not admit of it." When it was all over he said: "Now I can ride; I have got a pumpkin in each end of my bag." Later on he said: "I do not see how it could have been done better. I am sure it was right. If I had yielded to that storm, and dismissed Seward, the thing would have slumped over one way, and we should have been left with a scanty handful of supporters,"

———:o:———

Mr. Lincoln's Remedy for Baldness.

In 1864 Mr. Lincoln was greatly bothered by the well-meant but ill-advised efforts of certain good Northern men to bring about a termination of the war. An old gentleman from Massachusetts, very bland and entirely bald, was especially persistent and troublesome. Again and again he appeared before the President, and was got rid of by one and another ingenious expedient. One day when this angel of mercy had been boring Mr. Lincoln for half an hour to the interruption of important business, the President suddenly arose, went to a closet, and took out of it a large bottle. "Did you ever try this remedy for baldness?" he asked, holding up the bottle before his astonished visitor. No; the man was obliged to confess that he never had tried it. Mr. Lincoln called a servant, had the bottle wrapped up, and handed it to the bald philanthropist. "There," said he, "go and rub some of that on your head. Persevere. They say it will make your hair grow. Come back in about three months and report." And almost before he knew it the good man was outside of the door with the package under his arm.

In all the great emergencies of his closing years Mr. Lincoln's reliance upon Divine guidance and assistance was often extremely touching.

"I have been driven many times to my knees," he once remarked, "by the overwhelming conviction that I had nowhere else to go. My own wisdom, and that of all about me, seemed insufficient for that day."

WAR STORIES.

Story of Andy Johnson and His Doubtful Interest in Prayers.

Col. Moody, "the fighting Methodist parson," as he was called in Tennessee, while attending a conference in Philadelphia, met the President and related to him the following story, which we give as repeated by Mr. Lincoln to a friend.

"He told me," said Lincoln, "this story of Andy Johnson and General Buel which interested me intensely:

The Colonel happened to be in Nashville the day it was reported that Buel had decided to evacuate the city. The Rebels, strongly re-enforced, were said to be within two days' march of the capitol. Of course the city was greatly excited.

Moody said he went in search of Johnson, at the edge of the evening, and found him at his office closeted with two gentlemen, who were walking the floor with him, one on each side. As he entered, they retired, leaving him alone with Johnson, who came up to him, manifesting intense feeling, and said:

"Moody, we are sold out. Buel is a traitor. He is going to evacuate the city, and in forty-eight hours we will all be in the hands of the Rebels!"

Then he commenced pacing the floor again, twisting his hands and chafing like a caged tiger, utterly insensible to his friend's entreaties to become calm. Suddenly he turned and said:

"Moody, can you pray?"

"That is my business, sir, as a minister of the gospel, returned the Colonel.

"Well, Moody, I wish you would pray," said Johnson, and instantly both went down upon their knees, at opposite sides of the room.

As the prayer waxed fervent Johnson began to respond in true Methodist style. Presently he crawled over on his hands and knees to Moody's side and put his arm over him, manifesting the deepest emotion. Closing the prayer with a hearty "Amen" from each, they arose.

Johnson took a long breath and said with emphasis:

"Moody, I feel better."

Shortly afterwards he asked:

"Will you stand by me?"

"Certainly I will," was the answer.

"Well, Moody, I can depend upon you; you are one in a hundred thousand."

He then commenced pacing the floor again. Suddenly he wheeled, the current of his thought having changed, and said:

"Oh! Moody, I don't want you to think I have become a religious man because I asked you to pray. I am sorry to say it, I am not, and never pretended to be, religious. No one knows this better than you, but, Moody, there is one thing about it—I do believe in Almighty God! and I believe also in the Bible, and I say, d——n me if Nashville shall be surrendered!"

And Nashville was not surrendered.

———:o:———

A Soldier that Knew No Royalty.

Captain Mix, the commander at one period of the President's body-guard, told this story to a friend:

On their way to town one sultry morning, from the Soldiers' Home, they came upon a regiment marching into the city. A "stragler," very heavily loaded with camp equipage, was accosted by the President with the question:

"My lad, what is that?" referring to the designation of his regiment.

"It's a regiment," said the soldier curtly, plodding on, his gaze bent steadily upon the ground.

"Yes, I see that," responded the President, "but I want to know *what* regiment."

"——Pennsylvania," replied the man in the same tone, looking neither to the right nor the left.

As the carriage passed on, Mr. Lincoln turned to Captain Mix and said, with a merry laugh:

"It is very evident that fellow smells no blood of 'royalty' in this establishment."

———:o:———

A Little Soldier Boy.

"President Lincoln," says the Hon. W. D. Kell, "was a large and many-sided man, and yet so simple that no one, not even a child, could approach him without feeling that he had found in him a sympathizing friend. I remember that I apprised him of the fact that a lad, the son of one of my townsmen, had served a year on the gunboat Ottawa, and had been in two important engagements; in the first as a powder-monkey, when he had conducted himself with such coolness that he had chosen as captain's messenger in the second; and I suggested to the President that it was within his power to send to the Naval School annually three boys who had served at least a year in the navy.

He at once wrote on the back of a letter from the commander of the Ottawa, which I had handed him, to the Secretary of the Navy:

"If the appointments for this year have not been made, let this boy be appointed."

The appointment had not been made, and I brought it home with me. It directed the lad to report for examination at the school in July. Just as he was ready to start his father, looking over the law, discovered that he could not report until he was fourteen years of age, which he would not be until September following.

The poor child sat down and wept. He feared that he was not to go to the naval school. He was, however, soon consoled by being told that "the President could make it right."

It was my fortune to meet him the next morning at the door of the Executive Chamber with his father.

Taking by the hand the little fellow—short for his age, dressed in the sailor's blue pants and shirt—I advanced with him to the President, who sat in his usual seat, and said:

"Mr. President, my young friend, Willie Bladen, finds a difficulty about his appointment. You have directed him to appear at the school in July; but he is not yet fourteen years of age."

But before I got half of this out, Mr. Lincoln, laying down his spectacles, said:

"Bless me! Is that the boy who did so gallantly in those two great battles? Why, I feel that I should bow to him, and not he to me."

The little fellow had made his graceful bow.

The President took the papers at once, and as soon as a postponement until September would suffice, made the order that the lad should report in that month. Then, putting his hand on Willie's head, he said:

"Now, my boy go home and have good fun during the two months, for they are about the last holiday you will get."

The little fellow bowed himself out, feeling that the President of the United States, though a very great man, was one that he would nevertheless like to have a game of romps with.

———:o:———

Sallie Ward's Practical Philosophy.

When the telegram from Cumberland Gap reached Mr. Lincoln that "firing was heard in the direction of Knoxville," he remarked that he was "glad of it." Some person present, who had the perils of Burnside's position uppermost in his mind, could not see why Mr. Lincoln should be glad of it, and so expressed himself.

"Why, you see," responded the President, "it reminds me of Mrs. Sallie Ward, a neighbor of mine, who had a very large family. Occasionally one of her numerous progeny would be heard crying in some out-of-the-way place, upon which Mrs. Ward would exclaim:

'There's one of my children that isn't dead yet.'"

———:o:———

Pardons a Soldier.

The Hon. Mr. Kellogg, representative from Essex Co., N. Y., received a dispatch one evening from the army to the effect that a young townsman who had been induced to enlist through his instrumentality had, for a serious misdemeanor been convicted by a court-martial and was to be shot the next day. Greatly agitated, Mr. Kellogg went to the Secretary of War and urged, in the strongest manner, a reprieve. Stanton was inexorable.

"Too many cases of the kind had been let off," he said, "and it was time an example was made."

Exhausting his eloquence in vain, Mr. Kellogg said:

"Well, Mr. Secretary, the boy is not going to be shot, of that I give you fair warning!"

Leaving the War Department, he went directly to the White House, although the hour was late. The sentinel on duty told him that special orders had been issued to admit no one whatever that night.

After a long parley, by pledging himself to assume the responsibility of the act, the Congressman passed in. M. Lincoln had retired, but indifferent to etiquette or cerimony, Judge Kellogg pressed his way through all obstacles to his sleeping apartment. In an excited manner he stated that the dispatch announcing the hour of execution had but just reached him.

"This man must not be shot, Mr. President," said he. "I can't help what he may have done. Why, he is an old neighbor of mine; I can't allow him to be shot!"

Mr. Lincoln had remained in bed, quietly listening to the vehement protestations of his old friend (they were in Congress together). He at length said:

"Well, I don't believe shooting will do him any good. Give me that pen."

And so saying "red tape" was unceremoniously cut, and another poor fellow's life was indefinitely extended.

———:o:———

Lincoln's Vow.

The following incident, remarkable for its significant facts, is related by Mr. Carpenter, the artist:

Mr. Chase, said Mr. Carpenter, told me that at the Cabinet meeting immediately after the battle of Antietam and just prior to the issue of the September proclamation, the President entered upon the business before them by saying:

" The time for the annunciation of the emancipation proclamation could be no longer delayed. Public sentiment would sustain it—many of his warmest friends and supporters demanded it—and he had promised his God he would do it!"

The last part of this was uttered in a low tone, and appeared to be heard by no one but Secretary Chase, who was sitting near him. He asked the President if he correctly understood him. Mr. Lincoln replied:

"I made a solemn vow before God that if General Lee was driven back from Pennsylvania, I would crowm the result by the declaration of freedom to the slaves."

In February, 1865, a few days after the constitutional amendment, I went to Washington and was received by Mr. Lincoln with the kindness and familiarity which had characterized our previous intercourse.

I said to him at this time that I was very proud to have been the artist to have first conceived of the design of painting a picture commemorative of the Act of Emancipation; that subsequent occurrences had only confirmed my first judgment of that act as the most sublime moral event in our history.

"Yes," said he—and never do I remember to have noticed in him more earnestness of expression or manner—"as affairs have turned, it is the central act of my administration, and the great event of the nineteenth century.

———:o:———

"Borrowing the Army."

On a certain occasion the President said to a friend that he was in great distress; he had been to General McClellan's house and the General did not ask to see him; and as he must talk to somebody he had sent for General Franklin and my self, to obtain our opinions as to the possibility of soon commencing active operations with the army of tho Potomac. To use his own expression, if something was not done soon the bottom would fall out of the whole affair; and if General McClellan did not want to use the army, he would like to borrow it, provided he could see how it could be made to do something.

―――:o:―――

Lincoln's Politeness.

I was always touched, says Mr. Carpenter, by the President's manner of receiving a salute of the guard at the White House.

Whenever he appeared in the portico, on his way to or from the War or Treasury Departments, or on any excursion down the avenue, the first glimpse of him was, of course, the signal for the sentinel on duty to " present arms" and "call out the guard."

This was always acknowledged by Mr. Lincoln with a peculiar bow and touch of the hat, no matter how many times it might occur in the course of a day; and it always seemed to me as much of a compliment to the devotion of the soldiers, on his part, as it was the sign of duty and deference on the part of the guard.

―――:o:―――

His Visits to the Hospitals.

On the Monday before the assassination, when the President was on his way from Richmond, he stopped at City Point. Calling upon the head surgeon at that place, Mr. Lincoln told him that he wished to visit all the hospitals under his charge and shake hands with every soldier.

The surgeon asked if he knew what he was undertaking, there being five or six thousand soldiers at that place, and it would be quite a tax upon his strength to visit all the wards and shake hands with every soldier. Mr. Lincoln answered with a smile:

"He guessed he was equal to the task; at any rate he would try, and go as far as he could; he should never, probably, see the boys again, and he wanted them to know that he appreciated what they had done for their country."

Finding it useless to try to dissuade him, the surgeon began his rounds with the President, who walked from bed to bed, extending his hand to all, saying a few words of sympathy to some, making kind inquiries of others, and welcomed by all with the heartiest cordiality.

As they passed along they came to a ward in which lay a rebel who had been wounded and was a prisoner. As the tall figure of the kindly visitor appeared in sight, he was recognized by the rebel soldier, who, raising himself on his elbow in bed, watched Mr. Lincoln as he approached and extending his hand exclaimed, while tears ran down his cheeks:

" Mr. Lincoln, I have long wanted to see you, to ask your forgiveness for ever raising my hand against the old flag."

Mr. Lincoln was moved to tears. He heartily shook the hand of the repentant rebel and assured him of his good will, and with a few words of kind advice passed on.

After some hours the tour of the various hospitals was made, and Mr. Lincoln returned with the surgeon to his office. They had scarcely entered, however, when a messenger came saying that one ward had been omitted, and "the boys" wanted to see the President. The surgeon, who was thoroughly tired, and knew Mr. Lincoln must be, tried to dissuade him from going; but the good man said he must go back; he would knowingly omit no one, "the boys" would be so disappointed. So he went with the messenger, accompanied by the surgeon, and shook hands with the gratified soldiers, and then returned again to the office.

The surgeon expressed the fear that the President's arm would be lamed with so much hand-shaking, saying it certainly must ache.

Mr. Lincoln smiled, and saying something about his "strong muscles," stepped out at the open door, took up a very large, heavy axe which lay there by a log of wood, and chopped vigorously for a few moments, sending the chips flying in all directions; and then, pausing, he extended his right arm to its full length, holding the axe out horizontally, without its even quivering as he held it.

Stong men who looked on—men accustomed to manual labor—could not hold the same axe in that position for a moment. Returning to the office he took a glass of lemonade, for he would take no stronger beverage; and while he was within the chips he had chopped were gathered up and safely cared for by a hospital steward because they were " the chips that Father Abraham chopped."

Mr. Lincoln and a Clergyman.

At the semi-annual meeting of the New Jersey Historical Society, held in Newark, N. J., Rev. Dr. Sheldon, at Princeton, read a memorial of their late President, Rev. R. K. Rodgers, D. D., in which appears the following interesting incident concerning Mr. Lincoln and the war:

One day during the war Dr. Rodgers was called on by a man in his congregation, who, in the greatest distress, told him that his son, a soldier in the army, had just been sentenced to be shot for desertion, and begged the minister's interposition.

The Doctor went to Washington with the wife and infant child of the condemned man, and sent his card up to Mr. Lincoln. When admitted, the President said:

"You are a minister, I believe. What can I do for you, my friend?"

The reply was:

"A young man from my congregation in the army has so far forgotten his duty to his country and his God as to desert his colors, and is sentenced to die. I have come to ask you to spare him."

With characteristic quaintness the President replied:

"Then you don't want him hurt, do you?"

"Oh, no," said the petitioner, "I did not mean that; he deserves punishment, but I beg for him time to prepare to meet his God."

"Do you say he has father, wife and child?" said Mr. Lincoln.

"Yes."

"Where do you say he is?"

On being told, he turned to his secretary, said a few words in an undertone, of which that official made note, and added to Dr. Rodgers:

"You have your request. Tell his friends I have reprieved him."

With a "God bless you, Mr. President," Dr. Rodgers turned away to bear the glad news to the distressed family.

———:o:———

A Remarkable Letter.

The following remarkable letter from Lincoln to General Hooker was written after the latter had taken command of the Potomac, in January, 1863, and while the President yet retained it in his possession an intimate friend chanced to be in his Cabinet one night, and the President read it to him, remarking:

"I shall not read this to anybody else, but I want to know how it strikes you."

During the following April or May, while the Army of the Potomac lay opposite Fredericksburg, this friend accompanied the President to General Hooker's headquarters on a visit. One night General Hooker, alone with this gentleman in his tent, said:

"The President says that he showed you this letter," and he then took out that document, which was closely written on a sheet of letter-paper. The tears stood in the General's bright blue eyes as he added:

"It is such a letter as a father might have written to his son, and yet it hurt me."

And then, dashing the water from his eyes, he said:

"When I have been to Richmond, I shall have this letter published."

This was more than sixteen years ago, and the letter has just now seen the light of day. There are in it certain sharp passages which, after this long lapse of time, can not be verified by the memory of any who heard it read in 1863. There are others which seem missing. Nevertheless, the letter, which is herewith reprinted, must have been written by Lincoln:

EXECUTIVE MANSION, Washington, D, C., Jan, 26, 1863. Maj.-Gen. Hooker—General: I have placed you at the head of the Army of the Potomac. Of course I have done this upon what appears to me to be sufficient reasons; and yet I think it best for you to know that there are some things in regard to which I am not quite satisfied with you. I believe you to be a brave and skillful soldier—which, of course, I like. I also believe you do not mix politics with your profession—in which you are right. You have confidence in yourself—which is a valuable, if not an indispensable, quality. You are ambitious—which, within reasonable bounds, does good rather than harm; but I think that during General Burnside's command of the army, you have taken counsel of your ambition and thwarted him as much as you could, in which you did a great wrong to the country, and to a most meritorious and honorable brother-officer. I have heard, in such a way as to believe it, of your recently saying that both the army and the Government needed a Dictator. Of course, it was not for this, but in spite of it, that I have given you the command. Only those Generals who win victories can set up Dictators. What I now ask of you is military success, and I will risk the Dictatorship. The government will support you to the utmost of its ability—which is neither more nor less than it has done and will do for all commanders. I much fear that the spirit which you have aided to infuse into tne army, of criticising their commander and withholding confidence from him, will now turn upon you. I shall assist you as far as I can to put it down. Neither you nor Napoleon, if he were alive again, could get any good out of an army while such a spirit prevails in it. And now beware of rashness. Beware of rashness, but, with energy and sleepless vigilance, go forward and give us victories.

Yours, very truly,

A. LINCOLN.

A "Hen-Pecked" Husband.

When General Phelps took possession of Ship Island, near New Orleans, early in the war, it will be remembered that he issued a proclamation, somewhat bombastic in tone, freeing the slaves. To the surprise of many people, on both sides, the President took no official notice of this movement. Some time had elapsed, when one day a friend took him to task for his seeming indifference on so important a matter.

"Well," said Mr. Lincoln, "I feel about that a good deal as a man whom I will call Jones, whom I once knew, did about his wife. He was one of your meek men and had the reputation of being badly hen-pecked. At last, one day his wife was seen switching him out of the house. A day or two afterward a friend met him in the street and said: 'Jones I have always stood up for you, as you know; but I am not going to do it any longer. Any man who will stand quietly and take a switching from his wife, deserves to be horsewhipped,' Jones looked up with a wink, patting his friend on the back, "Now don't," said he, "why, it didn't hurt me any; and you've no idea what a power of good it did Sarah Ann?"

———:o:———

Lincoln's Curt Reply to a Clergyman.

No nobler reply ever fell from the lips of a ruler, than that uttered by President Lincoln in response to the clergyman who ventured to say, in his presence during the war, that he hoped "the Lord was on our side."

"I am not at all concerned about that," replied Mr.

Lincoln, "for I know that the Lord is always on the side of the right. But it is my constant anxiety and prayer that this nation should be on the Lord's side."

A Short Practical Sermon.

On a certain occasion, two ladies from Tennessee came before the President, asking the release of their husbands, held as prisoners of war at Johnson's Island. They were put off until the following Friday, when they came again, and were again put off until Saturday, At each of the interviews one of the ladies urged that her husband was a religious man. On Saturday, when the President ordered the release of the prisoner, he said to this lady:

"You say your husband is a religious man; tell him, when you meet him, that I say I am not much of a judge of religion, but that in my opinion the religion which sets men to rebel and fight against their Government because, as they think, that Government does not sufficiontly help some men to eat their bread in the sweat of other men's faces, is not the sort of religion upon which people can get to heaven."

A Celebrated Case.

The celebrated case of Franklin W. Smith and brother, was one of those which most largely helped to bring military tribunals into public contempt. Those two gentleman were arrested and kept in confinement, their papers seized, their business destroyed, their reputation damaged and a naval court-martial "organized to convict," pursued them unrelentingly till a wiser and juster hand arrested the malice of their prosecutors.

It is known that President Lincoln, after full investigation of the case, annulled the whole proceedings, but it is remarkable that the actual record of his decision could never be obtained from the Navy Department. An exact copy being withheld, the following was presented to the Boston Board of Trade as being very nearly the words of the late President:

"*Whereas*, Franklin W. Smith had transactions with the Navy Department to the amount of one million and a quarter of a million of dollars; and, *whereas*, he had the chance to steal a quarter of a million, and was only charged with stealing twenty-two hundred dollars—and the question now is about his stealing a hundred—I don't believe he stole anything at all. Therefore, the record and findings are disapproved—declared null and void, and the defendants are fully discharged."

"It would be difficult," says the New York Tribune, "to sum up the rights and wrongs of the business more briefly than that, or to find a paragraph more characteristically and unmistakably Mr. Lincoln's.

———:o,———

Recollections of the War President by Judge William Johnston.

"I rendered," says Judge Johnston, "Mr. Lincoln some service in my time. When I went to Washington I observed that among Congressmen and others in high places, Mr. Lincoln had very few friends. Montgomery Blair was the only one I heard speak of him for a second term.

"This was about the middle of his first administration. I went to Washington by way of Columbus, and G. Tod asked me to carry a verbal message to Mr. Lincoln, and that was to tell him that there were certain elements indispensable to the success of the war that would be seriously affected by any interference with McClellan.

"I suppose that the liberal translation of Tod's language would be thus:

" 'I am keeping the Democratic soldiers in the field, and if McClellan is interfered with I shall not be able to do it.' We all felt some trouble about it. McClellan had been relieved, and one bright moonlight night I saw a regiment, I suppose Pennsylvanians mostly, marching from the Capitol down Pennsylvania avenue, yelling at the top of their lungs, 'Hurrah for Little Mac!' and making a pause before the White House, they kept up that bawling and hurrahing for McClellan.

"I went to see Mr. Lincoln early the next morning, and asked him if he had witnessed the performance on the previous night. He said he had. I asked him what he thought of it. He said it was very perplexing. I told him I had come to make a suggestion. I told him I would introduce him to a young man of fine talents and liberal education, who had lost an arm in the service and I wanted him to tell one of his Cabinet Ministers to give that young man a good place in the Civil Service, and to avail himself of the occasion to declare that the policy of the Administration was, whenever the qualifications were equal, to give those who had been wounded or disabled in the service of the country the preference in the Civil department.

"He said it was an idea he would like to think of and asked me how soon I would wait upon him in the morning. I said any hour; and I went at 7 o'clock and found him in the hands of a barber.

Says he: "I have been thinking about your proposition, and I have a question to ask you; Did you ever know Colonel Smith, of Rockford, Ill?"

"I said I had an introduction to him when attending to the defense of of Governor Bebb."

"You know," said he, "that he was killed at Vicksburg; that his head was carried off by a shell. He was postmaster and his wife wants the place," and he inquired if that would come up to my idea; and thereupon he and I concocted a letter—I have the correspondence in my possession—to Postmaster General Blair, directing him to appoint the widow of Colonel Smith Postmistress, in the room of her deceased husband, who had fallen in battle, and stating that in consideration of what was due to the men who were fighting our battles, he had made up his mind that the families of those who had fallen and those disabled in the service, their qualifications being equal, should always have a preference in the Civil Service.

"I told him I was not personally acquainted with Mr. Blair, and he gave me a note of introduction to him with the letter. I told Blair that I proposed to take a copy of Mr. Lincoln's letter, which he had then made out by the clerk. I took the letter to the Chronicle office in Washington, in which paper it was published, and the next morning I jumped into an ambulance and went to the convalescing camp, where there were about 7,000 convalescents, a great many of them Ohio men, and when I made my appearance they called on me for a speech. I got upon a terrace and made them a few remarks, and coming round to the old saw, 'that Republics are always ungrateful,' I told them I could not vouch for the Republic, but I thought I could vouch for the chief man at the head of the Administration, and he had already spoken on that subject, and when I read Lincoln's letter the boys flung their hats into the air and made the welkin ring for a long while.

"I hurried back to the city, and with a pair of shears cut out Lincoln's letter, and then attached some editorial remarks, and that letter went around, and I believe was published in every friendly newspaper in the United States.

"About that time Congress passed a resolution to the same effect, that those disabled in the military service of the country, wherever qualified, ought to have a preference over others. This may have been a small matter, but it made a marvelous impression on the army.

———:o:———

A Church which God Wanted for the Union Soldiers.

Among the various applicants at the White House one day was a well-dressed lady, who came forward, without apparent embarrassment in her manner, and addressed the President. Giving her a very close and scrutinizing look, he said:

"Well, madam, what can I do for you?"

She proceeded to tell him that she lived in Alexandria; that the church where she worshiped had been taken for a hospital.

"What church, madam?" Mr. Lincoln asked, in a quick, nervous manner.

"The —— church," she replied; "and as there are only two or three wounded soldiers in it. I came to see if you would not let us have it, as we want it very much to worship God in."

"Madam, have you been to see the post surgeon at Alexandria about this matter?"

"Yes, sir; but we could do nothing with him."

"Well, we put him there to attend to just such business, and it is reasonable to suppose that he knows better what should be done under the circumstances than I do. See here; you say you live in Alexandria; probably you own property there. How much will you give to assist in building a hospital?"

"You know, Mr. Lincoln, our property is very much embarrassed by the war; so, really, I could hardly afford to give much for such a purpose.

"Well, madam, I expect we shall have another fight soon, and my candid opinion is, God wants that church for poor wounded Union soldiers, as much as he does for secesh people to worship in." Turning to his table, he said quite abruptly: "You will excuse me; I can do nothing for you. Good-day, madam."

———:o:———

How Lincoln Relieved Rosecrans.

General James B. Steedman, familiarly known as old "Old Chickamauga," relates the following:

Some weeks after the disastrous battle of Chickamauga, while yet Chattanooga was in a state of siege, General Steedman was surprised one day to receive a telegram from Abraham Lincoln to come to Washington. Seeking out Thomas, he laid the telegram before him, and was instructed to set out at once. Repairing to the White House, he was warmly received by Mr. Lincoln.

Mr. Lincoln's first question was abrupt and to the point:

"General Steedman, what is your opinion of General Rosecrans?"

General Steedman, hesitating a moment, said; "Mr. President, I would rather not express my opinion of my superior officer."

Mr. Lincoln said: "It is the man who does not want to express an opinion whose opinion I want. I am besieged on all sides with advice. Every day I get letters from army officers asking me to allow them to come to Washington to impart some valuable knowledge in their possession."

"Well, Mr. President," said Mr. Steedman, "you are the Commander-inChief of the Army, and if you order me to speak I will do so."

Mr. Lincoln said: "Then I will order an opinion."

General Steedman then answered:

"Since you command me, Mr. President, I will say General Rosecrans is a splendid man to command a victorious army."

"But what kind of a man is he to command a defeated army?" said Mr. Lincoln.

General Steedman in reply said, cautiously: "I think there are two or three men in that army that would be better."

Then, with quaint humor, Mr. Lincoln propounded this question:

"Who, besides yourself, General Steedman, is there in that army who would make a better commander?"

General Steedman promptly said;

"General George H. Thomas."

"I am glad to hear you say so," said Mr. Lincoln, "that is my own opinion exactly. But Mr. Stanton is against him, and it was only yesterday that a powerful New York delegation was here to protest against his appointment because he is from a rebel state and can not be trusted."

Said General Steedman:

"A man who will leave his own state (Thomas was a Virginian), his friends, all his associations, to follow the flag of his country, can be trusted in any position to which he may be called."

That night the order went forth from Washington relieving General Rosecrans of the command of the Army of the Cumberland and appointing General Thomas in his place.

———:o:———

An Interesting Incident Connected with Signing the Emancipation Proclamation.

The roll containing the Emancipation Proclamation was taken to Mr. Lincoln at noon on the first day of January, 1863, by Secretary Seward and his son Frederick. As it lay unrolled before him, Mr. Lincoln took a pen, dipped it in the ink, moved his hand to the place for the signature, held it a moment, and then removed his hand and dropped the pen. After a little hesitation he again took up the pen and went through the same movement as before. Mr. Lincoln then turned to Mr. Seward, and said:

"I have been shaking hands since nine o'clock this morning and my right arm is almost paralyzed. If my name ever goes into history it will be for this act, and my whole soul is in it. If my hand trembles when I sign the Proclamation, all who examine the document hereafter will say, 'He hesitated.'"

He then turned to the table, took up the pen again,

THE DAWN.

and slowly, firmly wrote "Abraham Lincoln," with which the whole world is now familiar. He then looked up, smiled, and said. "That will do!"

———:o:———

A Dream that was Portentous—What Lincoln said to General Grant about it.

At the Cabinet meeting held the morning of the day of the assassination, it was afterward remembered, a remarkable circumstance occurred. General Grant was present, and during a lull in the discussion the President turned to him and asked if he had heard from General

GEN. U. S. GRANT,
AFTER HIS RETURN FROM TOUR OF THE WORLD.

Sherman. General Grant replied that he had not, but was in hourly expectation of receiving despatches from him announcing the surrender of Johnson.

"Well," said the President, "you will hear very soon now, and the news will be important."

"Why do you think so?" said the General.

"Because," said Mr. Lincoln, "I had a dream last night; and ever since the war began, I have invariably had the same dream before any important military event occurred."

He then instanced Bull Run, Antietam, Gettysburg, etc., and said that before each of those events he had had the same dream; and turning to Secretary Wells, said: "It is in your line, too, Mr. Wells. The dream is that I saw a ship sailing very rapidly; and I am sure that it portends some important national event."

Later in the day, dismissing all business, the carriage was ordered for a drive. When asked by Mrs. Lincoln if he would like any one to accompany them, he replied:

"No; I prefer to ride by ourselves to-day."

Mrs. Lincoln subsequently said that she never saw him seem so supremely happy as on this occasion. In reply to a remark to this effect, the President said:

"And well I may feel so, Mary, for I consider this day the war has come to a close," And then added: "We must both be more cheerful in the future; between the war and the loss of our darling Willie, we have been very miserable."

———:o:———

The Serpent in Bed with Two Children.

A number of Kentuckians insisted that troops should not be sent through that state for the purpose of putting down the war in Tennessee. The President was hesitating what to do, and they were pressing immediate action.

"I am," he said, "a good deal like the farmer who, re-

turning to his home one winter night, found his two sweet little boys asleep with a hideous serpent crawling over their bodies. He could not strike the serpent without wounding or killing the children, so he calmly waited until it had moved away. Now, I do not want to act in a hurry about the matter; I don't want to hurt anybody in Kentucky; but I will get the serpent out of Tennessee.

"And he did march through Kentucky, to the aid of Andrew Johnson's mountaineer's."

Lincoln's Cutting Reply to the Confederate Commission.

At a so-called "peace conference" procured by the voluntary and irresponsible agency of Mr. Francis P. Blair, which was held on the steamer River Queen, in Hampton Roads, on the 3d of February, 1865, between President Lincoln and Mr. Seward, representing the government, and Messrs. Alexander H. Stephens, J. A. Campbell and Mr. Hunter, representing the rebel confederacy, Mr Hunter replied that the recognition of Jeff. Davis' power was the first and indispensable step to peace; and, to illustrate his point, he referred to the correspondence between King Charles the First and his Parliament, as a reliable precedent of a constitutional ruler treating with rebels. Mr. Lincoln's face wore that indescribable expression which generally preceded his hardest hits; and he remarked:

"Upon questions of history I must refer you to Mr. Seward, for he is posted in such things, and I don't profess to be: but my only distinct recollection of the matter is that Charles lost his head!"

Mr. Hunter remarked, on the same occasion, that the slaves, always accustomed to work upon compulsion, under an overseer, would, if suddenly freed, precipitate not only themselves, but the entire society of the South, into irremediable ruin. No work would be done, but blacks and whites would starve together. The President waited for Mr. Seward to answer the argument, but, as that gentleman hesitated, he said:

"Mr. Hunter, you ought to know a great deal better about this matter than I, for you have always lived under the slave system. I can only say, in reply to your statement of the case, that it reminds me of a man out in Illinois, by the name of Case, who undertook, a few years ago to raise a very large herd of hogs. It was a great trouble to feed them; and how to get around this was a puzzle to him. At length he hit upon the plan of planting an immense field of potatoes, and, when they were sufficiently grown, he turned the whole herd into the field and let them have full swing, thus saving not only the labor of feeding the hogs, but that also of digging the potatoes! Charmed with his sagacity, he stood one day leaning against the fence, counting his hogs, when a neighbor came along:

" 'Well, well,' said he, 'Mr. Case this is very fine. Your hogs are doing very well just now; but you know out here in Illinois the frost comes early, and the ground freezes a foot deep. Then what are they going to do?'

"This was a view of the matter which Mr. Case had not taken into account. Butchering time for hogs was away on in December or January. He scratched his head and at length stammered: 'Well, it may come pretty hard on their snouts, but I don't see but it will be root hog or die!'"

Lincoln and Judge Baldwin.

"Judge Baldwin, of California, being in Washington, called one day on General Halleck, and presuming upon a familiar acquaintance in California a few years before, solicited a pass outside of our lines to see a brother in Virginia, not thinking that he would meet with a refusal, as both his brother and himself were good Union men.

"We have been deceived too often," said General Halleck, 'and I regret I can't grant it."

Judge Baldwin then went to Stanton, and was very briefly disposed of, with the same result. Finally, he obtained an interview with Mr. Lincoln, and stated his case.

"Have you applied to General Halleck?" inquired the President.

"Yes, and met with a flat refusal," said Judge B.

" 'Then you must see Stanton,' continued the President.

" 'I have, and with the same result,' was the reply.

" 'Well, then,' said Mr. Lincoln, with a smile, 'I can do nothing; for you must know that I have very little influence with this Administration.' "

———:o:———

The Merciful President.

A personal friend of President Lincoln says: "I called on him one day in the early part of the war. He had just written a pardon for a young man who had been sentenced to be shot, for sleeping at his post, as a sentinel. He remarked as he read it to me:

" 'I could not think of going into eternity with the blood of the poor young man on my skirts.' Then he added: 'It is not to be wondered at that a boy, raised on a farm, probably in the habit of going to bed at dark, should, when required to watch, fall asleep; and I cannot consent to shoot him for such an act.' "

This story, with its moral, is made complete by Rev, Newman Hall, of London, who, in a sermon preached after and upon Mr. Lincoln's death, says that the dead body of this youth was found among the slain on the field of Fredericksburg, wearing next his heart a photograph of his preserver, beneath which the grateful fellow had written, "God bless President Lincoln!"

From the same sermon another anecdote is gleaned, of a similar character, which is evidently authentic. An officer of the army, in conversation with the preacher, said:

"The first week of my command, there were twenty-four deserters sentenced by court martial to be shot, and the warrants for their execution were sent to the President to be signed. He refused. I went to Washington and had an interview. I said:

" 'Mr. President, unless these men are made an example of, the army itself is in danger. Mercy to the few is cruelty to the many.'

"He replied: 'Mr. General, there are already too many weeping widows in the United States. For God's sake, don't ask me to add to the number, for I won't do it.' "

———:o:———

No Mercy for the Man Stealer.

Hon. John B. Alley, of Lynn, Massachusetts, was made the bearer to the President of a petition for pardon, by a person confined in the Newburyport jail for being engaged in the slave-trade. He had been sentenced to five years' imprisonment, and the payment of a fine of one thousand dollars. The petition was accompanied by a letter to Mr. Alley, in which the prisoner acknowledged his guilt and the justice of his sentence. He was very penitent—at least on paper—and had received the full measure of his punishment, so far as it related to the term of his imprisonment; but he was still held because he could not pay his fine. Mr. Alley read the letter to the President, who was much moved by its pathetic appeals; and when he had himself read the petition, he looked up and said: "My friend, that is a very touching appeal to our feelings. You know my weakness is to be, if possible, too easily moved by appeals for mercy, and, if this man were guilty of the foulest murder that the arm of man could perpetrate, I might forgive him on such an appeal; but the man who could go to Africa, and rob her of her children, and sell them into interminable bondage, with no other motive than that which is furnished by dollars and cents, is so much worse than the most depraved murderer, that he can never receive pardon at my hands. No! He may rot in jail before he shall have liberty by any act of mine." A sudden crime, committed under strong temptation, was venial in his eyes, on evidence of repentance; but the calculating, mercenary crime of man-stealing and man-selling, with all the cruelties that are essential accompaniments to the business, could win from him, as an officer of the people, no pardon.

―――:o:―――

How a Negro Argued the Point.

The following story is attributed to Mr. Lincoln upon the hurricane deck of one of our gun-boats:

An elderly darkey with a very philosophical and retrospective cast of countenance, squatted upon his bundle, toasting his shins against the chimney, and apparently plunged in a state of profound meditation. Finding, upon inquiry, that he belonged to the Ninth Illinois, one of the most gallantly behaved and heavy losing regiments at the Fort Donaldson battle, and a part of which was aboard, I began to interrogate him upon the subject:

"Were you in the fight?"

"Had a little taste of it, sa."

"Stood your ground, did you?"

"No sa; I runs."

"Run at the first fire, did you?"

"Yes sa, and would hab run soona had I knowd it war coming."

"Why, that wasn't very creditable to your courage.'

"Dat isn't my line, sa; cooking's my perfeshun."

"Well, but have you no regard for your reputation?"

"Reputation's nuffin to me by de side of life."

"Do you consider your life worth more than other people's?"

"It is worth more to me, sa."

"Then you must value it very highly?"

"Yes, sa, I does; more dan all dis wuld, more dan a million ob dollars, sa; for what wud dat be wuf to a man wid de bref out of him? Self-preserbation am de fust law wid me."

"But why should you act upon a different rule from other men?"

"Because different men set different values upon their lives; mine is not in de market."

"But if you lost it, you would have the satisfaction of knowing that you died for your country."

"What satisfaction would dat be to me when de power ob feelin' was gone?"

"Then patriotism and honor are nothing to you?"

"Nuffin whatever, sa; I regard them as among the vanities."

"If our soldiers were like you, traitors might have broken up the Government without resistance."

"Yes. sa; dar would hab been no help for it. I wouldn't put my life in de scale 'ginst any gobernment dat eber existed, for no gobernment could replace de loss to me."

"Do you think any of your company would have missed you if you had been killed?"

"Maybe not, sa; a dead man ain't much to dese sogers, let alone a dead nigga; but I'd a missed myself and dat was de pint wid me."

———:o:———

How Lincoln Associated His Second Nomination with a Very Singular Circumstance.

It appeared that the dispatch announcing Lincoln's renomination for President had been sent to his office from the War Department while he was at lunch. Afterward, without going back to the official chamber, he proceeded to the War Department. While there, the telegram came in announcing the nomination of Johnson.

"What!" said he to the operator, "do they nominate a Vice Pdesident before they do a President?"

"Why!" rejoined the astonished official, "have you not heard of your own nomination? It was sent to the White House two hours ago."

"It is all right," was the reply; "I shall probably find it on my return."

Laughing pleasantly over this incident, he said, soon

afterwards: "A very singular occurrence took place the day I was nominated at Chicago, four years ago, of which I am reminded to-night. In the afternoon of the day, returning home from down town, I went up-stairs to Mrs. Lincoln's reading-room. Feeling somewhat tired, I lay down upon a couch in the room, directly opposite a bureau, upon which was a looking-glass. As I reclined, my eye fell upon the glass, and I saw distinctly two images of myself, exactly alike, except that one was a little paler than the other. I arose, and lay down again, with the same result. It made me quite uncomfortable for a few moments, but some friends coming in, the matter passed out of my mind.

"The next day, while walking in the street, I was suddenly reminded of the circumstance, and the disagreeable sensation produced by it returned. I had never seen anything of the kind before, and did not know what to make of it.

"I determined to go home and place myself in the same position, and if the same effect was produced, I would make up my mind that it was the natural result of some principle of refraction of optics which I did not understand, and dismiss it. I tried the experiment, with a like result; and, as I had said to myself, accounting for it on some principle unkown to me, it ceased to trouble me. But," said he, "some time ago, I tried to produce the same effect here. by arranging a glass and couch in the same position, without success."

He did not say, at this time, that either he or Mrs. Lincoln attached any omen to the phenomenon, but it is known that Mrs. Lincoln regarded it as a sign that the President would be re-elected.

A Touching Incident in the Life of Lincoln.

A few days before the President's death, Secretary Stanton tendered his resignation of the War Department. He accompanied the act with a heartfelt tribute to Mr. Lincoln's constant friendship and faithful devotion to the country; saying, also, that he as Secretary had accepted the position to hold it only until the war should end, and that now he felt his work was done, and his duty was to resign.

BIRTHPLACE OF GENERAL U. S. GRANT.

Mr. Lincoln was greatly moved by the Secretary's words, and tearing in pieces the paper containing the resignation, and throwing his arms adout the Secretary, he said:

"Stanton, you have been a good friend and a faithful public servant, and it is not for you to say when you will no longer be needed here." Several friends of both parties were present on the occasion, and there was not a dry eye that witnessed the scene.

How Lincoln Illustrated What Might Be Done With Jeff. Davis.

One of the latest of Mr. Lincoln's stories was told to a party of gentlemen, who, among the tumbling ruins of the Confederacy, anxiously asked "what he would do with Jeff. Davis?"

"There was a boy in Springfield," replied Mr. Lincoln, who saved up his money and bought a 'coon,' which, after the novelty wore off, became a great nuisance.

"He was one day leading him through the streets, and had his hands full to keep clear of the little vixen, who had torn his clothes half off of him. At length he sat down on the curb-stone, completely fagged out. A man passing was stopped by the lad's disconsolate appearance, and asked the matter.

" 'Oh,' was the only reply, 'this coon is such a trouble to me.'

" 'Why don't you get rid of him then?" said the gentleman.

" 'Hush!' said the boy: 'don't you see he is gnawing his rope off? I am going to let him do it, and then I will go home and tell the folks that he got away from me!' "

—:o:—

The Great Thing About Gen. Grant as Lincoln Saw It.

Mr. Carpenter, the artist, made particular inquiry of the President, during the progress of the Battles of the Wilderness, how General Grant personally impressed him as compared to other officers of the army, and especially those who had been in command.

"The great thing about Grant," said he, "I take it, is his perfect coolness and persistency of purpose. I judge he is not easily excited, which is a great element in an officer, and has the grit of a bull-dog! Once let him get his 'teeth' in, and nothing can shake him off."

———:o:———

A Joke on Mr. Chase.

One day, while the Americau war was going on, and Secretary Chase was issuing the paper money, known as ,'greenbacks," in large quantities, he found upon a desk in his office a drawing of an ingenious invention for turning gold eagles into "greenbacks," with a portrait of himself feeding it with "yellor boys," at one end, while the government currency came out at the other end, flying about like leaves of autumn. While he was examining the drawing, President Lincoln came in, and recognizing the likeness of the secretary, exclaimed:

"Capital joke, isn't it, Mr. Chase?"

"A joke," said the irate financier, "I'd give a thousand dollars to know who left that here."

"Would you, indeed," said the President, "and which end would you pay from?"

The answer is not "recorded."

———:o:———

A Curious Story of Lincoln and the Spirits.

It is stated on the authority of the Boston Evening Gazette, that Abraham Lincoln once gave a spiritual soiree at the Presidential residence to test the wonderful alleged supernatural powers of one Mr. Charles E: Shockle. The party consisted of the President, Mrs.

Lincoln, Mr. Wells, Mr. Stanton and two other gentlemen.

For some half-hour the demonstrations were of a physical character—tables were moved, and a picture of Henry Clay, which hangs on the wall, was swayed more than a foot, and two candelabra, presented by the Dey of Algiers to President Adams, was twice raised nearly to the ceiling. At length loud rappings was heard directly beneath the President's feet, and Mr. Shockle stated that an Indian desired to communicate.

"I shall be happy to hear what his Indian majesty has to say," replied the President, "for I have very recently received a deputation of our red brethren, and it was the only delegation, black, white or blue, which did not volunteer some advice about the conduct of the war."

The medium then called for a pencil and paper, which were laid upon the table, and afterwards covered with a handkerchief. Presently knocks were heard and the paper was uncovered, To the surprise of all present, it read as follows:

'.Haste makes waste, but delays cause vexations. Give vitality by energy. Use every means to subdue. Proclamations are useless, Make a bold front and fight the enemy; leave traitors at home to the care of loyal men. Less note of preparation, less parade and policy-talk, and more action.—HENRY KNOX."

"That is not Indian talk, Mr. Shockle," said the President. "Who is Henry Knox?

The medium, speaking in a strange voice, replied, "The first Secretary of War."

"Oh, yes; General Knox," said the President. "Stanton, that message is for you; it is from your predecessor. I should like to ask General Knox to tell us when this rebellion will be put down."

The answer was oracularly indefinite. The spirit said that Napoleon thought one thing, Lafayette another. and that Franklin differed from both.

'Ah," exclaimed the President. "opinions differ among the saints as well as among the sinners. Their talk is very much like the talk of my cabinet. I wish the spirits would tell us how to catch the Alabama?"

The lights almost instantaneously became so dim that it was impossible to distinguish the features of any one in the room, and on the large mirror over the mantlepiece, there appeared a sea-view, the Alabama, with all steam up, flying from the pursuit of another large steamer. Two merchantmen in the distance were seen partially destroyed by fire.

The picture changed, and the Alabama was seen at anchor under the shadow of an English fort, from which an English flag was flying. The Alabama was floating idly, not a soul on board, and no signs of life visible about her. The picture vanished, and, in letters of purple. appeared: "The American people demand this of the English aristocracy."

"So England is to seize the Alabama, finally?" said the President. "It may be possible, but Mr. Wells, do not let one gunboat or one monitor less be constructed."

"Well, Mr. Shockle," continued he, "I have seen

strange things, and heard rather odd remarks, but nothing that convinces me, except the pictures, that there is anything very heavenly about all this. I should like, if possible, to hear what Judge Douglas says about this war."

After an interval of about three minutes, Mr. Shockle rose quickly from his chair and stood behind it. Resting his left hand on the back, his right into his bosom, he spoke in a voice such as no one could mistake who had ever heard Mr. Douglas. He urged the President to throw aside all advisers who hesitated about the policy to be pursued, and said that if victory were followed up by energetic action, all would be well.

"I believe that," said the President, "whether it comes from spirit or human. It needs not a ghost from 'the bourne from which no traveler returns' to tell that."

———:o:———

The President's Aversion to Bloodshed.

A striking incident in Mr. Lincoln's official life is related by Judge Bromwell, of Denver, who visited the White House in March, 1865. Mr. Seward and several other gentlemen were also present, and the President gradually came to talk on decisions of life and death.

All other matters submitted to him, he declared, were nothing in comparison to these, and he added:

"I reckon there never was a man raised in the country on a farm, where they are always butchering cattle and hogs and think nothing of it, that ever grew up with such an aversion to bloodshed as I have; and yet I've had more questions of life and death to settle in four years than all the men who ever sat in this chair put together.

"But I've managed to get along and do my duty, as I

[The Massacre.]

believe, and still save most of them, and there's no man knows the distress of my mind. But there have been some of them I couldn't save—there are some cases where the law must be executed.

"There was that man ———, who was sentenced for piracy and slave-trading on the high seas. That was a case where there must be an example, and you don't know how they followed and pressed to get him pardoned, or his sentence commuted; but there was no use of talking. It had to be done; I could not help the poor man.

"And then there was that ———, who was caught spying and recruiting within Pope's lines in Missouri. That was another case. They besieged me day and night but I couldn't give way.

"We had come to a point where something must be done that would put a stop to such work.

"And then there was the case of Beal on the lakes. That was a case where there had to be an example. They tried me every way. They wouldn't give up; but I had to stand firm on that, and I even had turned away his poor sister when she came and begged for his life, and let him be executed, and he was executed, and I can't get the distress out of my mind."

As the kindly man uttered these words the tears ran down his cheeks, and the eyes of the men surrounding him moistened in sympathy. There was a profound silence in which they rose to depart. Three weeks after, the President was killed.

How Lincoln Told a Secret.

When the Sherman expedition which captured Port Royal went out, there was great curiosity to know where it had gone. A person visiting President Lincoln at his official residence importuned him to disclose the destination.

"Will you keep it entirely secret?" asked the President.

"Oh yes, upon my honor."

"Well," said the President, "I will tell you." Assuming an air of great mystery, and drawing the man close to him, he kept him a moment awaiting the revelation with an open mouth and in great anxiety, and then said in a loud whisper, which was heard all over the room, "The expedition has gone to—sea,"

Two Hundred and Fifty Thousand Passes to Richmond.

A gentleman called upon President Lincoln before the fall of Richmond and solicited a pass for that place. "I should be very happy to oblige you," said the President, "if my passes were respected; but the fact is, I have, within the past two years given passes to two hundred and fifty thousand men to go to Richmond and not one has got there yet.

Hon. Leonard Swett's Reminiscences.

"I saw him," says the late Mr. Sweet, who was a most intimate friend of Lincoln, "early one morning, when the President, alluding to the proposed Emancipation Proclamation, invited me to sit down, as he wished to confer with me on the subject. The conference lasted until the time came for the Cabinet Council, and during the whole time Lincoln did all the talking. He did not really want my advice, he wanted simply to go over the ground with me.

"During the conference the President read a very able letter from Robert Dale Owen, urging reasons why the war could never be gone through successfully without the Emancipation Proclamation. As Lincoln read it he remarked, 'this is a very able paper,' at the same time stating that he had prepared a paper on the same subject but that Mr. Owen's paper was much the abler of the two.

The President then offered to read letters of another kind,—letters complaining of his administration, piling upon him the most frightful abuse for a do nothing in the Presidential chair. The reading of letters of this class occupied an hour, He also read a letter from the Frenchman Gasparin, who advised him to do nothing that was revolutionary, and urging the claims of legitimacy. He argued that the South were revolutionists, and asked whether a proclamation freeing the slaves might not render the Northerners revolutionists themselves.

Lincoln then reviewed the three kinds of letters, and also gave his own views as to the probable results of freeing the negroes, his great fear being that they might, thus freed, become an element of weakness to their liberators.

"Before the interview was ended, I, pondering upon what Mr. Lincoln had said about having written something upon the subject of emancipation, made a guess that he had in the drawer before him the proclamation ready written, and I asked the President to let me see what he had prepared on the subject. Lincoln asked me not to press the request, and I abstained from doing so, but three weeks afterward, when the proclamation had been issued, the President acknowledged to me that my guess had been a correct one, and that the document was, at the time of the interview, lying in the very spot I had mentioned.

As soon as Lincoln saw that the negro slave could become a soldier he saw that he had the material out of which the rebellion could be crushed, and it is my belief that from this time forward Lincoln had a clear sight of the victory that stood at the end of the war.

Speaking of Lincoln's habits, the Hon. Leonard Swett says:

"The martyr-President was used to work all his life, but never to its dissipations. With him morning meant 6 o'clock a. m., and, as a rule, he had finished breakfast and was at work at 7 o'olock. What tore his heart most of all during the war, was an approval of the death penalty. He had a horror of blood, and although he knew that under certain circumstances he could not avoid signing the death-warrant for desertion, it always caused him infinite pain to do so.

One morning Mr. Swett found him sitting in the "east room" before a pile of papers. They sat together, chatted and told stories. It was a Thursday, and Friday was always the day upon which deserters were shot. Suddenly Lincoln arose and said:

"Swett, go out of here; to-morrow is butcher's day, and I've got to go through these papers not to see if they are regular, but if I can't find something by which I can let them off."

———:o:———

Lincoln and the Colored People of Richmond.

G. F. Shepley gives the following interesting reminiscence:

After Mr. Lincoln's interview with Judge Campbell,

the President, about to return to the Wabash, I took him and Admiral Porter in my carriage. An immense concourse of colored people thronged the streets, accompanied and followed the carriage, calling upon the President with the wildest exclamations of gratitude and delight.

He was the Moses, the Messiah, to the slaves of the South. Hundreds of colored women tossed their hands high in the air and then bent down to the ground weeping for joy. Some shouted songs of deliverance, and sang the old plantation refrains, which had prophesied the coming of a deliverer from bondage. "God bless you, Father Abraham!" went up from a thousand throats.

Those only who have seen the paroxysmal enthusiasm of a religious meeting of slaves can form an adequate conception of the way in which the tears and smiles, and shouts of these emancipated people evinced the frenzy of their gratitude to their deliverer. He looked at all attentively, with a face expressive only of a sort of pathetic wonder.

Occasionally its sadness would alternate with one of his peculiar smiles, and he would remark on the great proportion of those whose color indicated a mixed lineage from the white master and the black slave; and that reminded him of some little story of his life in Kentucky, which he would smilingly tell; aud then his face would relapse again into that sad expression which all will remember who saw him during the last few weeks of the rebellion. Perhaps it was a presentiment of his impending fate.

I accompanied him to the ship, bade him farewell and left him to see his face no more. Not long after, the bullet of the assassin arrested the beatings of one of the kindest hearts that ever throbbed in human bosom.

———:o:———

Lincoln's First Convictions of War.—His Great Sadness.

The Hon. Leonard Swett, in an address before the Union Veteran Club at Chicago, gives the following interesting reminiscence:

I remember well the first time that the belief that war was inevitable took hold of Lincoln's mind. Some time after the election Lincoln asked me to write a letter to Thurlow Weed to come to Springfield and consult with him (Lincoln). Mr. Weed came, and he, the President-elect, and myself had a meeting, in which Lincoln for the first time acknowledged that he was in possession of facts that showed that the South meant war.

These facts consisted of the steps which the disaffected States were taking to spirit away the arms belonging to the Government, and, taking them into consideration, Lincoln was forced to the belief that his Administration was to be one of blood.

As he made this admission his countenance rather than his words demonstrated the sadness which it occasioned, and he wanted to know if there was not some way of avoiding the disaster. He felt as if he could not go forward to an era of war, and these days were to him a sort of forty days in the wilderness, passed under great stress of doubt and, perhaps to him, of temptations of weakness. Finally, however, he seemed quietly to put on the armor and prepare himself for the great responsibility and struggle before him.

Gen C. H. Howard's Reminiscences.

Gen. Howard in the Northwestern Christian Advocate says:

It was soon after the battle of Antietam, and while our army was resting and refitting with clothing and other needed supplies in the vicinity of Harper's Ferry, that I first saw Abraham Lincoln. He visited the different corps and divisions, reviewed the troops and held brief interviews with the leading officers. It need not be stated that he was warm in his commendation of the valor and endurance of the troops. Cheer upon cheer greeted him as he passed from brigade to brigade, and sometimes he had a few words of encouragement for a single regiment which had distinguished itself.

Subordinate officers, when asked about the condition of their soldiers, were not backward in speaking of the need of shoes and other clothing, and of the decimated condition of many of the regiments resulting from the diseases and hard campaigning of the Chickahominy swamps scarcely less from the numerous battles in which they had taken a noble part. The fact that a campaign or a battle had been badly conducted and was disastrous was neither proof that the troops had not done their duty nor that their losses had not been great. President Lincoln expressed in the most kindly and feeling way his sympathy with the rank and file of the army. There was a gentle and serious expression of countenance which seemed to comport with his known character for truth and serenity of heart.

Nearly two years elapsed when I had another interview with Abraham Lincoln which it is the purpose of this paper to mention. The writer had been transferred to the Western department, and had taken part in the Atlanta campaign and in Sherman's famous "March to the Sea." On the first day of January, 1865, he had left Savannah to go via steamship to New York, and thence by rail to Washington with official dispatches. Sherman had sent his unique telegram to the President on Christmas eve announcing as a Christmas present the capture of Savannah. Owing to the fact that the railroads had been destroyed this dispatch had been sent by special steamer to Fortress Monroe and thence by telegraph to Washington. But President Lincoln had not yet seen any person who had marched through Georgia with Sherman.

It was early in the day when my card was given to the messenger in the ante-room of the White House. He shook his head and pointed to the crowds in waiting, filling the ante-room and thronging even the lower hall and the stairway. He called my attention to the fact that there were congressmen of the number who were supposed to have precedence in calling upon the President. Nevertheless, I requested him to give the President the card which indicated that I had dispatches from Sherman's army. The messenger returned within a few minutes and invited me in. First, we entered a room occupied by the President's secretaries, and there I saw one or two senators in waiting, and passing through this room I was ushered into a smaller room, where I saw President Lincoln standing at a glass shaving himself. He paused a moment, came to me with a droll look, heightened no doubt by the half-lathered, half-shaved face, gave me his hand, and asked me to take a seat on the sofa, saying, as he returned to the mirror, that he could not even wait till he had finished shaving when an officer from Sherman's army had come. Of course the youthful staff officer was somewhat abashed in coming into the presence of the President of the United States, his commander-in-chief, and the now world-renowned Abraham Lincoln. But the President's frank and cordial manner when, on the completion of his toilet, he came and took the right hand of his visitor between both of his large hands and then sat down beside him on the sofa, immediately put him at his ease. Naturally, the President had many questions to ask concerning the "March to the Sea." It was apparent he had been very anxious, as no doubt had the entire North, during the thirty days or more when nothing was heard from the vanquished army. He was interested to know in detail the daily operations.

―――:o:―――

Getting at the Pass-Word.

An amusing story is attributed to the late President Lincoln about the Iowa First, and the changes which a certain pass-word underwent about the time of the battle of Springfield.

One of the Dubuque officers, whose duty it was to furnish the guards with a pass-word at night, gave the word "Potomac."

A German on guard, not comprehending distinctly the difference between B's and P's, understood it to be "Bottomic," and this, on being transferred to another, was corrupted into "Buttermilk."

Soon afterward the officer who had given the word wished to return through the lines, and on approaching the sentinel was ordered to halt, and the word demanded. He gave the word "Potomac."

"Nicht right; you don't pass mit me dis way."

"But this is the word, and I will pass."

"No, you stan'," at the same time placing a bayonet at his breast, in a manner that told the officer that "Potomac" didn't pass in Missouri.

"What is the word then?"

"Buttermilk."

"Well, then, buttermilk."

"Dat is right; now you pass mit yourself all about your piziness."

There was then a general overhauling of the password, and the difference between Potomac and Buttermilk being understood, the joke became one of the laughable incidents of the campaign.

———:o:———

Lincoln and a Clergyman.

At the semi-annual meeting of the New Jersey Historical Society,, held in Newark, N. J., Rev. Dr. Sheldon, of Princeton, read a memorial of their late President, Rev. R. R. Rodgers, D. D., in which occurs the following incident concerning Mr. Lincoln, and the war.

One day during the war, Dr. Rodgers was called on by a man in his congregation, who, in great distress, told him that his son, a soldier in the army, had just been sentenced to be shot for desertion, and begged the minister's interposition.

The Doctor went to Washington with the wife and infant child of the condemned man, and sent his card up to Mr. Lincoln. When admitted, the President said:

"You are a minister, I believe. What can I do for you, my friend?"

'The reply was: "A young man from my congregation in the army has so far forgotten his duty to his country and his God as to desert his colors, and is sentenced to die. I have come to ask you to spare him.'

With characteristic quaintness the President replied: 'Then you don't want him hurt, do you?'

'Oh, no,' said the petitioner, 'I did not mean that; he deserves punishment, but I beg for him time to prepare to meet his God.'

'Do you say he has father, wife and child?' said Mr. Lincoln.

'Yes.'

'Where do you say he is?'

On being told, he turned to his secretary, said a few words in an undertone, of which that official made note, and added to Dr. Rodgers, 'You have your request. Tell your friends I have reprieved him.'

With a 'God bless you, Mr. President,' Dr. Rodgers turned away to bear the glad news to the distressed family."

———:o:———

The President Advises Secretary Stanton to Prepare for Death.

The imperious Stanton, when Secretary of War, took a fancy one day for a house in Washington that Lamon had just bargained for. Lamon not only did not vacate, but went to Stanton and said he would kill him if he interfered with the house. Stanton was furious at the threat, and made it known at once to Lincoln. The latter said to the astonished War Secretary:

"Well, Stanton, if Ward has said he will kill you, he certainly will, and I'd advise you to prepare for death without further delay."

The President promised, however, to do what he could to appease the murderous Marshal, and this was the end of Stanton's attempt on the house.

———:o:———

"A Great Deal of Shuck for a Little Nubbin."

At the peace conference which occured in February, 1865, at Fortress Monroe, President Lincoln and Secretary Seward were on one side, and Alexander H. Stephens, John A Campbell and R. M. T. Hunter on the other. The attenuation of Mr. Stephens has so long been a matter of such general notoriety that it is not offensive to speak of it. It seems that Mr. Lincoln had never seen Mr. Stephens before. At that time a kind of cloth was worn by Southern gentlemen, nearly the shade of ordinary corn husk, and Mr. Stephens' great coat was made of that material. But Mr. Stephens, who always had been a frail man, wore many other garments beneath to protect him against the raw wind of Hampton Roads; and Mr. Lincoln watched with much interest the process of shedding until the man was finally reached. At last Mr. Stephens stood forth in his physical entity, ready for business. Mr. Lincoln, giving Gov. Seward one of his most comical looks, and pointing to the discarded coats, said:

"Well, I never saw as much shuck for as little a nubbin in my life."

———:o:———

"Tad's" Rebel Flag.

One of the prettiest incident's in the closing days of the civil war occurred when the troops "marching home again" passed in grand form, if with well-worn uniforms and tattered bunting, before the White House, says Harper's Young People.

Naturally, an immense crowd had assembled on the streets, the lawns, porches, balconies, and windows, even those of the executive mansion itself being crowded to excess. A central figure was that of the President, Abraham Lincoln, who, with bared head, unfurled and waved our nation's flag in the midst of lusty cheers.

But suddenly there was an unexpected sight.

A small boy leaned forward and sent streaming to the air the banner of the boys in gray. It was an old flag which had been captured from the Confederates, and which the urchin, the President's second son, Tad, had obtained possession of and considered an additional triumph to unfurl on this all-important day.

Vainly did the servant who had followed him to the window plead with him to desist. No, Master Tad, the Pet of the White House, was not to be prevented from adding to the loyal demonstration of the hour.

To his surprise, however, the crowd viewed it differently. Had it floated from any other window in the capital that day, no doubt it would have been the target of contempt and abuse; but when the President, understanding what had happened, turned, with a smile on his grand, plain face and showed his approval by a gesture and expression, cheer after cheer rent the air.

It was, surely enough, the expression of peace and good will which, of all our commanders, none was better pleased to promote than our commander-in-chief.

———:o:———

A Position That Lincoln Wanted.

A gentleman named Farquhar of York, Pa., did not enlist because he was a Quaker. In the course of the war General Early marched before York and threatened to burn the houses of its peaceful citizens unless a ransome of $25,000 was forthcoming.

Mr. F—— was foremost in arranging matters and struck a bargain with the Confederates which, while they were near, seemed very clever to his fellow-townsmen, but when they marched away, brought forth many bitter complaints.

The whole matter set Mr. F—— thinking. The war ought to be ended. So he set out for Washington to offer his services to the government. He called upon Mr. Lincoln, told him how he felt, and said he wished to help his country.

"Well," said Mr. Lincoln, "come with me to the Secretary of war and I will give you a position which I would gladly take myself."

They were soon in Mr. Stanton's office. Lincoln made a sign to the Secretary, who produced a Bible and proceeded to swear Mr. F—— into the United States service.

The ceremony had not gone very far when he discovered that the position Mr. Lincoln coveted was that of a a private soldier. Mr. F—— showed alarm and the President laughingly released him.

———:o:———

A Lincoln Story About Little Dan Webster's Soiled Hands!—How Dan Escaped a Flogging.

Mr. Lincoln on one occasion narrated to Hon. Mr. Odell and others, with much zest, the following story about young Daniel Webster:

When quite young, at school, Daniel was one day guilty of a gross violation of the rules. He was detected in the act, and called up by the teacher for punishment. This was to be the old fashioned "feruling" of the hand. His hands happened to be very dirty. Knowing this, on the way to the teacher's desk, he spit upon the palm of his right hand, wiping it off upon the side of his pantaloons.

"Give me your hand, sir," said the teacher, very sternly.

Out went the right hand, partly cleansed. The teacher looked at it a moment, and said:

"Daniel! if you will find another hand in this schoolroom as filthy as that, I will let you off this time!"

Instantly from behind the back came the left hand. "Here it is sir," was the ready reply.

"That will do," said the teacher, " for this time; you can take your seat, sir."

———:o:———

Lincoln and the Little Baby — A Touching Story.

"Old Daniel," who was one of the White House ushers, is responsible for the following touching story:

A poor woman from Philadelphia had been waiting with a baby in her arms for several days to see the President. It appeared by her story, that her husband had furnished a substitute for the army, but some time afterward, in a state of intoxication, was induced to enlist. Upon reaching the post assigned his regiment, he deserted, thinking the Government was not entitled to his services. Returning home, he was arrested, tried, convicted and sentenced to be shot. The sentence was to be executed on a Saturday. On Monday his wife left home with her baby to endeavor to see the President.

Said Daniel, "She had been waiting here three days, and there was no chance for her to get in. Late in the afternoon of the third day, the President was going through the passage to his private room to get a cup of tea. On the way he heard the baby cry. He instantly went back to his office and rang the bell.

"Daniel," said he, "is there a woman with a baby in the ante-room?"

I said there was, and if he would allow me to say it, it was a case he ought to see; for it was a matter of life and death.

"Said he. "Send her to me at once."

She went in, told her story, and the President pardoned her husband.

As the woman came out from his presence, her eyes

were lifted and her lips moving in prayer, the tears streaming down her cheeks.

Said Daniel, "I went up to her, and pulling her shawl, said, 'Madam, it was the baby that did it.' "

———:o:———

DWIGHT L. MOODY.

D. L. Moody's Story of Lincoln's Compassion —What a Little Girl Did With Mr. Lincoln to Save Her Brother.

During the war, says D. L. Moody, I remember a young man, not twenty, who was court-martialed at the front and sentenced to be shot. The story was this:

The young fellow had enlisted. He was not obliged to, but he went off with another young man. They were what we would call "chums."

One night his companion was ordered out on picket duty, and he asked the young man to go for him. The next night he was ordered out himself; and having been awake two nights, and not being used to it, fell asleep at his post, and for the offense he was tried and sentenced to death. It was right after the order issued by the President that no interference would be allowed in cases of this kind. This sort of thing had become too frequent, and it must be stopped.

When the news reached the father and mother in Vermont it nearly broke their hearts. The thought that their son should be shot was too great for them. They had no hope that he could be saved by anything that they could do.

But they had a little daughter who had read the life of Abraham Lincoln, and knew how he loved his own children, and she said:

"If Abraham Lincoln knew how my father and mother loved my brother he wouldn't let him be shot."

The little girl thought this matter over and made up her mind to see the President.

She went to the White House, and the sentinel, when he saw her imploring looks, passed her in, and when she came to the door and told the private secretary that she wanted to see the President, he could not refuse her. She came into the chamber and found Abraham Lincoln surrounded by his generals and counselors, and when he saw the little country girl the asked her what she wanted.

The little maid told her plain, simple story—how her brother, whom her father and mother loved very dearly, had been sentenced to be shot; how they were mourning for him, and if he was to die in that way it would break their hearts.

The President's heart was touched with compassion, and he immediately sent a dispatch canceling the sentence and giving the boy a parole so that he could come home and see his father and mother. I just tell you this to show you how Abraham Lincoln's heart was moved by compassion for the sorrow of that father and mother, and if he showed so much do you think the Son of God will not have compassion upon you, sinner, if you only take that crushed, bruised heart to him?

———:o:———

Honorable Frederick Douglas' Reminiscences.

The well-known Frederick Douglas in the Northwestern Advocate says:

I saw and conversed with this great man for the first time in the darkest hours of the military situation when the armies of the rebellion seemed more confident, defiant and aggressive than ever.

I had never before had an interview with a President of the United States, and though I felt I had something important to say, considering his exalted position and my lowly origin and the people whose cause I came to plead, I approached him with much trepidation as to how this great man might receive me; but one word and look from him banished all my fears and set me perfectly at ease. I have often said since that meeting it was much easier to see and converse with a great man than a small man.

On that occasion he said:

"Douglas, you need not tell me who you are, Mr. Seward has told me all about you."

I then saw that there was no reason to tell him my personal story, however interesting it might be to myself or others, so I told him at once the object of my visit. It was to get some expression from him upon three points.

1. Equal pay to colored soldiers.

2. Their promotion when they had earned it on the battlefield.

3. Should they be taken prisoners and enslaved or hanged, as Jefferson Davis had threatened, an equal number of Confederate prisoners should be executed within our lines.

A declaration to that effect I thought would prevent the execution of the rebel threat. To all but the last President Lincoln assented, He argued, however, that neither equal pay nor promotion could be granted at once. He said that in view of existing prejudices it was a great step forward to employ colored troops at all; that it was necessary to avoid everything that would offend this prejudice and increase opposition to the measure.

He detailed the steps by which white soldiers were reconciled to the employment of colored troops; how these were first employed as laborers; how it was thought they should not be armed or uniformed like white soldiers; how they should only be made to wear a peculiar uniform; how they should be employed to hold forts and arsenals in sickly locations, and not enter the field like other soldiers.

With all these restrictions and limitations he easily made me see that much would be gained when the colored man loomed before the country as a full-fledged United States soldier to fight, flourish or fall in defense of a united republic. The great soul of Lincoln halted only when he came to the point of retaliation.

The thought of hanging men in cold blood, even though the rebels should murder a few of the colored prisoners, was a horror from which he shrunk.

"Oh, Douglas! I cannot do that. If I could get hold of the actual murderers of colored prisoners, I would retaliate; but to hang those who had no hand in such murders, I cannot."

The contemplation of such an act brought to his countenance such an expression of sadness and pity that it made it hard for me to press my point, though I told him it would tend to save rather than destroy life. He, however, insisted that this work of blood once begun would be hard to stop; that such violence would beget violence. He argued more like a disciple of Christ than a commander-in-chief of the army and navy of a warlike nation already involved in a terrible war.

How sad and strange the fate of this great and good man, the savior of his country, the embodiment of human charity, whose heart, though strong, was as tender as the heart of childhood; who always tempered justice with mercy; who sought to supplant the sword with the counsel of reason, to suppress passion by kindness and moderation; who had a sigh for every human grief and a tear for every human woe, should at last perish by the hand of a desperate assassin, against whom no thought of malice had ever entered his heart.

Dr. Edwards Bumping the President.

The popular editor of the Northwestern Advocate, Dr. Arthur Edwards, is responsible for the following, which we take from the editorials of his excellent paper:

Early in the war it became this writer's duty, for a brief period, to carry certain reports to the War Department in Washington, at about nine in the morning. Being late one morning, we were in a desperate hurry to deliver the papers in order to be able to catch the train returning to camp.

On the winding, dark staircase of the old War Department, which many will remember, it was our misfortune, while taking about three stairs at a time, to run a certain head like a catapult into the body of the President, striking him in the region of the right lower vest pocket.

The usual surprised and relaxed human grunt of a man thus assailed came promptly. We quickly sent an apology in the direction of the dimly seen form, feeling that the ungracious shock was expensive, even to the humblest clerk in the department.

A second glance revealed to us the President as the victim of the collision. Then followed a special tender of "ten thousand pardons," and the President's reply:

"One's enough; I wish the whole army would charge like that."

Lincoln "Taking Up a Collection."

While the army of the Potomac was near Falmouth, on the river opposite Fredericksburg, Va., early in the war, Mr. Lincoln reviewed, says Dr. Edwards in the Northwestern Advocate, and inspected that splendid body of troops, 100,000 strong. Those who were present remember the quiet Dobbin ridden by the President. The steed proceeded soberly, as if he had been put upon his equine honor to be kind to his illustrious rider.

During a part of the formality when the reviewing officer or personage is specially the center of all eyes, Mr. Lincoln carried his tall "plug hat" in his hand, and, as he bumped up and down in his saddle, bowed right and left to the magnificent military lines. The right arm was extended almost horizontally, and the hand grasped the hat's ample brim.

The whole aspect of the now historic man abundantly justified the suggestion of a certain Methodist who was present, to the effect that "the dear old gentleman looks as if he were about to take up a collection."

The joker was discounted on the ground that he was indulging in his Methodfst traditions as far as the collection was concerned, but the second look at the horse and rider aided many a kindly smile. It was said at the time that Mr. Lincoln's visit to the army was in part to enable him to escape the importunities of office-seekers and industrious advisers in Washington.

An Inauguration Incident.

Noah Brooks, in his "Reminiscences," relates the following incident:

While the ceremonies of the second inauguration were in progress, just as Lincoln stepped forward to take the oath of office, the sun, which had been obscured by rain-clouds, burst forth in splendor. In conversation the next day, the President asked:

"Did you notice that sun-burst? It made my heart jump."

Later in the month, Miss Anna Dickinson, in a lecture delivered in the hall of the House of Representatives, eloquently alluded to the sun-burst as a happy omen. The President sat directly in front of the speaker, and from the reporter's gallery, behind her, I had caught his eye, soon after he sat down. When Miss Dickinson referred to the sunbeam, he looked up to me, involuntarily, and I thought his eyes were suffused with moisture. Perhaps they were; but the next day he said:

"I wonder if Miss Dickinson saw me wink at you?"

---:o:---

The Brigadier Generals and the Horses.

When President Lincoln heard of the rebel raid at Fairfax, in which a brigadier-general and a number of valuable horses were captured, he gravely observed:

"Well, I am sorry for the horses."

"Sorry for the horses, Mr. President!" exclaimed the Secretary of War, raising his spectacles, and throwing himself back in his chair in astonishment.

"Yes," replied Mr. Lincoln, "I can make a brigadier-general in five minutes, but it is not easy to replace a hundred and ten horses."

———:o:———

Lincoln and Stanton Fixing up Peace Between the Two Contending Armies.

"On the night of the 3d of March, the Secretary of War, with others of the Cabinet, were in the company of the President, at the Capitol, awaiting the passage of the final bills of Congress. In the intervals of reading and signing these documents, the military situation was considered—the lively conversation tinged by the confident and glowing account of General Grant, of his mastery of the position, and of his belief that a few days more would see Richmond in our posession, and the army of Lee either dispersed utterly or captured bodily—when the telegram from Grant was received, saying that Lee had asked an interview with reference to peace. Mr. Lincoln was elated, and the kindness of his heart was manifest in intimations of favorable terms to be granted to the conquered Rebels.

"Stanton listened in silence, restraining his emotion but at length the tide burst forth. 'Mr. President,' said he, 'to-morrow is inauguration day. If you are not to be the President of an obedient and united people, you had better not be inaugurated. Your work is already done, if any other authority than yours is for one moment to be recognized, or any terms made that do not signify you are the supreme head of the nation. If generals in the field are to negotiate peace, or any other chief magistrate is to be acknowledged on this continent, then you are not needed, and you had better not take the oath of office.'

GENERAL GRANT'S MONUMENT AT LINCOLN PARK, CHICAGO.

[240]

"'Stanton, you are right!' said the President, his whole tone changing, 'Let me have a pen.'

"Mr. Linclon sat down at the table, and wrote as follows:

"'The President directs me to say to you that he wishes you to have no conference with General Lee, unless it be for the capitulation of Lee's army, or on some minor or purely military matter. He instructs me to say that you are not to decide, discuss, or confer upon any political question. Such questions the President holds in his own hands, and will submit them to no military conferences or conventions. In the meantime you are to press to the utmost your military advantages.'

"The President read over what he had written, and then said:

"'Now, Stanton, date and sign this paper, and send it to Grant, We'll see about this peace business.'

"The duty was discharged only too gladly by the energetic Secretary.

———:o:———

MISCELLANEOUS STORIES, ETC.

Attending Henry Ward Beecher's Church.

Mr. Nelson Sizer, one of the gallery ushers of Henry Ward Beecher's church in Brooklyn, told a friend that about the time of the Cooper Institute speech, Mr. Lincoln was twice present at the morning services of that church. On the first occasion he was accompanied by his friend, George B. Lincoln, Esq., and occupied a prominent seat in the center of the house. On a subsequent Sunday morning, not long afterwards, the church was packed, as usual, and the services had proceeded to the announcement of the text, when the gallery door at the right of the organ-loft opened, and the tall figure of

Mr. Lincoln entered, alone. Again in the city over Sunday, he started out by himself to find the church, which he reached considerably behind time. Every seat was occupied; but the gentlemanly usher at once surrendered his own, and, stepping back, became much interested in watching the effect of the sermon upon the western orator. As Mr. Beecher developed his line of argument, Mr. Lincoln's body swayed forward, his lips parted, and he seemed at length entirely unconscious of his surroundings—frequently giving vent to his satisfaction, at a well-put point or illustration, with a kind of involuntary Indian exclamation—"*ugh!*"—not audible beyond his immediate presence, but very expressive! Mr. Lincoln henceforward had a profound admiration for the talents of the famous pastor of Plymouth Church. He once remarked to the Rev. Henry M. Field, of New York, that "he thought there was not upon record, in ancient or modern biography so productive a mind as had been exhibited in the career of Henry Ward Beecher!"

———:o:———

Lincoln's Love for Little Tad.

No matter who was with the President, or how intently absorbed, his little son Tad was always welcome. He almost always accompanied his father. Once on the way to Fortress Monroe, he became very troublesome. The President was much engaged in conversation with the party who accompanied him, and he at length said:

"Tad, if you will be a good boy, and not disturb me any more till we get to Fortress Monroe, I will give you a dollar.

The hope of reward was effectual for a while in securing silence, but, boy-like, Tad soon forgot his promise, and was as noisy as ever. Upon reaching their destination, however, he said, very promptly, "Father, I want my dollar."

Mr. Lincoln looked at him half reproachfully for an instant, and then taking from his pocket-book a dollar note, he said: "Well, my son, at any rate, I will keep my part of the bargain."

While paying a visit to Commodore Porter of Fortress Monroe, on one occasion, an incident occurred, subsequently related by Lieutenant Braine, one of the officers on board the flag-ship, to the Rev. Dr. Ewer, of New York. Noticing that the banks of the river were dotted with spring blossoms, the President said, with the manner of one asking a special favor:

"Commodore, Tad is very fond of flowers; won't you let a couple of your men take a boat and go with him for an hour or two along shore, and gather a few? It will be a great gratification to him."

———:o:———

Lincoln at the Five Points' House of Industry in New York.

When Mr. Lincoln visited New York in 1860, he felt a great interest in many of the institutions for reforming criminals and saving the young from a life of crime. Among others he visited, unattended, the Five Points House of Industry, and the superintendent of the Sabbath-school there gave the following account of the event:

"One Sunday morning I saw a tall, remarkable-looking man enter the room and take a seat among us. He listened with fixed attention to our exercises, and his couhtenance expressed such genuine interest that I approached him and suggested that he might be willing to say something to the children. He accepted the invitation with evident pleasure, and coming forward began a simple address, which at once fascinated every little hearer and hushed the room into silence. His language was strikingly beautiful, and his tones musical with in-intense feeling. The little faces would droop into sad conviction as he uttered sentences of warning, and would brighten into sunshine as he spoke cheerful words of promise. Once or twice he attempted to close his remarks, but the imperative shout of 'Go on! Oh, do go on!' would compel him to resume.

As I looked upon the gaunt and sinewy frame of the stranger, and marked his powerful head and determined features, now touched into softness by the impressions of the moment, I felt an irrepressible curiosity to learn something more about him, and while he was quietly leaving the room I begged to know his name. He courteously replied: 'It is Abraham Lincoln, from Illinois.'"

———:o:———

Lincoln and His New Hat.

Mr. G. B. Lincoln tells of an amusing circumstance which took place at Springfield soon after Mr. Lincoln's nomination in 1860. A hatter in Brooklyn secretly obtained the size of the future President's head, and made for him a very elegant hat, which he sent by his townsman, Lincoln, to Springfield. About the time it was presented, various other testimonials of a similar char-

character had come in from different sections. Mr. Lincoln took the hat, and after admiring its texture and workmanship, put it on his head and walked up to a looking-glass. Glancing from the reflection to Mrs. Lincoln he said, with a peculiar twinkle of his eye, "Well, wife, there is one thing likely to come out of this scrape, any how. We are going to have some new clothes!"

―――:o:―――

Lincoln's Failure as a Merchant—He, However, Six Years Later Pays the "National Debt."

It is interesting to recall the fact that at one time Mr. Lincoln seriously took into consideration the project of learning the blacksmith's trade. He was without means, and felt the immediate necessity of undertaking some business that would give him bread. It was while he was entertaining this project that an event occurred which in his undeterminded state of mind seemed to open a way to success in another quarter

A man named Reuben Radford, the keeper of a small store in the village of New Salem, had somehow incurred the displeasure of the Clary's Grove Boys, who had exercised their "regulating" derogatives by irregularly breaking his windows. William G. Greene, a friend of young Lincoln, riding by Radford's store soon afterward, was hailed by him, and told that he intended to sell out. Mr. Greene went into the store, and looking around offered him at random four hundred dollars for his stock. The offer was immediately accepted.

Lincoln happening in the next day, and being familiar with the value of the goods, Mr. Greene proposed to him to take an inventory of the stock, and see what sort of a bargain he had made. This he did, and it was found that the goods were worth six hundred dollars. Lincoln then made him an offer of a hundred and twenty-five dollars for his bargain, with the proposition that he and a man named Berry, as his partner, should take his (Greene's) place in the notes given to Radford. Mr. Greene agreed to the arrangement, but Radford declined it, except on condition that Greene would be their security, and this he at last assented to.

Berry proved to be a dissipated, trifling man, and the business soon became a wreck. Mr. Greene was obliged to go in and help Lincoln close it up, and not only do this but pay Radford's notes. All that young Lincoln won from the store was some very valuable experience, and the burden of a debt to Greene which, in conversations with the latter, he always spoke of as the national debt. But this national debt, unlike the majority of those which bear the title, was paid to the utmost farthing in after years.

Six years afterwards Mr. Greene, who knew nothing of the law in such cases, and had not troubled himself to inquire about it, and who had in the meantime removed to Tennessee, received notice from Mr. Lincoln that he was ready to pay him what he had paid for Berry —he (Lincoln) being legally bound to pay the liabilities of his partner.

Lincoln's Feat at the Washington Navy Yard With an Axe.

One afternoon during the summer of 1862, the President accompanied several gentlemen to the Washington

Navy Yard to witness some experiments with a newly-invented gun. Subsequently the party went aboard of one of the steamers lying at the wharf. A discussion was going on as to the merits of the invention, in the midst of which Mr. Lincoln caught sight of some axes hanging up outside of the cabin. Leaving the group, he quietly went forward, and taking one down, returned with it, and said:

"Gentlemen, you may talk about your 'Raphael repeaters' and 'eleven-inch Dahlgrens,' but here is an institution which I guess I understand better than either of you." With that he held the axe out at arm's length by the end of the handle, or "helve," as the wood-cutters call it—a feat not another person in the party could perform, though all made the attempt.

In such acts as this, showing that he neither forgot nor was ashamed of his humble origin, the good President exhibited his true nobility of character. He was a perfect illustration of his favorite poet's words:

"The rank is but the guinea's stamp,
The man's the gold, for a' that!"

———:o:———

An Amusing Illustration.

One of Mr. Lincoln's illustrations given by him on one occasion was that of a man who, in driving the hoops of a hogshead to "head" it up, was much annoyed by the constant falling in of the top. At length the bright idea struck him of putting his little boy inside to "hold it up." This he did; it never occurring to him till the job was done, how he was to get his child out. "This," said Lincoln, "is a fair sample of the way some people always do business."

LINCOLN'S FATHER'S MONUMENT, NEAR ROCKPORT, IND.

Funeral Services of Lincoln's Mother.—The Old Pastor and Young Abraham.

Several months after the death of Lincoln's mother, which occurred when he was but a few years old, child as he was, he wrote to Parson Elkin who had been their pastor when residing in Kentucky, begging him to come to Indiana and preach her funeral sermon.

This was asking a great favor of their former minister, for it would require him to ride on horseback a hundred miles through the wilderness; and it is something to be remembered to the humble itinerant's honor that he was willing to pay this tribute of respect to the woman who had so thoroughly honored him and his sacred office. He replied to Abraham's invitation that he would preach the sermon on a certain future Sunday, and gave him liberty to notify the neighbors of the promised service.

As the appointed day approached notice was given to the whole neighborhood, embracing every family within twenty miles. Neighbor carried the notice to neighbor. It was scattered from every little school. There was probably not a family that did not receive intelligence of the anxiously-anticipated event.

On a bright Sabbath morning the settlers of the region started for the cabin of the Lincolns, and as they gathered in they presented a picture worthy the pencil of the worthiest painter. Some came in carts of the rudest construction, their wheels consisting of sections of the huge boles of forest trees, and every other member the product of the axe and auger: some came on horseback, two or three upon a horse; others came in wagons drawn by oxen, and still others came on foot. Two hundred persons in all were assembled when Parson Elkin came out from the Lincoln cabin, accompanied by the little family, and proceeded to a tree under which the precious dust of a wife and mother were buried.

The congregation, seated upon stumps and logs around the grave, received the preacher and the mourning family in silence, broken only by the songs of birds, and the murmur of insects, or the creaking cart of some late comer. Taking his stand at the foot of the grave, Parson Elkin lifted his voice in prayer and sacred song, and then preached a sermon.

The occasion, the eager faces around him, and all the sweet influences of the morning, inspired him with an unusual fluency and fervor; and the flickering sunlight, as it glanced through the wind-parted leaves, caught many a tear upon the bronzed cheeks of his auditors, while father and son were overcome by the revival of their great grief. He spoke of the precious Christian woman who had gone with the warm praise which she deserved, and held her up as an example to true womanhood.

Those who knew the tender and reverent spirit of Abraham Lincoln later in life, will not doubt that he returned to his cabin-home deeply impressed by all that he had heard. It was the rounding up for him of the influences of a Christian mother's life and teachings. It recalled her sweet and patient example, her assiduous efforts to inspire him with pure and noble motives, her simple instructions in divine truth, her devoted love for him, and the motherly offices she had rendered him during all his tender years. His character was planted in this Christian mother's life. Its roots were fed by this Christian mother's love: and those that have wondered at the truthfulness and earnestness of his mature character have only to remember that the tree was true to the soil from which it sprung.

Not many years ago a monument was raised over Mrs. Nancy Lincoln's grave, and also over the grave of Abraham Lincoln's father, near Rockport, Ind.

———:o:———

Something Concerning Mr. Lincoln"s Religious Views.

The Rev. Mr. Willets, of Brooklyn, gives an account of a conversation with Mr. Lincoln, on the part of a lady of his acquaintance, connected with the "Christian Commission,", who in the prosecution of her duties had several interviews with him.

The President, it seemed, had been much impressed with the devotion and earnestness of purpose manifested by the lady, and on one occasion, after she had discharged the object of her visit, he said to her:

"Mrs. ———, I have formed a high opinion of your Christian character, and now, as we are alone, I have a mind to ask you to give me, in brief, your idea of what constitutes a true religious experience."

The lady replied at some length, stating that, in her judgment, it consisted of a conviction of one's own sinfulness and weakness, and personal need of the Saviour for strength and support; that views of mere doctrine might and would differ, but when one was really brought to feel his need of Divine help, and to seek the aid of the Holy Spirit for strength and guidance, it was satisfactory evidence of his having been born again. This was the substance of her reply.

When she had concluded Mr. Lincoln was very thoughtful for a few moments; He at length said, very earnestly: "If what you have told me is really a correct view of this great subject, I think I can say with sincerity that I hope I am a Christian. I had lived," he continued, "until my boy Willie died, without realizing fully these things. That blow overwhelmed me. It showed me my weakness as I had never felt it before, and if I can take what you have stated as a *test*, I think I can safely say that I know something of that *change* of which you speak; and I will further add, that it has been my intention for some time, at a suitable opportunity, to make a public religious profession."

———:o:———

Thurlow Weed's Recollections.

In a letter to the New York Lincoln Club, Thurlow Weed remarked; I went to the Whig National Convention, at Chicago, in 1860, warmly in favor of and confidently expecting the nomination of Governor Seward. That disappointment of long-cherished hopes was a bitter one. I then accepted, very reluctantly, an invitation to visit Mr. Lincoln at his residence in Springfield, where, in an interesting conversation, even while smarting under the sense of injustice to Mr. Seward, confidence in Mr. Lincoln's good sense, capacity and fidelity was inspired.

A campaign programme was agreed upon, and, returning to Albany, I went to work as zealously and as cheerfully as I should have done with Mr. Seward as our Presidential nominee. Mr. Lincoln's inauguration simultaneously inaugurated rebellion. Events soon proved that the Chicago Convention had been wisely if not providentially guided, The country in its greatest emergency had, what it so greatly needed, the services of two, instead of one, of its greatest and best men. With Lincoln as President and Seward as Secretary of State, the right men were in the right places.

With ample opportunities to study the character of Abraham Lincoln, I never hesitated in declaring that his sense of public and private duty and honor was as high and his patriotism as devoted as that of George Washington.

Their names and their memories should descend to future generations as examples worthy of imitation.

———:o:———

How Lincoln Took His Altitude—A Prophetic Bowl of Milk.

Soon after Mr. Lincoln's nomination for the Presidency, the Executive Chamber, a large fine room in the State House at Springfield was set apart for him, where he met the public until after his election.

As illustrative of the nature of many of his calls, the following brace of incidents were related to Mr. Holland by an eye witness: "Mr. Lincoln, being in conversation with a gentleman one day, two raw, plainly-dressed young 'Suckers' entered the room, and bashfully lingered near the door. As soon as he observed them, and apprehended their embarrassment, he rose and walked to them, saying, "How do you do, my good fellows ? What can I do for you ? Will you sit down ?" The spokesman of the pair, the shorter of the two, declined to sit, and explained the object of the call thus: he had had a talk about the relative height of Mr. Lincoln and his companion, and had asserted his belief that they were of exactly the same height. He had come in to verify his judgment. Mr. Lincoln smiled, went and got his cane, and, placing the end of it upon the wall, said:

"Here, yonng man, come under here."

The young man came under the cane, as Mr. Lincoln held it, and when it was perfectly adjusted to his height, Mr. Lincoln said:

"Now, come out, and hold up the cane."

This he did while Mr. Lincoln stepped under. Rubbing his head back and forth to see that it worked easily under the measurement, he stepped out, and declared to the sagacious fellow who was curiously looking on, that he had guessed with remarkable accuracy—that he and the young man were exactly the same height. Then he shook hands with them and sent them on their way. Mr. Lincoln would just as soon have thought of cutting off his right hand as he would have thought of turning those boys away with the impression that they had in any way insulted his dignity.

They had hardly disappeared when an old and modestly dressed woman made her appearance. She knew Mr. Lincoln, but Mr. Lincoln did not at first recognize her. Then she undertook to recall to his memory certain incidents connected with his rides upon the circuit—especially his dining at her house upon the road at different times. Then he remembered her and her home. Having fixed her own place in his recollection, she tried to recall to him a certain scanty dinner of bread and milk that he once ate at her house. He could not remember it—on the contrary, he only remembered that he had always fared well at her house.

"Well," said she, one day you came along after we had

got through dinner, and we had eaten up everything, and I could give you nothing but a bowl of bread and milk and you ate it; and when you got up you said it was good enough for the President of the United States !"

The good woman had come in from the country, making a journey of eight or ten miles, to relate to Mr. Lincoln this incident, which, in her mind, had doubtless taken the form of prophecy. Mr. Lincoln placed the honest creature at her ease, chatted with her of old times, and dismissed her in the most happy and complacent frame of mind.

———:o:———

How Lincoln Won the Nomination for Congress.

Old-time politicians, says a correspondent, will readily recall the heated political campaign of 1843 in the neighboring State of Illinois.

The chief interest of the campaign lay in the race for Congress in the Capital district, which was between Hardin—fiery, eloquent and impetuous Democrat, and Lincoln—plain, practical and ennobled Whig. The world knows the result. Lincoln was elected.

It is not so much with his election as with the manner in which he secured his nomination with which we have to deal. Before that ever-memorable spring Lincoln vacilated between the courts of Springfield, rated as a plain, honest, logical Whig, with no ambition higher politically than to occupy some good home office. Late in the fall 1842 his name began to be mentioned in connection with Congressional aspirations, which fact greatly annoyed the leaders of his political party, who had already selected as

258   LINCOLN'S STORIES AND SPEECHES.

the whig candidate, one Baker, afterward the gallant Colonel who fell so bravely and died such an honorable death on the battlefield of Ball's Bluff in 1842. Despite all efforts of his opponents within his party the name of the "gaunt rail-splitter" was hailed with acclaim by the

TRIUMPHAL ARCH.

masses, to whom he had endeared himself by his witticisms, honest tongue and quaint philosophy when on the stump or mingling with them in their homes.

The convention, which met in early spring in the city of Springfield, was to be composed of the usual number of delegates. The contest for the nomination was spirited and exciting.

A few weeks before the meeting of the convention the fact was found by the leaders that the advantage lay with Lincoln, and that unless they pulled some very fine wires nothing could save Baker.

They attempted to play the game that has so often won, by "convincing" delegates under instructions for Lincoln to violate them and vote for Baker. They had apparently succeeded.

"The plans of mice and men aft gang aglee;" so it was in this case. Two days before the convention Lincoln received an intimation of this, and late at night indited the following letter.

The letter was addressed to Martin Morris, who resides at Petersburg, an intimate friend of his, and by him circulated among those who were instructed for him at the county convention.

It had the desired effect. The convention met, the scheme of the conspiritors miscarried, Lincoln was nominated, made a vigorous canvass, and was triumphantly elected, thus paving the way for his more extended and brilliant conquests.

This letter, Lincoln has often told his friends, gave him ultimately the Chief Magistracy of the nation. He has also said that had he been beaten before the convention he would have been forever obscured. The following is a verbatim copy of the epistle:

"APRIL 14, 1843.

Friend Morris: I have heard it intimated that Baker is trying to get you or Miles, or both of you, to violate the instructions of the meeting that appointed you, and to go for him. I have insisted, and still insist, that this cannot be true.

Surely Baker would not do the like. As well might Hardin ask me to vote for him in the convention.

Again, it is said there will be an attempt to get up instructions in your county requiring you to go for Baker. This is all wrong. Upon the same rule why might I not fly from the decision against me in Sangamon and get up instructions to their delegates to go for me. There are at least 1,200 Whigs in the county that took no part, and yet I would as soon stick my head in the fire as to attempt it.

Besides, if any one should get the nomination by such extraordinary means, all harmony in the district would inevitably be lost. Honest Whigs (and very nearly all of them are honest), would not quietly abide such enormities.

I repeat, such an attempt on Baker's part cannot be true. Write me at Springfield how the matter is. Don't show or speak of this letter.

A. LINCOLN."

Mr. Morris did show the letter, and Mr. Lincoln always thanked his stars that he did.

Old Relics.

The following is a copy of an autograph letter of Abraham Lincoln which was received by Capt. A. H. Parker, President of the Englewood Soldiers' Memorial Association, from W. H. Herndon, former law partner of President Lincoln.

SPRINGFIELD, ILL., Oct. 10, 1860.

Dear William: I cannot give you details, but it is entirely certain that Pennsylvania and Indiana have gone Republican very largely. Penn. 25,000, & Ia. 5 to 10,-000. Ohio of course is safe.

Yours as ever, A. LINCOLN,

Accampanying the above is a leaf from Mr. Lincoln's boy copy-book. The two relics are explained in full by a letter from Mr. Herndon to Capt. Parker, of which the following is a copy:

SPRINGFIELD, ILL., Nov. 9, 1881.

Mr. Parker—My Dear Sir: Enclosed is a genuine let-

[The original Fort Dearborn, as built in 1804.]

ter from Lincoln, addressed to myself, dated the 10th day of October, 1860, a few days before Mr. Lincoln's election to the Presidency.

The history of the letter is as follows:

I was in Petersburg on the day the letter is dated, and in the evening, say at 7 o'clock, I was speaking to a large audience in the court-house urging Lincoln's election. I had spoken about thirty minutes when a runner handed me a letter, and I opened it in dead silence, thinking possibly that bad news had come to me, possibly Lincoln's defeat.

However, the dead silence was soon broken by the reading of the letter, first to myself and then aloud, as loud as I could, and then there went up such yells, huzzas, such noise, such banging and thumping as were never heard in that house of justice before. The joy of the crowd, the noise of the yells, etc., were more eloquent than I was, and I got off the stand and quit my jabber in the presence of the general joy.

When Lincoln wrote the letter he knew that he was elected to the Presidential chair. He must have been grateful to the people and happy. I can see his feelings in his handwriting; he trembled a little, was full of emotion, joy and happiness.

I hate to part with this letter. It is the last one I have, and no money could get it. I willingly give it to you for the purposes it is given—namely: to the Soldiers' Memorial Association of Englewood, Ill., and its uses, etc., etc. To me there is a long history in the letter and its glorious recollections.

Again, I send you a leaf of Mr. Lincoln's boy copybook—a book in which Mr. Lincoln put down his arithmetical sums worked out.

I was collecting the facts of Mr. Lincoln's life in 1865-6 and went into Coles County, Illinois, to see his stepmother; found the motherly, good old lady, and took down the testimony, etc., as material of his life, etc.

During her examination she let drop in her conversation the fact that Mr. Lincoln when a boy had two copybooks in which he set down the sums worked out, and wrote out in his literary one what seemed strong, beautiful or good. We, the Lincoln family and myself, commenced the search and found the arithmetical book, but not the other; it is gone, and gone forever.

I willingly send you a leaf of said copybook for the uses and purposes above, and for no other. I say this of the letter and the leaf. I would not spare them under any other consideration. God bless the soldier and his friends.

To keep the pieces, get two glasses and put the letter between them; have it framed, and the letter thus framed will last for ages hung on the wall.

To keep the leaf and letter, get two glasses, say 6x7 inches for the latter, and 10x12 for the leaf—clean and clear glass like perfect window glass—put the paper and the leaf between the two glasses, hang up in the hall, and it will last for ages; keep a watch out that too much light does not exhaust the ink; dry it out or up, etc.

Hurriedly your friend,
W. H. HERNDON.

How Lincoln Won a Case from his Partner—Laughable Toilet Ignorance.

While Judge Logan, of Springfield, Ill., was Lincoln's partner, two farmers, who had a misunderstanding respecting a horse trade, went to law. By mutual consent the partners in law became antagonists in this case On the day of the trial Mr. Logan, having bought a new shirt, open in the back, with a huge standing collar, dressed himself in extreme haste, and put on the shirt with the bosom at the back, a linen coat concealing the blunder. He dazed the jury with his knowledge of "horse points" and as the day was sultry, took off his coat and summed up in his shirt-sleeves.

Lincoln, sitting behind him, took in the situation, and when his turn came, remarked to the jury:

"Gentlemen, Mr. Logan has been trying for over an hour to make you believe he knows more about a horse than these honest old farmers who are witnesses. He

has quoted largely from his 'horse doctor,' and now, gentlemen, I submit to you, (here he lifted Logan out of his chair, and turned him with his back to the jury and the crowd, at the same time flipping up the enormous standing collar) what dependence can you place in his horse knowledge when he has not sense enough to put on his shirt?"

The roars of laughter that greeted this exhibition, and the verdict that Lincoln got soon after, gave Logan a permanent prejudice against "bosom shirts."

———:o:———

Lincoln's Life as Written by Himself—The Whole Thing in a Nut Shell.

The compiler of the "Dictionary of Congress" states that while preparing the work for publication in 1858, he sent to Mr. Lincoln the usual request for a sketch of his life, and received the following reply:

Born February 12, 1809, in Hardin, County, Kentucky."

"Education Defective." "Profession a Lawyer." "Have been a Captain of Volunteers in Black Hawk War." "Postmaster at a very small office." "Four times a member of the Illinois Legislature, and was a member of the Lower House of Congress.

Yours, etc.,
"A. LINCOLN."

———:o:———

Lincoln as a Lover.

A writer to the Springfield Republican gives the following exceedingly interesting account of the early loves of Abraham Lincoln:

The death of Mrs. Lincoln at the home of that sister

where she was first met and courted by her future husband, closes the family life of the great President.

She was not his first or his deepest love. That distinction belongs to Ann Rutledge, whose father was the founder of New Salem, on the Sangamon, a village which is now deserted.

Rutledge was one of the famous South Carolina families, and his daughter, four years younger than Lincoln, seems to have impressed the whole community as a lovely and refined girl, unaffected, "a blonde in complexion, with golden hair, cherry-red lips, and a bonny blue eye," says McNamara.

McNamara was the lover who first won her heart. He went to New York to take West his parents, but was detained some years in New York. In the meantime Lincoln pressed his suit, and the girl's parents doubted whether McNamara would ever come back; she gave her love to Lincoln, but insisted on waiting for a formal release from McNamara before marriage. The waiting told upon her sensitive organism, her health declined, and she died of what was called brain fever on August 25, 1835.

This was the great grief of Lincoln's youth. His reason was unsettled and his friend, Bowlin Greene, had to take him off to a lonely log cabin and keep him until he recovered his sanity. Then was when he learned the poem beginning:

"Oh, why should the spirit of mortal be proud?"

An old friend who asked him after his election to the Presidency if it was true that he loved and courted Ann Rutledge, got this reply:

"It is true—true; indeed I did. I have loved the name

of Rutledge to this day. It was my first. I loved the woman dearly. She was a handsome girl; would have made a good, loving wife; was natural and quite intellectual, though not highly educated. I did honestly and truly love the girl, and think often, often of her now."

McNamara returned soon after her death, lived near the little .burying ground. and in 1866 pointed out the grave of Ann Rutledge to Mr. Herndon. This affair had a marked effect upon Lincoln's life, and added to its somber tone; but it probably had also a deeper meaning in purifying and ennobling his inner nature

Mr. Lincoln, who by this time was a member of the legislature, and about 27, next "paid attentions" to a Miss Owens, a smart young woman of some avoirdupois, who once told him that she thought he was "lacking in the smaller attentions, those little links which made up the great chain of woman's happiness," because he dangled along by her side once when they were going up a hill, and allowed her friend, Mrs. Bowlin Greene, to "carry a big, fat child, and crossly disposed," up the hill.

A still more untoward incident happened once at Mrs. Able's, a sister of Miss Owens. Lincoln had sent word to Able's that he was coming down to see Miss Owens. She, girl fashion, to test her lover, went off "to Graham's," about a mile and a half. When Lincoln came and was so informed, he asked if Miss Owens did not know he was coming.

Mrs. Able said no, but one of her *enfantes terribles* promptly replied:

"Yes, ma, she did, for I heard Sam tell her so."

"Lincoln sat awhile and then went about his business," says Lamon's account. Letters exist from Lincoln to Miss Owens in 1836 and 1839, in one of which he says:

"If you feel yourself in any degree bound to me, I am now willing to release you, provided you wish it; while, on the other hand, I am willing and even anxious to bind you faster, if I can be convinced that it will, in any considerable degree, add to your happiness. Nothing would make me more miserable than to believe you miserable —nothing more happy than to know you were so."

This is the language of an honorable man, a cool lover, and a practiced hand in the English language. Miss Owens lived to marry another man at her home in Kentucky, and have two sons in the rebel army.

Lamon prints also a letter of Lincoln to Mrs. O. H. Browning, in 1838, reviewing this affair in terms, it must be confessed, brutally derogatory to the young woman's personal appearance and parts. Lamon speaks of its defective spelling, but there are only one or two misspelled words in it, and these, likely enough, by accident. Lincoln was evidently mortified by his rejection and ignobly attempted to represent to Mrs. Browning (the wife of his new-found legislative friend), that the object of his affections had been unworthy of them.

It was not two years (1839) before another Springfield

matron, Mrs Ninian W. Edwards, had a Kentucky sister to live with her, Mary Todd, daughter of Robert S. Todd, of Lexington. Miss Todd was of distinguished family in both States, her mother had died young, and she had been educated by "a French lady." She had a keen sense of the ridiculous, was sharp, ambitious, high-tempered; according to Lamon, "high-bred, proud, brilliant, witty, and with a will that bent everyone else to her purpose, she took Lincoln captive the moment she considered it expedient to do so.

She was ambitious to be the wife of a president, and was courted by Douglas until she dismissed him for his bad morals. She said of one of her mates who had married a wealthy old gentleman, "I would rather marry a good man, a man of mind, with hope and bright prospects ahead for position, fame and power, than to marry all the horses, gold and bones in the world."

Lincoln and Miss Todd became engaged, though a pretty sister of Edwards, came near shipwrecking this match.

Pretty girls must have been distressingly thick in those days, when Kentucky was sending her best blood into Illinois. Lincoln felt the Edwards attachment so strongly that he begged to be released by Miss Todd (the Edwards girl married another man, for Lincoln never mentioned it to her), and he "ran off the track" again, to use the expression by which he once described his attack of insanity.

He was "crazy as a loon" for nearly a year, and did not attend the session of the legislature of 1841-42, to which he had been chosen. They had to keep knives and razors away from him. As he came out of it, the Edwards' advised Abe and Mary not to marry, as they were unfitted to each other, and probably in consequence of that advice they—went and married on "one or two hours' notice."

Lincoln said to Matheney, who made out the license, "Jim, I shall have to marry that girl," and he "looked as if he was going to the slaughter," and said he was "driven into it" by the Edwards family. But, perhaps, these expressions ought not to be taken too seriously.

Lamon prints letters from Lincoln to Speed earlier in the year, indicating his embarrassing position, and his "great agony," as Lamon calls it.

The "Shield's duel" was fought a month or two before the marriage, and was occasioned by Miss Todd's satirical sketches in The Sangamon Journal. These sketches were dated from the "Lost Township," a humorous expression of indefiniteness of locality which had a local point, and were written in vernacular and signed "Rebecca." The last one was in verse and signed "Cathleon,"

That Miss Todd was no green Western girl is evinced

by the spirit of these sketches of local life, which are reproduced in "Lamon's Life of Lincoln." She teased Shields in them, and he demanded to know the author. Lincoln accepted the responsibility.

―――:o:―――

Didn't Know His Own House—How Mrs. Lincoln Surprised Her Husband.

A funny story is told of how Mrs. Lincoln made a little surprise for her husband.

In the early days it was customary for lawyers to go from one county to another on horseback, a journey which often required several weeks. On returning from one of these jaunts, late one night, Mr. Lincoln dismounted from his horse at the familiar corner and then turned to go into the house, but stopped; a perfectly unknown structure was before him. Surprised, and thinking there must be some mistake, he went across the way and knocked at a neighbor's door. The family had retired and so called out:

"Who's there?"

"Abe Lincoln," was the reply. "I am looking for my house. I thought it was across the way, but when I went away, a few weeks ago, there was only a one-story house there, and now there is two. I think I must be lost."

The neighbors then explained that Mrs. Lincoln had added another story during his absence. And Mr. Lincoln laughed and went to his remodeled house.

―――:o:―――

Lincoln's Foster-Mother—Her Romantic Marriage to Thomas Lincoln.

Abraham Lincoln was 7 or 8 years old when his father, Thomas Lincoln, removed from Kentucky to Indiana, where, in a year or two, his wife died. The year following her death, says a writer in the Christain Union, Mr. Lincoln returned to Elizabethtown to search out, if possible, a former neighbor and friend, Mrs. Sally Johnston, whom, upon inquiry, he found still a widow, and to whom he at once made a proposal of marriage.

On entering Mrs. Johnston's humble dwelling, Mr. Lincoln asked if she remembered him.

"Yes," said she, "I remember you very well, Tommy Lincoln. What has brought you back to old Kentucky?"

"Well," he said in answer, "my wife, Nancy, is dead."

"Why, you don't say so!"

"Yes," said Mr. Lincoln, "she died more than a year ago, and I have come back to Kentucky to look for another wife. Do you like me, Mrs. Johnston¿"

"Yes," replied Mrs. Johnston, "I like you Tommy Lincoln."

"Do yo like me well enough to marry me?"

"Yes," she said, "I like you, Tommy Lincoln, and I like you well enough to marry you, but I can't marry you now."

"Why not?" said he.

"Because I am in debt, and I could never think of burdening the man I marry with debt; it would not be right."

"What are those debts?" said he.

THE LINCOLN FAMILY REMOVING FROM KENTUCKY TO INDIANA IN 1816.

She told him of the sums, "Which," said she, "I have all down here in my account book."

On looking it over, he saw that her debts ranged from fifty cents to a dollar and a quarter, and amounted in the gross to something less than twelve dollars; not a very startling thing even in those days of small things.

He succeeded in putting the little book into his coat pocket without attracting her attention, and went out, looked up the various parties, and paid off all the little sums according to the memorandum, and returned in the afternoon with the acknowledgments of payments in full. On his returning the account book to her, she exclaimed:

"Why, Tommy Lincoln, have you gone and paid off all my debts?"

"Yes," he said, "and you will marry me now?"

"Yes," said she, and they were married the next morning at 9 o'clock. Mr. Haycraft, the narrator of the story, was present at the ceremony.

———:o:———

Little Lincoln Stories.

AN old Englishman who resided in Springfield, Ill., hearing the result of the Political Convention at Chicago, could not contain his astonishment. "What!" said he, "Abe Lincoln nominated for President of the United States? Can it be possible! A man that buys a ten-cent beefsteak for his breakfast, and carries it home himself!"

MR. LINCOLN being asked by a friend how he felt when the returns came in that insured his defeat, replied that "he felt, he supposed, very much like the stripling who had stumped his toe; too badly to laugh and too big to cry."

A YOUNG man bred in Springfield speaks of a vision that has clung to his memory very vividly, of Mr. Lincoln as he appeared in those days. His way to school led by the lawyer's door. On almost any fair summer morning, he could find Mr. Lincoln on the sidewalk, in front of his house, drawing a child back and forth, in a baby carriage.

In the old country church near the Lincoln place, near Rockport, Indiana, is a pulpit which was made by Abe Llncoln and his father. There is a book case in the Evansville Custom House made by the same carpenters and taken there for preservation. Near where the old house stood is a dilapidated corn crib with a rail floor, the rails for which were split by young Lincoln.

In South Starksboro, Addison County, Vt., says the Burlington Free Press, there are residing triplets, sons of Leonard Haskins, born May 24, 1864, and named by President Lincoln. They have in their hand a letter from the martyr-President, and the names given were Abraham Lincoln, Gideon Welles and Simon Cameron. They are the ehildren of American parents.

Mr. Lincoln never made his profession lucrative to himself. It was very difficult for him to charge a heavy fee to anybody, and still more difficult for him to charge his friends anything at all for his professional services. To a poor client, he was as apt to give money as to take it from him. He never encouraged the spirit of litigation. Henry McHenry, one of his old clients, says that he went to Mr. Lincoln with a case to prosecute, and that Mr. Lincoln refused to have anything to do with it, because he was not strictly in the right. "You can give the other party a great deal of trouble," said the lawyer, "and perhaps beat him, but you had better let the suit alone."

In one of Lincoln's early speeches against slavery he said: "My distinguished friend, Stephen A. Douglas, says, it is an insult to the emigrants to Kansas and Nebraska to suppose they are not able to govern themselves. We must not slur over an argument of this kind because it happens to tickle the ear. It must be met and answered. I admit that the emigrant to Kansas and Nebraska is competent to govern himself, but (the speak-

er rising to his full height), *I deny his right to govern any other person without that person's consent,"* That touched the very marrow of the matter, and revealed the whole difference between Lincoln and Douglas.

An old gentleman in Rockport, near the early home of the Lincoln's in Indiana, lives to tell of the last time he saw Lincoln. He was visiting the Lincoln homestead, and as he was coming away they found a trespassing cow hanging about the gate. The cow had given the Lincolns much annoyance by entering their garden and committing depredations. Young Abe was dressed in a suit of jeans, without any coat, as it was summer time, and on his head he wore a broad-brimmed white straw hat, part of which was cracked and broken. Finding the cow standing hypocritically meek at the gate, young Abe leaped astride of her back, and, digging his bare heels into her sides, the astonished animal broke away down the road in a lumbering gallop. "The last I saw of Abe

Lincoln," the old gentleman relates fondly, "he was swinging his hat, shouting at the top of his voice, galloping down the road on that thunderstruck cow."

FROM the original manuscript of one of Mr. Lincoln's speeches, these words were transferred: "Twenty-two years ago, Judge Douglas and I first became acquainted. We were both young then—he a trifle younger than I. Even then we were both ambitious,—I, perhaps, quite as much so as he. With me, the race of ambition has been a failure—a flat failure; with him, it has been one of splendid success. His name fills the nation, and is not unknown even in foreign lands. I affect no contempt for the high eminence he has reached. So reached that the oppressed of my species might have shared with me in the elevation, I would rather stand on that eminence than wear the richest crown that ever pressed a monarch's brow.

———:o:———

Lincoln's Last Story and Last Written Words and Conversation.

The last story written by Mr. Lincoln was drawn out by a circumstance which occurred just before the interview with Messrs. Colfax and Ashmun, on the evening of the assassination.

Marshal Lamon, of Washington, had called upon him with an application for the pardon of a soldier. After a brief hearing the President took the application, and, when about to write his name upon the back of it he looked up and said:

"Lamon, have you ever heard how the Patagonians eat oysters? They open them and throw the shells out of the window until the pile gets higher than the house, and then they move;" adding:

"I feel to-day like commencing a new pile of pardons, and I may as well begin it just here."

At the subsequent interview with Messrs. Colfax and Ashmun, Mr. Lincoln was in high spirits. The uneasiness felt by his friends during his visit to Richmond was dwelt upon, when he sportively replied that "he supposed he should have been uneasy also, had any other man been President and gone there; but as it was he felt no apprehension of danger whatever." Turning to speaker Colfax, he said:

"Sumner has the 'gavel' of the Confederate Congress, which he got at Richmoud, and intended giving it to the Secretary of War, but I insisted he must give it to you, and you tell him from me to hand it over."

Mr. Ashmun, who was the presiding officer of the Chicago Convention in 1860, alluded to the "gavel" used on that occasion, saying he had preserved it as a valuable memento.

Mr. Ashmun then referred to a matter of business connected with a cotton claim, preferred by a client of his, and said that he desired to have a "commission appointed to examine and decide upon the merits of the case. Mr. Lincoln replied, with a considerable warmth of manner:

"I have done with 'commissions.' I believe they are contrivances to cheat the Government out of every pound of cotton they can lay their hands on."

Mr. Ashmun's face flushed, and he replied that he hoped the President meant no personal imputation.

Mr. Lincoln saw that he had wounded his friend, and he instantly replied:

"You do not understand me, Ashmun. I did not mean what you inferred. I take it all back."

Subsequently he said:

"I apoligize to you, Ashmun."

He then engaged to see Mr. Ashmun early the next morning, and, taking a card, he wrote:

"Allow Mr, Asmun and friend to come in at 9 A. M. to-morrow.

A. LINCOLN."

These were his last written words. Turning to Mr. Colfax, he said:

"You will accompany Mrs. Lincoln and me to the theater, I hope?"

Mr. Colfax pleaded other engagements—expecting to start on his Pacific trip the next morning. The party passed out on the portico together, the President saying at the very last:

"Colfax, don't forget to tell the people of the mining regions what I told you about the development when peace comes;" and then shaking hands with both gentlemen, he followed Mrs. Lincoln into the carriage, leaning forward at the last moment, to say as they were driven off, "I will telegraph you, Colfax, at San Francisco,"— passing thus forth for the last time from under that roof into the creeping shadows which were to settle before another dawn into a funeral pall upon the orphaned heart of the nation.

———:o:———

Abraham Lincoln's Death — Walt Whitman's Vivid Description of the Scene at Ford's Theater.

The day (April 14, 1865) seems to have been a pleasant one throughout the whole land—the moral atmosphere pleasant, too— the long storm, so dark, so fratricidal, full of blood and doubt and gloom, over and ended at last by the sunrise of such an absolute National victory, and utter breaking down of secessionism—we almost doubted our senses! Lee had capitulated beneath the apple tree at Appommatox. The other armies, the flanges of the revolt, swiftly followed.

And could it really be, then? Out of all the affairs of this world of woe and passion, of failure and disorder and dismay, was there really come the confirmed, unerring sign of peace, like a shaft of pure light—of rightful rule—of God?

But I must not dwell on assessories. The deed hastens. The popular afternoon paper, the little Evening Star, had scattered all over its third page, divided among the advertisements in a sensational manner in a hundred different places:

"The President and his lady will be at the theater this evening."

Lincoln was fond of the theater. I have myself seen him there several times. I remember thinking how funny it was that he, in some respects the leading actor in greatest and stormiest drama known to real history's stage, through centuries, should sit there and be so completely interested in those human jack-straws, moving about with their silly little gestures, foreign spirit, and flatulent text.

So the day, as I say, was propitious. Early herbage, early flowers, were out. I remember where I was stopping at the time, the season being advanced, there were many lilacs in full bloom. By one of those caprices that enter and give tinge to events without being a part at all of them, I find myself always reminded of the great tragedy of this day by the sight and odor of these blossoms. It never fails.

On this occasion the theater was crowded, many ladies in rich and gay costumes, officers in their uniforms, many well-known citizens, young folks, the usual clusters of gas.lights, the usual magnetism of so many people, cheerfull with perfumes, music of violins and flutes—and over all, that saturating, that vast, vague wonder, Victory, the Nation's victory, the triumph of the Union, filling the air, the thought, the sense, with exhiliration more than all perfumes.

The President came betimes, and, with his wife, witnessed the play, from the large stage boxes of the second tier, two thrown into one, and profusely draped with the

National flag. The acts and scenes of the piece—one of those singularly witless compositions which have at least the merit of giving entire relief to an audience engaged in mental action or business excitements and cares during the day, as it makes not the slightest call on either the moral, emotional, esthetic or spiritual nature—a piece ("Our American Cousin") in which, among other characters so called. a Yankee, certainly such a one as was never seen, or at least like it ever seen in North America, is introduced in England, with a varied fol-de-rol of talk, plot, scenery, and such phantasmagoria as goes to make up a modern popular drama—had progressed through perhaps a couple of its acts, when in the midst of this comedy, or tragedy, or non-such, or whatever it is to be called, and to offset it, or finish it out, as if in Nature's and the Great Muse's mockery of these poor mimies, comes interpolated that scene, not really or exactly to be described at all (for on the many hundreds who were there it seems to this hour to have left little but a passing blur, a dream, a blotch)—and yet partially described as I now proceed to give it:

There is a scene in the play representing the modern parlor, in which two unprecedented ladies are informed by the unprecedented and impossible Yankee that he is not a man of fortune, and therefore undesirable for marriage catching purposes; after which, the comments being finished, the dramatic trio make exit, leaving the stage clear for a moment.

There was a pause, a hush, as it were. At this period came the death of Abraham Lincoln.

Great as that was, with all it manifold train circling around it, and stretching into the future for many a century, in the politics, history, art, etc., of the New World in point of fact, the main thing, the actual murder, transpired with the quiet and simplicity of any commonest occurrence—the bursting of a bud or pod in the growth of vegetation, for instance.

Through the general hum followiug the stage pause, with the change of positions, etc., came the muffled sound of a pistol shot, which not one-hundredth part of the audience heard at the time—and yet a moment's hush—somehow, surely a vague, startled thrill—and then, through the ornamented, drapereied, starred, and striped space-way of the President's box, a sudden figure, a man, raises himself with hands and feet, stands a moment on the railing, leaps below to the stage (a distance perhaps of 14 or 15 feet), falls out of position catching his boot-heel in the copious drapery (the American flag), falls on one knee, quickly recovers himself, rises as if nothing had happened (he really sprains his ankle, but unfelt then)—and the figure, Booth, the murderer, dressed in plain, black broadcloth, bare-headed, with a full head of glossy, raven hair, and his eyes, like some mad animal's flashing with light and resolution, yet with a certain strange calmness, holds aloft in one hand a large knife—walks along not much back of the foot-lights —turns fully towards the audience his face of statuesque beauty, lit by those basilisk eyes, flashing with desperation, perhaps insanity—launches out in a firm and steady voice the words *Sic Semper Tyrannis*—and then walks with neither slow nor very rapid pace diagonally across to the back of the stage, and disappears.

(Had not all this terrible scene—making the mimic

ones preposterous—had it not all been rehearshed, in blank, by Booth, beforehand?)

A moment's hush, incredulous—a scream—a cry of murder—Mrs. Lincoln leaning out of the box, with ashy cheeks and lips, with involuntary cry, pointing to the retreating figure, "He has killed the President."

And still a moment's strange, incredulous suspense—and then the deluge!—then that mixture of horror, noises, uncertainty—(the sound, somewhere back, of a horse's hoofs clattering with speed) the people burst through chairs and railings, and break them up—that noise adds to the queerness of the scene—there is extricable confusion and terror—women faint—quite feeble persons fall, and are trampled on—many cries of agony are heard—the broad stage suddenly fills to suffocation with a dense and motley crowd, like some horrible carnival—the audience rush generally upon it—at least the strong men do—the actors and actresses are there in their play costumes and painted faces, with moral fright showing through the rouge—some trembling, some in tears—the screams and calls, confused talk—redoubled, trebled—two or three manage to pass up water from the stage to the President's box, others try to clamber up, etc., etc,

In the midst of all this the soldiers of the President's Guard, with others, suddenly drawn to the scene, burst in—some 200 altogether—they storm the house, through all the tiers, especially the upper ones—inflamed with fury, literally charging the audience with fixed bayonets, muskets and pistols, shouting "Clear out! clear out! you sons of b——!"

Such the wild scene, or a suggestion of it rather, inside the play house that night.

Outside, too, in the atmosphere of shock and craze, crowds of people, filled with frenzy, ready to seize any outlet for it, came near committing murder several times on innocent individuals.

One such case was particularly exciting. The infuriated crowd, through some chance, got started against one man, either for words he uttered, or perhaps without any cause at all, and were proceeding to hang him at once to a neighboring lamp-post, when he was rescued by a few heroic policemen, who placed him in their midst and fought their way slowly and amid great peril toward the station house.

It was a fitting episode of the whole affair. The crowd rushing and eddying to and fro, the night, the yells, the pale faces, many frightened people trying in vain to extricate themselves, the attacked man, not yet freed from the jaws of death, looking like a corpse; the silent, resolute half-dozen policemen, with no weapons but their little clubs; yet stern and steady through all those eddying swarms; made indeed a fitting side scene to the grand tragedy of the murder. They gained the station house with the protected man, whom they placed in security for the night, and discharged him in the morning.

And in the midst of that night pandemonium of senseless hate, infuriated soldiers, the audience and the crowd—the stage, and all its actors and actresses, its paint pots, spangles and gas-light—the life-blood from those veins, the best and sweetest of the land, drips slowly

[Mr. Lincoln was removed from the theater to this adjacent building where he soon passed away.]

down, and death's ooze already begins its little bubbles on the lips.

Such, hurriedly sketched, were the accompaniments of the death of President Lincoln. So suddenly, and in murder and horror unsurpassed, he was taken from us. But his death was painless.

———:o:———

LINCOLN'S FAVORITE POEM.

Oh! Why Should the Spirit of Mortal be Proud?

The evening of March 22nd, 1864, says F. B. Carpenter, was a most interesting one to me. I was with the President alone in his office for several hours. Busy with pen and papers when I went in, he presently threw them aside and commenced talking to me of Shakspeare, of whom he was very fond. Little "Tad," his son, coming in, he sent him to the library for a copy of the plays, and then read to me several of his favorite passages. Relapsing into a sadder strain, he laid the book aside, and leaning back in his chair, said:

"There is a poem which has been a great favorite with me for years, which was first shown to me when a young man by a friend, and which I afterwards saw and cut from a newspaper and learned by heart. I would," he continued, "give a great deal to know who wrote it, but I have never been able to ascertain." Then, half-closing his eyes, be repeated the verses to me, as follows:

Oh! why should the spirit of mortal be proud?—
Like a swift-fleeting meteor, a fast-flying cloud,
A flash of the lightning, a break of the wave,
He passeth from life to his rest in the grave.

The leaves of the oak and the willow shall fade,
Be scattered around, and together be laid;
And the young and the old, and the low and the high,
Shall moulder to dust, and together shall lie.

The infant a mother attended and loved;
The mother, that infant's affection who proved,
The husband, that mother and infant who blessed—
Each, all, are away to their dwellings of rest.

The maid on whose cheek, on whose brow, in whose eye,
Shone beauty and pleasure—her triumphs are by;
And the memory of those who loved her and praised,
Are alike from the minds of the living erased.

The hand of the king, that the sceptre hath borne,
The brow of the priest, that the mitre hath worn,
The eye of the sage, and the heart of the brave,
Are hidden and lost in the depths of the grave.

The peasant, whose lot was to sow and to reap,
The herdsman, who climbed with his goats up the steep,
The beggar, who wandered in search of his bread,
Have faded away like the grass that we tread.

The saint, who enjoyed the communion of heaven,
The sinner, who dared to remain unforgiven,
The wise and the foolish, the guilty and just,
Have quietly mingled their bones in the dust.

So the multitude goes—like the flower or the weed,
That withers away to let others succeed;
So the multitude comes—even those we behold,
To repeat every tale that has often been told:

For we are the same our fathers have been;
We see the same sights our fathers have seen;
We drink the same stream, we view the same sun,
And run the same course our fathers have run.

The thoughts we are thinking, our fathers would think;
From the death we are shrinking, our fathers would shrink;
To the life we are clinging, they also would cling—
But it speeds from us all like a bird on the wing.

The loved—but the story we cannot unfold;
They scorned—but the heart of the haughty is cold;
They grieved—but no wail from their slumber will come;
They joyed—but the tongue of their gladness is dumb.

They died—aye, they died—and we things that are now,
That walk on the turf that lies o'er their brow,
And make in their dwellings a transient abode,
Meet the things that they met on ther pilgrimage road.

Yea! hope and despondency, pleasure and pain,
Are mingled together in sunshine and rain;
And the smile and the tear, the song and the dirge,
Still follow each other, like surge upon surge.

'Tis the wink of an eye,—'tis the draught of a breath;
From the blossom of health to the paleness of death,
From the gilded saloon to the bier and the shroud:—
Oh! why should the spirit of mortal be proud?

[This poem was written by Wm. Knox, a Scotchman.]

LINCOLN'S SPEECHES.

1832—1865.

CHRONOLOGICALLY ARRANGED.

LINCOLN'S FIRST POLITICAL SPEECH.

Mr. Lincoln made his first political speech in 1832, at the age of twenty-three, when he was a candidate for the Illinois Legislature. His opponent had wearied the audience by a long speech, leaving him but a short time in which to present his views. He condensed all he had to say into a few words, as follows:

"GENTLEMEN, FELLOW-CITIZENS:—I presume you know who I am. I am humble Abraham Lincoln. I have been solicited by my friends to become a candidate for the legislature. My politics can be briefly stated. I am in favor of the Internal Improvement system, and a High Protective Tariff. These are my sentiments and political principles. If elected, I shall be thankful. If not, it will be all the same.

MONUMENT OF ABRAHAM LINCOLN AT LINCOLN PARK.

SHOWING HIS HAND.

Delivered at New Salem, Ill., June 13, 1836, to the voters of Sangamon County, Ill., after being called upon to "show his hand."

FELLOW CITIZENS:—The candidates are called upon, I see, to show their hands. Here is mine. I go for all sharing the privileges of government who assist in bearing its burdens. Consequently, I go for admitting all the whites to the right of suffrage who pay taxes or bear arms, by no means excluding the females.

If elected, I shall consider the whole people of Sangamon County my constituents, as well those who oppose as those who support me.

While acting as their Representative, I shall be governed by their will on all subjects upon which I have the means of knowing what their will is, and upon all others I shall do what my judgment tells me will best advance their interests.

Whether elected or not, I go for distributing the proceeds of the sales of the public lands to the several States, to enable our State, in common with others, to dig canals and construct railroads without borrowing money and paying the interest on it.

If alive on the first day in November, I shall vote for Hugh L. White for President.

FORQUER'S LIGHTNING ROD IS STRUCK.

Lincoln's opponent for the Legislature in 1836 was the Hon. George Forquer, of Springfield, Ill., wno was celebrated for having "changed his coat" politically, and as having introduced the first and only lightning-rod in Springfield at this time. He said in a speech in Lincoln's presence, "this young man would have to be taken down, and I am sorry the task devolves upon me;" and then proceeded to try and "take him down." Mr. Lincoln made a reply, and in closing, turned to the crowd and made these remarks:

FELLOW-CITIZENS:—It is for you, not for me, to say whether I am up or down. The gentleman has alluded to my being a young man; I am older in years than I am in the tricks and trades of politicians. I desire to live, and I desire place and distinction as a politician; but I would rather die now than, like the gentleman, live to see the day that I would have to erect a lightning rod to protect a guilty conscience from an offended God!

THE PERPETUITY OF OUR FREE INSTITUTIONS.

Delivered before the Springfield, Ill., Lyceum, in January, 1837, when 28 years of age. Coming, as he did upon this occasion, before a literary society, Mr. Lincoln's Websterian diction is more observable.

Ladies and Gentlemen:—In the great journal of things happening under the sun, we, the American people, find our account running under date of the nineteenth century of the Christian era. We find ourselves in the peaceful possession of the fairest portion of the earth as regards extent of territory, fertility of soil and salubrity of climate.

We find ourselves under the government of a system of political institutions conducing more essentially to the ends of civil and religious liberty than any of which history of former times tell us.

We, when mounting the stage of existence, found ourselves the legal inheritors of these fundamental blessings. We toiled not in the acquisition or establishment of them; they are a legacy bequeathed to us by a once hardy, brave and patriotic, but now lamented and departed race of ancestors.

Theirs was the task (and nobly they performed it) to possess themselves, and, through themselves, us, of this goodly land to uprear upon its hills and valleys a political edifice of liberty and equal rights; 'tis ours to transmit these—the former unprofaned by the foot of an intruder, the latter undecayed by the lapse of time and untorn by usurpation—to the generation that fate shall permit the world to know. This task, gratitude to our fathers, justice to ourselves, duty to posterity—all imperatively require us faithfully to perform.

How, then, shall we perform it? At what point shall we expect the approach of danger? Shall we expect that

BEN FRANKLIN.

some trans-Atlantic military giant to step the ocean and crush us at a blow?

Never! All the armies of Europe, Asia and Africa combined, with all the treasures of the earth (our own excepted) in their military chest, with a Bonaparte for a commander, could not, by force, take a drink from the Ohio, or make a track on the blue ridge, in a trial of a thousand years.

At what point, then, is this approach of danger to be

expected? I answer, if ever it reach us, it must spring up amongst us. It cannot come from abroad. If destruction be our lot, we must ourselves be its author and finisher. As a nation of freeman, we must live through all time or die by suicide.

I hope I am not over-wary; but, if I am not, there is even now something of ill-omen amongst us. I mean the increasing disregard for law which pervades the country, the disposition to substitute the wild and furious passions in lieu of the sober judgment of courts, and the worse than savage mobs for the executive ministers of justice.

This disposition is awfully fearful in any community, and that it now exists in ours, though grating to our feelings to admit it, it would be a violation of truth and an insult to deny.

Accounts of outrages committed by mobs form the every day news of the times. They have pervaded the country from New England to Louisiana; they are neither peculiar to the eternal snows of the former, nor the burning sun of the latter.

They are not the creatures of climate, neither are they confined to the slave-holding or non-slave-holding States. Alike they spring up among the pleasure-hunting masters of southern slaves and the order-loving citizens of the land of steady habits. Whatever, then, their cause may be, it is common to the whole country.

Many great and good men, sufficiently qualified for any task they may undertake, may ever be found, whose ambition would aspire to nothing beyond a seat in Congress, a gubernatorial or presidential chair; but such belong not to the family of the lion, or the tribe of the eagle.

What! Think you these places would satisfy an Alexander, a Cæsar or a Napoleon? Never! Towering genius disdains a beaten path. It seeks regions hitherto unexplored.

It seeks no distinction in adding story to story upon the monuments of fame, erected to the memory of others. It denies that it is glory enough to serve under any chief. It scorns to tread in the footpaths of any predecessor, however illustrious. It thirsts and burns for distinction, and, if possible, it will have it, whether at the expense of emancipating the slaves or enslaving freemen.

Another reason which once was, but which to the same extent is now no more, has done much in maintaining our institutions thus far. I mean the powerful influence which the interesting scenes of the Revolution had upon the passions of the people, as distinguished from their judgment.

But these histories are gone. They can be read no more forever. They were a fortress of strength. But what the invading foeman could never do, the silent artillery of time has done—the levelling of the walls. They were a forest of giant oaks, but the all-resisting hurricane swept over them and left only here and there a lone trunk, despoiled of its verdue, shorn of its foliage, unshading and unshaded, to murmur in a few more gentle breezes and to combat with its multiplied limbs a few more rude storms, then to sink and be no more. They were the pillars of the temple of liberty, and now that they have crumbled away, that temple must fall, unless

GEORGE WASHINGTON,
First President of the United States.

we, the descendants, supply the places with pillars hewn from the same solid quarry of sober reason.

Passion has helped us, but can do so no more. It will in future be our enemy.

Reason—cold, calculating, unimpassioned reason—must furnish all the materials for our support and defense. Let those materials be molded into general intelligence, sound morality, and in particular, a reverence for the constitution and the laws; and then our country shall continue to improve, and our nation, revering his name, and permitting no hostile foot to pass or desecrate his resting place, shall be that to hear the last trump that shall awaken our Washington.

Upon these let the proud fabric of freedom rest as the rock of its basis, and as truly as has been said of the only greater institution, "the gates of hell shall not prevail against it."

———:o:———

LINCOLN'S FIRST SPEECH IN THE SUPREME COURT.

The case being called, Mr. Lincoln appeared for appellant, and, according to Judge Treat, spoke as follows:

YOUR HONOR:—This is the first case I ever had in this court, and I have examined it with great care. As the court will perceive by looking at the abstract of the record, the only question in the case is one of authority. I have not been able to find any authority sustaining my side of the case, but I have found several cases directly in point on the other side. I will now give the citations and then submit the case.

———:o:———

EXCULPATING THE WHIGS.

Being so much as is on record of a reply to Col. Dick Taylor, a Democrat, who had characterized the Whigs as being "pretentious lords," and very aristocratic, etc., delivered, says Hon. Ninian W. Edwards, in 1840.

GENTLEMEN:—While he (Col. Taylor) was making these charges against the Whigs riding in fine carriages, wearing ruffled shirts, kid gloves, massive gold watch chains, with large seals, and flourishing a heavy gold-headed cane, I (Lincoln) was a poor boy, hired on a flatboat at eight dollars a month, and had only one pair of breeches, and they were buckskin—and if you know the nature of buckskin, when wet and dried by the sun, they shrink—and mine kept shrinking until they left several inches of my legs bare between the tops of my socks and the lower part of my breeches; and whilst I was growing taller they were growing shorter, and so much tighter, that they left a blue streak around my legs that can be seen to this day. If you call this aristocracy, I plead guilty to the charge.

———:0:———

NATIONAL BANK vs. SUB-TREASURY.

Delivered in the Second Presbyterian Church, Springfield, Illinois, and published in the Sangamon Journal, March 6, 1840. The debaters on the question were Messrs. Logan, Baker, Browning and Lincoln, against Douglas, Calhoun, Lamborn and Thomas.

FELLOW-CITIZENS:—It is peculiarly embarrassing to me to attempt a continuance of the discussion, on this evening, which has been conducted in this hall on several preceding ones.

It is so, because on each of these evenings there was a much fuller attendance than now, without any reason for its being so except the greater interest the community feel in the speaker who addressed them then than they do in him who addresses them now.

I am, indeed, apprehensive that the few who have attended have done so more to spare me of mortification than in the hope of being interested in anything I may be able to say.

This circumstance casts a damp upon my spirits which I am sure I shall be unable to overcome during the evening.

The subject heretofore and now to be discussed is the sub-treasury scheme of the present administration, as a means of collecting, safe-keeping, transferring and disbursing the revenues of the nation as contrasted with a national bank for the same purpose.

Mr. Douglas has said that we (the Whigs) have not

dared to meet them (the Locos) in argument on this question.

I protest against this assertion. I say we have again and again during this discussion urged facts and arguments against the sub-treasury which they have neither dared to deny nor attempted to answer.

But lest some may be led to believe that we really wish to avoid the question, I now propose, in my humble way, to urge these arguments again, at the same time begging the audience to mark well the positions I shall take and the proof I shall offer to sustain them, and that they will not allow Mr. Douglas or his friends to escape the force of them by a round of groundless assertions that we dare not meet them in argument.

First. It will injuriously affect the community by its operation on the circulating medium.

Second. It will be a more expensive fiscal agent.

Third. It will be a less secure depository for the public money.

Mr. Lamborn insists that the difference between the Van Buren party and the Whigs is, that although the former sometimes err in practice, they are always correct in principle, whereas the latter are wrong in principle; and the better to impress this proposition he uses a figurative expression in these words:

"The Democrats are vulnerable in the heel, but they are sound in the heart and head."

The first branch of the figure—that the Democrats are vulnerable in the heel—I admit is not merely figurative, but literally true. Who that looks for a moment at their Swartwouts, their Prices, their Harringtons, and their hundreds of others scampering away with the public money to Texas, to Europe, and to every spot on earth where a villian may hope to find refuge from justice, can at all doubt that they are most distressingly affected in their heels with a species of running itch.

It seems this malady of the heels operates on the sound headed and honest hearted creatures very much like the cork leg in the comic song did on its owner, which when he had once got started on it, the more he tried to stop it the more it would run away.

At the hazard of wearing this point threadbare, I will

INDUSTRIAL EXPOSITION.

relate an anecdote which is too strikingly in point to be omitted:

A witty Irish soldier was always boasting of his bravery when no danger was near, who invariably retreated without orders at the first charge of the engagement, being asked by the captain why he did so, replied, "Captain I have as brave a heart as Julius Cæsar ever had, but somehow or other, when danger approaches, my cowardly legs will run away with it!"

So with Mr. Lamborn's party.

They take the public money into their own hands for the most laudable purpose that wise heads and willing hearts can dictate; but, before they can possibly get it out again, their rascally vulnerable heels will run away with them.

Mr. Lamborn refers to the late elections in the States, and from the result predicts that every State in the Union will vote for Mr. Van Buren at the next Presidential election.

Address that argument to cowards and knaves; with the free and the brave it will affect nothing. It may be true; if it must, let it. Many free countries have lost their liberty, and ours may lose hers; but if she shall, be it my proudest plume, not that I was the last to desert, but that I never deserted her.

I know that the great volcano at Washington, aroused by the civil spirits that reign there, is belching forth the laws of polilical corruption in a current broad and deep, which is sweeping with frightful velocity over the whole length and breadth of the land, bidding fair to leave unscathed no green spot or living thing; while on its bosom are riding, like demons on the wave of hell, the imps of that evil spirit fiendishly taunting all those who dare resist its destroying course with hopelessness of their efforts; and knowing this, I cannot deny that all may be swept away. Broken by it, I, too, may be; bow to it, I never will.

The probability that we may fall in the struggle ought not to deter us from the support of a course we believe to be just. It shall not deter me.

If ever I feel the soul within me elevate and expand to those dimensions, not wholly unworthy of its Almighty architect, it is when I contemplate the cause of my country deserted by all the world beside, and I standing up boldly alone, hurling defiance at her victorious opposers.

Here, without contemplating the consequences, before heaven and in the face of the world, I swear eternal fealty to the just cause, as I deem it, of the land of my life, my liberty, and my love.

And who that thinks with me will not fearlessly adopt that oath that I take? Let none falter who thinks he is right, and we may succeed. But if after all we may fail, be it so; we shall still have the proud consolation of saying to our conscience, and to the departed shade of our country's freedom, that the cause approved of our judgment and adored of our hearts in disaster, in chains, in torture, in death, we never faltered in defending.

LINCOLN'S TEMPERANCE SPEECH.

Originally Printed as "An Address by Abraham Lincoln, Esq."

[Delivered before the Springfield Washingtonian Temperance Society, at the Second Presbyterian Church, on the 22nd day of February, 1842,

Although the temperance cause has been in progress for nearly twenty years, it is apparent to all that it is just now being crowned with a degree of success hitherto unparalleled.

The list of its friends is daily swelled by the additions of fifties, hundreds and thousands. The cause itself seems suddenly transformed from a cold, abstract theory to a living, breathing, active and powerful chieftain, going forth "conquering and to conquer." The citadels of his great adversary are daily being stormed and dismantled: his temples and his altars, where the rites of his idolatrous worship have long been performed, and where human sacrifices have long been wont to be made, are daily desecrated and deserted. The tramp of the conqueror's fame is sounding from hill to hill, from sea to sea, and from land to land, and calling millions to his standard at a blast.

For this new and splendid success we heartily rejoice. That that success is so much greater now, than heretofore, is doubtless owing to rational causes; and if we would have it continue, we shall do well to inquire what those causes are.

The warfare heretofore waged against the demon intemperance has, somehow or other, been erroneous. Either the champions engaged or the tactics they adopted have not been the most proper. These champions, for the most part, have been preachers, lawyers and hired agents; between these and the mass of mankind, there is a want of approachability, if the term be admissable, partial at least, fatal to their success. They are supposed to have no sympathy of feeling or interest with those very persons whom it is their object to convince and persuade.

And again, it is so easy and so common to ascribe motives to men of these classes other than those they profess to act upon. The preacher, it is said, advocates temperance because he is a fanatic; and desires a union of the Church and State; the lawyer from his pride and vanity of hearing himself speak; and the hired agent for his salary.

But when one who has long been known as a victim of intemperance bursts the fetters that have bound him, and appears before his neighbors "clothed in his right mind," a redeemed specimen of long-lost humanity, and stands up with tears of joy trembling in his eyes to tell of the miseries once endured, now to be endured no more forever; of his once naked and starving children, now fed and clad comfortably; of a wife long weighed down with woe, weeping and a broken heart, now restored to health, happiness, and a renewed affection, and how

easily it is all done, once resolved to be done; how simple his language; there is a logic and an eloquence in it that few with human feelings can resist.

They cannot say that he desires a union with Church and State, for he is not a church member; they cannot say he is vain of hearing himself speak, for his whole demeanor shows he would gladly avoid speaking at all; they cannot say he speaks for pay, for he receives none. Nor can his sincerity in any way be doubted, or his sympathy for those he would persuade to imitate his example be denied.

In my judgment it is to the battles of this new class of champions that our late success is greatly, perhaps chiefly, owing. But had the old school champions themselves been of the most wise selecting? Was their system of tactics the most judicious? It seems to me it was not.

Too much denunciation against dram-sellers and dram-drinkers was indulged in. This, I think, was both impolitic, and unjust: It was impolitic, because it is not much in the nature of man to be driven to any thing, still less to be driven about that which is exclusively his own business; and least of all, where such driving is to be submitted to at the expense of pecuniary interest, or burning appetite.

When the dram-seller and drinker were incessanlty told, not in the accents of entreaty and persuasion, diffidently addressed by erring man to an erring brother, but in the thundering tones of anathema and denunciation, with which the lordly judge often groups together all the crimes of the felon's life and thrusts them in his face just ere he passes sentence of death upon him, that they were the authors of all the vice and misery and crime in the land; that they were the manufacturers and material of all the thieves and robbers and murderers that infest the earth; that their houses were the workshops of the devil, and that their persons should be shunned by all the good and virtuous as moral pestilences.

I say, when they were told all this, and in this way, it is not wonderful that they were slow, very slow, to acknowledge the truth of such denunciations, and to join the ranks of their denouncers in a hue and cry against themselves.

To have expected them to do otherwise than they did —to have expected them not to meet denunciation with denunciation, crimination with crimination, and anathema with anathema—was to expect a reversal of human nature, which is God's decree, and can never be reversed.

When the conduct of men is designed to be influenced persuasion, kind, unassuming persuasion, should ever be adopted. It is an old and a true maxim, "that a drop of honey catches more flies than a gallon of gall." So with men.

If you would win a man to your cause, first convince him that you are his sincere friend. Therein is a drop of honey that catches his heart; which, say what he will, is the great high road to his reason, and which, when once gained, you will find but little trouble in convincing his judgment of the justice of your cause, if, indeed, that cause really be a just one. On the contrary, assume to dictate to his judgment, or to command his action, or to mark him as one to be shunned and despised, and he will retreat within himself, close all the avenues to his head and his heart, and though your cause be the naked truth itself, transformed to the heaviest lance, harder than steel, and sharper than steel can be made, and though you throw it with more than herculean force and precision, you shall be no more able to pierce him than to penetrate the hard shell of a tortoise with a rye straw. Such is man, and so must he be understood by those who would lead him, even to his own best interest.

On this point the Washingtonians greatly excel the temperance advocates of former times. Those whom they desire to convince and persuade are their old friends and companions. They know they are not demons, not even the worst of men; they know that generally they are kind, generous and charitable, even beyond the example of their more staid and sober neighbors. They are practical philanthropists; and they glow with a generous and brotherly zeal, that mere theorizers are incapable of feeling. Benevolence and charity possess their hearts entirely; and out of the abundance of their hearts their tongues give utterance: "Love through all their actions run, and all their words are mild;" in this spirit they speak and act, and in the same they are heard and regarded. And when such is the temper of the advocate, and such of the audience, no good cause can be unsuccessful. But I have said that denunciations against dram-sellers and dram-drinkers are unjust as well as impolitic. Let us see.

I have not inquired at what period of time the use of intoxicating liquors commenced, nor is it important to know. It is sufficient that to all of us who now inhabit the world the practice of drinking them is just as old as the world itself—that is, we have seen the one just as long as we have seen the other. When all such of us have now reached the years of maturity first opened our eyes upon the stage of existence we found intoxicating liquors recognized by everybody, used by everybody, repudiated by nobody. It commonly entered into the first draught of the infant and the last of the dying man.

From the sideboard of the parson down to the ragged pocket of the homeless loafer it was constantly found. Physicians prescribed it in this, that, and the other disease; Government provided it for soldiers and sailors; and to have a rolling or raising, a husking or hoe-down anywhere about without it was positively insufferable.

So, too, it was everywhere a respectable article of manufacture and of merchandise. The making of it was regarded as an honorable livelihood, and he who could make most was the most enterprising and respectable. Manufactories of it were everywhere erected, in which all the earthly goods of their owners were invested. Wagons drew it from town to town, boats bore it from clime to clime, and the winds wafted it from nation to nation; and merchants bought and sold it by wholesale and retail with precisely the same feelings on the part of the seller, buyer, and by-stander as are felt at the selling and buying of plows beef, bacon, or any other of the real necessaries of life. Universal public opinion not only tolerated but recognized and adopted its use.

It is true that even then it was known and acknowledged that many were greatly injured by it; but none seemed to think that the injury arose from the use of a bad thing, but from the abuse of a very good thing. The victims of it were to be pitied and compassionated, just as are the heirs of consumption and other hereditary diseases. The failing was treated as a misfortune, and not as a crime.

If then what I have been saying is true, is it wonderful that some should think and act now as all thought and acted twenty years ago; and is it just to assail, condemn, or despise them for doing so? The universal sense of mankind, on any subject, is an argument, or at least an influence not easily overcome.

The success of the argument in favor of the existence of an overruling Providence mainly depends upon that sense; and men ought not, in justice, be denounced for yielding to it in any case, or giving it up slowly, especially when they are backed by interest, fixed habits, or burning appetites.

Another error, as it seems to me, into which the old reformers fell, was the position that all habitual drunkards were utterly incorrigible, and therefore must be turned adrift and damned without remedy, in order that the grace of temperance might abound, to the temperate then, and to all mandkind some hundreds of years thereafter.

There is in this something so repugnant to humanity, so uncharitable, so cold-blooded and feelingless, that it never did, nor never can, enlist the enthusiasm of a popular cause. We could not love the man who taught it—

we could not hear him with patience. The heart could not throw open its portals to it; the generous man could not adopt it: it could not mix with his blood. It looked so fiendishly selfish, so like throwing fathers and brothers overboard to lighten the boat for our security, that the noble minded shrank from the manifest meanness of the thing: And besides this, the benefits of a reformation to be effected by such a system were too remote in point of time to warmly engage many in its behalf.

Few can be induced to labor exclusively for posterity, and none will do it enthusiastically. Posterity has done nothing for us; and theorize on it as we may, practically we shall do very little for it unless we are made to think we are, at the same time, doing something for ourselves.

What an ignorance of human nature does it exhibit to ask or expect a whole community to rise up and labor for the temporal happiness of others, after themselves shall be consigned to the dust, a majority of which community take no pains whatever to secure their own eternal welfare at no greater distant day. Great distance in either time or space has wonderful power to lull and render quiescent the human mind. Pleasures to be enjoyed, or pains to be endured, after we shall be dead and gone, are but little regarded, even in our own cases, and much less in the cases of others.

Still, in addition to this, there is something so ludicrous in promises of good or threats of evil a great way off, as to render the whole subject with which they are connected easily turned into ridicule. "Better lay down that spade you're stealing, Paddy—if you don't you'll pay for it at the day of judgment." "Be the powers, if ye'll credit me so long, I'll take another jist."

By the Washingtonians this system of consigning the habitual drunkard to hopeless ruin is repudiated. They adopt a more enlarged philanthropy. They go for pressent as well as future good. They labor for all now living, as well as hereafter to live. They teach hope to all —despair to none. As applying to their cause, they deny the doctrine of unpardonable sin. As in Christianity it is taught, so in this they teach:

> "While the lamp holds out to burn,
> The vilest sinner may return."

And, what is a matter of the most profound congratulations, they, by experiment upon experiment and example upon example, prove the maxim to be no less true in the one case than in the other. On every hand we behold those who but yesterday were the chief of sinners, now the chief apostles of the cause. Drunken devils are cast out by ones, by sevens, by legions, and their unfortunate victims, like the poor possessed who was redeemed from his long and lonely wanderings in the tombs, are publishing to the ends of the earth how great things have been done for them.

To these new champions and this new system of tactics our late success is mainly owing, and to them we must mainly look for the final consummation. The ball is now rolling gloriously on, and none are so able as they to increase its speed and its bulk, to add to its momentum and magnitude, even though unlearned in letters, for this task none are so well educated. To fit them for this work they have been taught in the true school. They have been in that gulf from which they would teach others the means of escape. They have passed that

THE DANCE AND THE "GULF."

[319]

prison wall which others have long declared impassable, and who that has not shall dare to weigh opinions with them as to the mode of passing?

But if it be true, as I have insisted, that those who have suffered by intemperance personally and have reformed are the most powerful and efficient instruments to push the reformation to ultimate success, it does not follow that those who have not suffered have no part left them to perform. Whether or not the world would be vastly benefited by a total and final banishment from it of all intoxicating drinks seems to me not now an open question. Three-fourths of mankind confess the affirmative with their tongues, and I believe all the rest acknowledge it in their hearts.

Ought any, then, to refuse their aid in doing what the good of the whole demands? Shall he who cannot do much be for that reason excused if he do nothing? "But," says one, "what good can I do by signing the pledge? I never drink, even without signing." This question has already been asked and answered more than a million of times. Let it be answered once more. For the man, suddenly or in any other way, to break off from the use of drams who has indulged in them for a long course of years, and until his appetite for them has grown ten or a hundred-fold stronger and more craving than any natural appetite can be, requires a most powerful moral effort. In such an undertaking he needs every moral support and influence that can possibly be brought to his aid and thrown around him. And not only so, but every moral prop should be taken from whatever argument might rise in his mind to lure him to his backsliding. When he casts his eyes around him he should be able to see all that he respects, all that he admires, all that he loves, kindly and anxiously pointing him onward, and none beckoning him back to his former miserable "wallowing in the mire."

But it is said by some that men will think and act for themselves; that none will disuse spirits or any thing else because his neighbors do; and that moral influence is not that powerful engine contended for. Let us examine this. Let me ask the man who could maintain this position most stiffly what compensation he will accept to go to church some Sunday and sit during the sermon with his wife's bonnet upon his head? Not a trifle, I'll venture. And why not? There would be nothing irreligious in it, nothing immoral, nothing uncomfortable—then why not? Is it not because there would be something egregiously unfashionable in it? Then it is the influence of fashion; and what is the influence of fashion but the influence that other people's actions have on our own actions—the strong inclination each of us feels to do as we see all our neighbors do? Nor is the influence of fashion confined to any particular thing or class of things. It is just as strong on one subject as another. Let us make it as unfashionable to withhold our names from the temperance pledge as for husbands to wear their wives' bonnets to church, and instances will be just as rare in the one case as the other.

"But," say some, "we are no drunkards, and we shall not acknowledge ourselves such by joining a reformed drunkard's society, whatever our influence might be." Surely no Christian will adhere to this objection.

If they believe as they profess, that Omnipotence condescended to take on Himself the form of sinful man, and as such to die an ignominious death for their sakes, surely they will not refuse submission to the infinitely lesser condescension for the temporal and perhaps eternal salvation of a large, erring, and unfortunate class of their fellow creatures. Nor is the condescension very great. In my judgment such of us as have never fallen victims have been spared more from the absence of appetite than from any mental or moral superiority over those who have. Indeed, I believe, if we take habitual drunkards as a class, their heads and their hearts will bear an advantageous comparison with those of any other class.

There seems ever to have been a proneness in the brilliant and warm-blooded to fall into this vice—the demon of intemperance ever seems to have delighted in sucking the blood of genius and generosity. What one of us but can call to mind some relative more promising in youth than all his fellows who has fallen a sacrifice to his rapacity? He ever seems to have gone forth like the Egyptian angel of death, commissioned to slay, if not the first, the fairest born of every family. Shall he now be arrested in his desolating career? In that arrest all can give aid that will, and who shall be excused that can and will not? Far around as human breath has ever blown, he keeps our fathers, our brothers, our sons, and our friends prostrate in the chains of moral death. To all the living everywhere we cry: "Come, sound the moral trump, that these may rise and stand up an exceeding great army." "Come from the four winds, O breath! and breathe upon these slain, that they may live." If the relative grandeur of revolutions shall be estimated by the great amount of human misery they alleviate, and

THE WAITING WIFE.

the small amount they inflict, then, indeed, will this be the grandest the world shall ever have seen.

Of our political revolution of 1776 we are all justly proud. It has given us a degree of political freedom far exceeding that of any other nations of the earth. In it the world has found a solution of the long-mooted problem as to the capability of man to govern himself. In it was the germ which has vegetated, and still is to grow and expand into the universal liberty of mankind.

But with all these glorious results, past, present, and to come, it had its evils too. It breathed forth famine, swam in blood, and rode in fire; and long, long after, the orphans' cry and the widows' wail continued to break the sad silence that ensued. These were the price, the inevitable price, paid for the blessings it bought.

Turn now to the temperance revolution. In it we shall find a stronger bondage broken, a viler slavery manumitted, a greater tyrant deposed—in it, more of want, supplied, more disease healed, more sorrow assuaged. By it, no orphans starving, no widows weeping; by it, none wounded in feeling, none injured in interest. Even the dram-maker and dram-seller will have glided into other occupations so gradually as never to have felt the change, and will stand ready to join all others in the universal song of gladness. And what a noble ally this to the cause of political freedom; with such an aid, its march cannot fail to be on and on, till every son of earth shall drink in rich fruition the sorrow-quenching draughts of perfect liberty! Happy day, when, all appetities controlled, all passions subdued, all matter subjugated, mind, all-conquering mind, shall live and move, the monarch of the world! Glorious consummation! Hail, fall of fury! Reign of reason, all hail!

And when the victory shall be complete—when there shall be neither a slave nor a drunkard on the earth—how proud the title of that *Land*, which may truly claim to be the birthplace and the cradle of both those revolutions that shall have ended in that victory. How nobly distinguished that people who shall have planted and nurtured to maturity both the political and moral freedom of their species.

This is the one hundred and tenth anniversary of the birthday of Washington. We are met to celebrate this day. Washington is the mightiest name of earth—long since mightiest in the cause of civil liberty, still mightiest in moral reformation. On that name a eulogy is expected. It cannot be. To add brightness to the sun or glory to the name of Washington is alike impossible. Let none attempt it. In solemn awe pronounce the name, and in its naked, deathless splendor leave it shining on.

A GREAT CONGRESSIONAL SPEECH.

Abraham Lincoln on the Presidency and General Politics.

Delivered in the House of Representatives, Washington, D. C., July 27, 1848.

MR. SPEAKER:—Our Democratic friends seem to be in great distress because they think our candidate for the Presidency don't suit us. Most of them can not find out that General Taylor has any principles at all, some, however, have discovered that he has one, but that one is entirely wrong. This one principle is his position on the veto power.

The gentleman from Tennessee (Mr. Stanton), who has just taken his seat, indeed, has said there is very little if any difference on this question between General Taylor and all the Presidents; and he seems to think it sufficient detraction from General Taylor's position on it, that it has nothing new in it. But all others, whom I have heard speak, assail it furiously.

A new member from Kentucky (Mr. Clarke), of very considerable ability, was in particular concern about it. He thought it altogether novel and unprecedented for a President, or a Presidential candidate, to think of approving bills whose Constitutionality may not be entirely clear to his own mind. He thinks the ark of our safety is gone, unless Presidents shall always veto such bills as, in their judgment, may be of doubtful Constitutionality. However clear Congress may be of their authority to pass any particular act, the gentleman from Kentucky thinks the President must veto if he has doubts about it.

Now I have neither time nor inclination to argue with the gentleman on the veto power as an original question; but I wish to show that General Taylor, and not he, agrees with the earliest statesmen on this question. When the bill chartering the first Bank of the United States passed Congress, its Constitutionality was questioned; Mr. Madison, then in the House of Representatives, as well as others, opposed it on that ground. General Washington, as President, was called on to approve or reject it. He sought and obtained, on the Constitutional question, the separate written opinion of Jefferson, Hamilton and Edmund Randolph, they then being respectively Secretary of State, Secretary of the Treasury, and Attorney General. Hamilton's opinion was for the power; while Randolph's and Jefferson's were both against it. Mr. Jefferson, after giving his opinion decidedly against the Constitutionality of that bill, closed his letter with the paragraph I now read:

"It must be admitted, however, that unless the President's mind, on a view of everything which is urged for and against this bill, is tolerably clear that it is unauthorized by the Constitution, if the pro and the con hang so even as to balance his judgment, a just respect for the wisdom of the Legislature would naturally decide the balance in favor of their opinion; it is chiefly for cases where they are clearly misled by error, ambition or interest, that the Constitution has placed a check in the negative of the President. THOMAS JEFFERSON.

"February 15, 1791."

Gen. Taylor's opinion, as expressed in his Allison letter, is as I now read:

"The power given by the veto is a high conservative power; but, in my opinion, should never be exercised, except in cases of clear violation of the Constitution, or manifest haste and want of consideration by Congress."

It is here seen that, in Mr. Jefferson's opinion, if on the Constitutionality of any given bill, the President doubts, he is not to veto it, as the gentleman from Kentucky would have him to do, but is to defer to Congress and approve it. And if we compare the opinions of Jefferson and Taylor, as expressed in these paragraphs, we shall find them more exactly alike than we can often find any two expressions having any literal difference. None but interested fault-finders can discover any substantial variation.

THE NATIONAL ISSUE.

But gentlemen on the other side are unanimously agreed that General Taylor has no other principle. They are in utter darkness as to his opinions on any of the questions of policy which occupy the public attention. But is there any doubt as to what he will do on the prominent questions, if elected? Not the least. It is not possible to know what he will, or would do in every imaginable case; because many questions have passed away, and others doubtless will arise which none of us have yet thought of; but on the prominent questions of currency, tariff, internal improvements, and Wilmot proviso, General Taylor's course is at least as well defined as is General Cass. Why, in their eagerness to get at General Taylor, several Democratic members here have desired to know whether, in case of his election, a bankrupt law is to be established. Can they tell us General Cass' opinion on this question? (Some member answered: "He's against it.") Aye, how do you know he is? There is nothing about it in the platform, or elsewhere, that I have seen. If the gentleman knows anything which I do not, he can show it. But to return: General Taylor, in his Allisan letter, says:

"Upon the subject of the tariff, the currency, the improvement of our great highways, rivers, lakes, and harbors, the will of the people, as expressed through their Representatives in Congress, ought to be respected and carried out by the Executive."

A PRESIDENCY FOR THE PEOPLE.

Now, this is the whole matter—in substance it is this: The people say to General Taylor:

"If you are elected, shall we have a National Bank?"
He answers: "Your will, gentlemen, not mine."
"What about the tariff?"
"Say yourselves."
"Shall our rivers and harbors be improved?"

"Just as you please. If you desire a bank, an alteration of the tariff, internal improvements, any or all, I will not hinder you. Send up your members to Congress from the various districts, with opinions according to your own, and if they are for these measures, or any of them, I shall have nothing to oppose; if they are not for them, I shall not, by any appliance whatever, attempt to dragoon them into their adoption."

Now can there be any difficulty in understanding this? To you, Democrats, it may not seem like principle; but surely you can not fail to perceive the position plainly enough. The distinction between it and the position of your candidate is broad and obvious, and I admit you have a clear right to show it is wrong, if you can; but you have no right to pretend you cannot see it at all. We see it, and to us it appears like principle, and the best sort of principle at that—the principle of allowing the people to do as they please with their own business.

My friend from Indiana (Mr. C. B. Smith) has aptly asked: "Are you willing to trust the people!" Some of of you answered, substantially: "We are willing to trust the people; but the President is as much the representative of the people as Congress." In a certain sense, and to a certain extent, he is the representative of the people. He is elected by them, as well as Congress is. But can he, in the nature of things, know the wants of the people as well as three hundred other men coming from all the various localities of the nation? If so, where is the propriety of having a Congress? That the Constitution gives the President a negative on legislation all know; but that this negative should be so combined with platforms and other appliances as to enable him, and in fact, almost compel him, to take the whole of legislation into his own hands, is what we object to—is what General Taylor objects to—and is what constitutes the broad distinction between you and us. To thus transfer legislation is clearly to take it from those who understand with minuteness the interest of the people, and give it to one who does not and cannot so well understand it.

I understand your idea, that if a Presidential candidate avow his opinion upon a given question, or rather upon all questions, and the people, with full knowledge of this, elect him, they thereby distinctly approve all those opinions. This, though plausible, is a most pernicious deception. By means of it measures are adopted or rejected, contrary to the wishes of the whole of one party, and often nearly half of the other. The process is this Three, four, or ·a half dozen questions are prominent at a given time; the party selects its candidate, and he takes his position on each of these questions. On all but one of his positions have already been indorsed at former elections, and his party fully committed to them; but that one is new, and a large portion of them are against it. But what are they to do ? The whole are strung together, and they must take all or reject all. They can not take what they like and leave the rest. What they are already committed to, being the majority, they shut their eyes and gulp the whole. Next election still another is introduced in the same way.

If we run our eyes along the line of the past, we shall see that almost, if not quite, all the articles of the present Democratic creed have been at first forced upon the party in this very way. And just now, and just so, opposition to internal improvements is to be established if General Cass shall be elected. Almost half the Democrats here are for improvements, but they will vote for Cass, and if if he succeeds, their votes will have aided in closing the doors against improvements. Now, this is a process which we think is wrong. We prefer a candidate who, like General Taylor, will allow the people to have their own way regardless of his private opinion; and I should think the internal-improvement Democrats at least, ought to prefer such a candidate. He would force nothing on them which they don't want, and he would allow them to have improvements, which their own candidate, if elected, will not.

GEN TAYLOR AND THE WILMOT PROVISO.

Mr. Speaker, I have said that General Taylor's position is as well defined as is that of General Cass. In saying this, I admit I do not certainly know what he would do on the Wilmot Proviso. I am a Northern man, or rather a Western-free State man, with a consituency I believe to be, and with personal feelings I know to be, against the extension of slavery. As such, and with what information I have, I hope, and believe, General Taylor, if elected, would not veto the proviso, but I do not know it. Yet, if I knew he would I still would vote for him. I should do so, because in my judgment his election alone can defeat General Cass; and because should slavery thereby go into the territory we now have, just so much will certainly happen by the election of Cass; and in addition, a course of policy leading to new wars, new acquisitions of territory, and still further extension of slavery. One of the two is to be President; which is preferable?

But there is as much doubt about of Cass on improvements as there is of Taylor on the proviso. I have no doubt of General Cass on this question, but I know the Democrats differ among themselves as to his position. My internal improvement colleague (Mr. Wentworth) stated on this floor the other day, that he was satisfied Cass was for improvements, because he had voted for all the bills that he (Mr. W.) had. So far so good. But Mr. Polk vetoed some of these very bills; the Baltimore Convention passed a set of resolutions, among other things, approving these vetoes, and Cass declares in his letter accepting the nomination, that he has carefully read these resolutions, and that he adheres to them as firmly as he approves them cordially. In other words, General Cass voted for the bills, and thinks the President did right to veto them; and his friends here are amiable enough to consider him as being on one side or the other, just as one or the other may correspond with their own respective inclinations.

My colleague admits that the platform declares against the Constitutionality of a general system of improvements, and that General Cass indorses the platform; but he still thinks General Cass is in favor of some sort of improvements. Well, what are they? As he is against general objects, those he is for must be particular and local. Now, this is taking the subject precisely by the wrong end. Particularity—expending the money of the whole people for an object which will benefit only a portion of them, is the greatest objection to improvements, and has been so held by General Jackson, Mr. Polk, and all others, I believe, till now. But now behold, the objects most general, nearest free from this objection, are to be rejected, while those most liable to it are to be embraced. To return: I cannot help believing that General Cass, when he wrote his letter of acceptance, well understood he was to be claimed by the advocates of both sides of this question, and that he then closed the doors against all further expressions of opinion, purposely to retain the benefits of that double position. His subsequent equivocation at Cleveland, to my mind, proves such to have been the case.

PLATFORMS.

One word more, and I shall have done with this branch of the subject. You Democrats, and your candidate, in the main are in favor of laying down, in advance, a platform—a set of party positions, as a unit; and then of enforcing the people, by every sort of appliance. to ratify them, however unpalatable some of them may be. We, and our candidate, are in favor of making Presidential elections and the legislation of the country distinct matters; so that the people can elect whom they please, and afterward legislate just as they please, without any hindrance, save only so much as may guard against infractions of the Constitution, undue haste, and want of consideration.

The difference between us is clear as noon-day. That we are right we cannot doubt. We hold the true Republican position. In leaving the people's business in their hands, we cannot be wrong. We are willing, and even anxious, to go to the people on this issue.

MR. CLAY'S DEFEAT AND DEMOCRATIC SYMPATHIES.

But I suppose I cannot reasonably hope to convince you that we have any principles. The most I can expect is, to assure you that we think we have, and are quite contented with them.

The other day, one of the gentlemen from Georgia (Mr. Iverson), an eloquent man, and a man of learning, so far as I can judge, not being learned myself, came down upon us astonishingly. He spoke in what the Baltimore American calls the "scathing and withering style."

At the end of his second severe flash I was struck blind, and found myself feeling with my fingers for an assurance of my continued physical existence. A little of the bone was left, and I gradually revived. He eulogized Mr. Clay in high and beautiful terms, and then declared that we had deserted all our principles, and had turned Henry Clay out, like an old horse, to root. This is terribly severe. It cannot be answered by argument; at least I cannot so answer it.

I merely wish to ask the gentleman if the Whigs are the only party he can think of who sometimes turn old horses out to root! Is not a certain Martin Van Buren an old horse, which your party turned out to root? and is he not rooting to your discomfort about now? But in not nominating Mr. Clay, we deserted our principles, you say. Ah! in what? Tell us, ye men of principle, what principle we violated? We say you did violate principle in discarding Van Buren, and we can tell you how. You violated the primary, the cardinal, the one great living principle of all Democratic representative government—the principle that the representative is bound to carry out the known will of his constituents.

A large majority of the Baltimore Convention of 1844 were, by their constituents, instructed to procure Van Buren's nomination if they could. In violation, in utter, glaring contempt of this, you rejected him—rejected him, as the gentleman from New York (Mr. Birdsall), the other day, expressly admitted, for availability—that same "general availability" which you charge on us, and daily chew over here, as something exceedingly odious and unprincipled.

But the gentleman from Georgia (Mr, Iverson), gave

us a second speech yesterday, all well considered and put down in writing, in which Van Buren was scathed and withered a "few" for his present position and movements. I can not remember the gentleman's precise language, but I do remember he put Van Buren down, down, till he got him where he was finally to "sink" and "rot."

LINCOLN'S DESCRIPTION OF HIMSELF AS A MILITARY HERO.

By the way, Mr. Speaker, did you know I am a military hero? Yes, sir, in the days of the Black Hawk war I fought, bled, and came away. Speaking of General Cass' career, reminds me of my own. I was not at Stillman's defeat, but I was about as near it as Cass to Hull's surrender; and like him, I saw the place very soon afterward. It is quite certain I did not break my sword, for I had none to break; but I bent a musket pretty badly on one occasion. If Cass broke his sword, the idea is, he broke it in desperation; I bent the musket by accident. If General Cass went in advance of me in picking whortleberries, I guess I surpassed him in charges upon wild onions. If he saw any live, fighting Indians, it was more than I did, but I had a good many bloody struggles with the mosquitos; and although I never fainted from loss of blood, I can truly say I was often very hungry.

Mr. Speaker, if I should ever conclude to doff whatever our Democratic friends may suppose there is of black-cockade Federalism about me, and, thereupon, they should take me up as their candidate for the Presidency, I protest they shall not make fun of me as they have of General Cass, by attempting to write me into a military hero.

CASS ON THE WILMOT PROVISO.

While I have General Cass in hand, I wish to say a word about his political principles. As a specimen, I take the record of his progress on the Wilmot Proviso. In the Washington Union, of March 2, 1847, there is a report of the speech of General Cass, made the day before in the Senate, on the Wilmot Proviso, during the delivery of which Mr. Miller, of New Jersey, is reported to have interrupted him as follows, to-wit:

"Mr. Miller expressed his great surprise at the change in the sentiments of the Senator from Michigan, who had been regarded as the great champion of freedom in the Northwest, of which he was a distinguished ornament. Last year the Senator from Michigan was understood to be decidedly in favor of the Wilmost Proviso; and, as no reason had been stated for the change, he (Mr. Miller) could not refrain from the expression of his extreme surprise."

To this General Cass is reported to have replied as follows, to-wit:

Mr. Cass said that the course of the Senator from New Jersey was most extraordinary. Last year he (Mr. Cass) should have voted for the proposition had it come up. But circumstances had altogether changed. The honorable Senator then read several passages from the remarks given above, which he had committed to writing in order to refute such a charge as that of the Senator from New Jersey.

In the "remarks above committed to writing," is one numbered 4, as follows, to-wit:

"4th. Legislation would now be wholly imperative,

because no territory hereafter to be acquired can be governed without an act of Congress providing for its government. And such an act, on its passage, would open the whole subject, and leave the Congress, called on to pass it, free to exercise its own discretion, entirely uncontrolled by any declaration found in the statute book.'

In Niles' Register, vol. 73, page 293, there is a letter of General Cass to A. O. P. Nicholson, of Nashville, Tennessee, dated December 25, 1847, from which the following are correct extracts:

The Wilmot Proviso has been before the country some time. It has been repeatedly discussed in Congress, and by the public press. I am strongly impressed with the opinion that a great change has been going on in the public mind upon this subject—in my own as well as others; and that doubts are resolving themselves into convictions, that the principle it involves should be kept out of the National Legislature, and left to the people of the Confederacy in their respective local governments.

"'Briefly, then, I am opposed to the exercise of any jurisdiction by Congress over this matter; and I am in favor of leaving the people of any territory which may be hereafter acquired, the right to regulate it themselves, under the general principles of the Constitution. Because,

"'I do not see in the Constitution any grant of the requisite power to Congress; and I am not disposed to extend a doubtful precedent beyond its necessity—the establishment of territorial governments when needed—leaving to the inhabitants all the rights compatible with the relations they bear to the Confederation.'

AN OBEDIENT DEMOCRAT.

These extracts show, in 1846, General Cass was for the Proviso at once; that, in March, 1847, he was still for it but not just then; and, that in December, 1847, against it altogether. This is a true index to the whole man. When the question was raised in 1846, he was in a blustering hurry to take ground for it. He sought to be in advance, and to avoid the uninteresting position of a mere follower; but soon he began to see a glimpse of the great Democratic ox-gad waving in his face, and to hear indistinctly a voice saying, "back, back, sir; back a little." He shakes his head and bats his eyes, and blunders back to his position of March, 1847; and still the gad waves and the voice grows more distinct, and sharper still—back, sir! back, I say! further back! and back he goes to the position of December, 1847; at which the gad is still, and the voice soothingly says, "So! stand still at that."

Have no fears, gentlemen of your candidate, he exactly suits you, and we congratulate you upon it. However much you may be distressed about our candidate you have all cause to be contented and happy with your own. If elected he may not maintain all, or even any of his positions previously taken; but he will be sure to do whatever the party exigency, for the time being, may require; and that is precisely what you want. He and Van Buren are the same "manner of men;" and like Van Buren, he will never desert you till you first desert him.

WONDERFUL PHYSICAL CAPACITIES OF GENERAL CASS.

But I have introduced General Cass' accounts here, chiefly to show the wonderful physical capacities of the man. They show that he not only did the labor of several men at the same time, but that he often did it at several places many hundred miles apart, at the same time. And at eating, too, his capacities are shown to be quite as wonderful. From October, 1821, to May, 1822, he ate ten rations a day in Michigan, ten rations a day here in Washington, and near five dollars' worth a day besides, partly on the road between the two places.

And then there is an important discovery in his example—the art of being paid for what one eats, instead of having to pay for it. Hereafter, if any nice man shall owe a bill which he can not pay in any other way, he can just board it out.

Mr; Speaker, we have all heard of the animal standing in doubt between two stacks of hay, and starving to death; the like of that would never happen to General Cass. Place the stacks a thousand miles apart, he would stand stock-still, midway between them, and eat both at once; and the green grass along the line would be apt to suffer some, too, at the same time. By all means, make him President, gentlemen. He will feed you bounteously —if—if there is any left after he shall have helped himself.

But as General Taylor, is, par excellence, the hero of the Mexican war; and, as you Democrats say we Whigs have always opposed the war, you think it must be very awkward and embarrassing for us to go for General Taylor.

THE MEXICAN WAR.

The declaration that we have always opposed the war is true or false acco.ding as one may understand the term "opposing the war." If to say ''the war was un-

GEN. TAYLOR'S ARMY NEAR POPOCATAPTL, IN MEXICO.

necessarily and unconstitutionally commenced by the President," be opposing the war, then the Whigs have very generally opposed it. Whenever they have spoken at all they have said this; and they have said it on what has appeared good reason to them: The marching of an army into the midst of a peaceful Mexican settlement, frightning the inhabitants away, leaving their growing crops and other property to destruction, to you may appear a perfectly amiable, peaceful, unprovoking procedure; but it does not appear so to us. So to call such an act, to us appears no other than a naked, impudent absurdity, and we speak of it accordingly. But if, when the war had begun, and become the cause of the country, the giving of our money and our blood, in common with yours, was support of the war, then it is not true that we have always opposed the war. With few individual exceptions, you have constantly had our votes here for all the necessary supplies.

And, more than this, you have had the services, the blood, and the lives of our political brethren in every trial and on every field. The beardless boy and the mature man—the humble and the distinguished, you have had them. Through suffering and death, by disease, and in battle they have endured, and fought, and fallen with you. Clay and Webster each gave a son, never to be returned.

From the State of my own residence, besides other worthy but less known Whig names, we sent Marshall, Morrison, Baker, and Hardin; they all fought, and one fell, and in the fall of that one, we lost our best Whig man. Nor were the Whigs few in number, or laggard in the day of danger. In that fearful, bloody, breathless struggle at Buena Vista, where each man's hard task was to beat back five foes, or die himself, of the five high officers who perished, four were Whigs.

In speaking of this, I mean no odious comparison between the lion-hearted Whigs and Democrats who fought there. On other occasions, I doubt not the proportion was different. I wish to do justice to all. I think of all those brave men as Americans, in whose proud fame, as an American, I, too, have a share. Many of them, Whigs and Democrats, are my constituents and personal friends; and I thank them—more than thank them—one and all, for the high, imperishable honor they have conferred on our common State.

AN IMPORTANT DISTINCTION.

But the distinction between the cause of the President in beginning the war, and the cause of the country after it was begun, is a distinction which you can not perceive. To you, the President and the country seem to be all one. You are interested to see no distinction between them; and I venture to suggest that possibly your interest blinds you a little.

We see the distinction, as we think, clearly enough; and our friends, who have fought in the war, have no difficulty in seeing it also. What those who have fallen would say, were they alive and here, of course we can never know; but with those who have returned there is no difficulty.

Colonel Haskell and Major Gaines, members here, both fought in the war; and one of them underwent extraordinary perils and hardships; still they, like all other Whigs here, vote on the record that the war was unnecessarily and unconstitutionally commenced by the President.

And even General Taylor, himself, the noblest Roman of them all, has declared that, as a citizen, and particularly as a soldier, it is sufficient for him to know that his country is at war with a foreign nation, to do all in his power to bring it to a speedy and honorable termination, by the most vigorous and energetic operations, without inquiring about its justice, or anything else connected with it.

Mr. Speaker, let our Democratic friends be comforted with the assurance that we are content with our position, content with our company, and content with our candidate; and that although they, in their generous sympathy, think we ought to be miserable, we really are not, and that they may dismiss the great anxiety they have on our account.

"THE AGE IS NOT DEAD."

[Delivered in the Court House at Springfield, Ill, in 1855, to only three persons. Mr. Herndon got out huge posters, announcing the event, employed a band to parade the streets and drum up a crowd, and bells were rung, but only three persons were present. Mr. Lincoln was to have spoken on the slavery question.]

GENTLEMEN:—This meeting is larger than I knew it would be, as I knew Herndon, (Lincoln's partner) and myself would come, but I did not know that any one else would be here, and yet another has come—you John Paine, (the Janitor.)

These are bad times, and seem out of joint. All seems dead, dead, DEAD; but the age is NOT yet dead; it liveth as sure as our Maker liveth. Under all this seeming want of life and motion, the world does move nevertheless. Be hopeful. And now let us adjourn and appeal to the people!

―――:o:―――

THE BALLOT vs. THE BULLET.

[Delivered to a delegation at Springfield, Ill., that proposed to visit Kansas Territory in the physical defense of freedom, in 1856. Hon. W. H. Herndon was in this delegation.]

FRIENDS:—I agree with you in Providence. I believe in the providence of the most men, the largest purse, and the longest cannon. You are in the minority—in a sad minority; and you can't hope to succeed, reasoning from all human experience. You would rebel against the Government, and redden your hands in the blood of your countrymen. If you are in the minority, as you are, you can't succeed. I say again and again, against the Government, with a great majority of its best citizens backing it, and when they have the most men, the longest purse, and the biggest cannon you can't succeed. If you have the majority, as some say you have, you can succeed with the ballot, throwing away the bullet. You can peaceably then redeem the Government. and preserve the liberties of mankind, through your votes and voice and moral influence.

Let there be peace. In a democracy, where a majority rule by the ballot through the forms of law, these physicial rebellions and bloody resistances, are radically wrong; unconstitutional, and are treason. Better bear the ills you have than to fly to those you know not of. Our own Declaration of Independence says that governments long established, for trival causes should not be resisted. Revolutionize through the ballot-box, and restore the Government once more to the affections and hearts of men, by making it express, as it was intended to do, the highest spirit of justice and liberty.

Your attempt, if there be such, to resist the laws of Kansas by force, is criminal and wicked; and all your feeble attempts will be follies, and end in bringing sorrow on your heads, and ruin the cause you would freely die to preserve.

———:o:———

LINCOLN "LINKED TO TRUTH."

[Spoken in the Library of the State House at Springfield, Illinois, to a few friends who wanted the sentence, "A house divided against itself cannot stand," expunged from the great speech known now as the "House Divided Against Itself Speech." Mr. Lincoln had submitted the manuscript for their criticism before the great speech was delivered.]

FRIENDS:—I have thought about this matter a great deal, have weighed the question well from all corners, and am thoroughly convinced the time has come when it should be uttered; and if it must be that I must go down because of this speech, then let me go down linked to truth, die in the advocacy of what is right and just. This nation cannot live on injustice, "A house divided against itself cannot stand." I say again and again; the proposition is true and has been true for six thousand years, and I will deliver it as it is written.

[This celebrated speech is given in full, commencing on the following page.

Mr. Herndon told Mr. Lincoln privately that it was all true, but he doubted whether it was good policy to give it utterance at that time. "That makes no difference," responded Mr. Lincoln. "It is the truth, and the nation is entitled to it." Then, alluding to a quotation which he had made from the Bible—"A house divided against itself cannot stand," he said that he wished to give an illustration familiar to all, "that he who runs may read."]

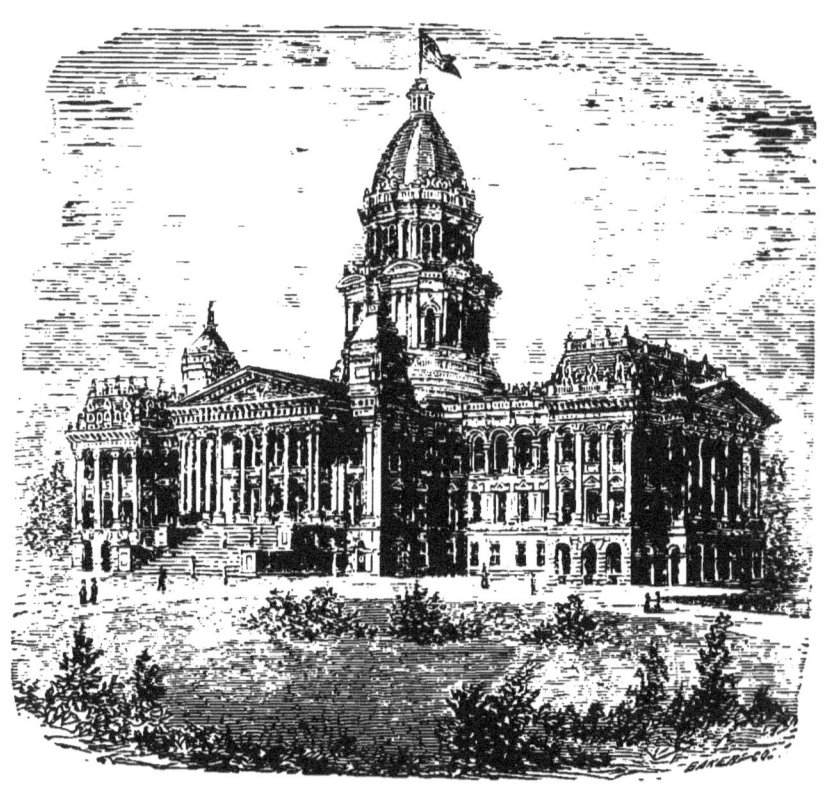

CAPITOL AT SPRINGFIELD, ILL.

LINCOLN'S FIRST SPEECH IN THE SENATORIAL CAMPAIGN.

"The House Divided Against Itself Speech."

(Delivered at Springfield, Ill., June 16, 1858, before the Republican State Convention. It is known as one of Lincoln's greatest speeches.)

Gentlemen of the Convention:—"If we could first know where we are, and whither we are tending, we could better judge what to do, and how to do it. We are now far into the fifth year, since a policy was initiated with the avowed object and confident promise of putting an end to slavery agitation. Under the operation of that policy, that agitation has not ceased, but has constantly augmented. In my opinion, it will not cease until a crisis shall have been reached and passed. "A house divided against itself cannot stand." I believe this government cannot endure permanently half slave and half free. I do not expect the Union to be dissolved—I do not expect the house to fall—but I do expect it will cease to be divided. It will become all one thing, or all the other. Either the opponents of slavery will arrest the further spread of it, and place it where the public mind shall rest in the belief that it is in the course of ultimate extinction; or its advocates will push it forward, till it shall become alike lawful in all the States, old as well as new—North as well as South.

"Have we no tendency to the latter condition?

"Let anyone who doubts, carefully contemplate that now almost complete legal combination—piece of machinery, so to speak—compounded of the Nebraska doctrine and the Dred Scott decision. Let him consider not only what work the machinery is adapted to do, and how well adapted; but also let him study the history of its construction, and trace, if he can, or rather fail, if he can, to trace the evidence of design and concert of action among its chief architects, from the beginning.

A FEW IMPORTANT FACTS.

"The new year of 1844 found slavery excluded from more than half the States by State Constitutions, and from most of the national territory by Congressional prohibition. Four days later, commenced the struggle which ended in repealing that Congressional prohibition. This opened all the national territory to slavery, and was the first point gained.

"But, so far, Congress had acted; and an indorsement by the people, real or apparent, was indispensable, to save the point already gained, and give chance for more.

"This necessity had not been overlooked; but had been provided for, as well as might be, in the notable argument of 'squatter sovereignty,' otherwise called 'sacred right of self-government,' which latter phrase, though expressive of the only rightful basis of any government, was so perverted in this attempted use of it as to amount to just this:

"That if any one man choose to enslave another, no third man shall be allowed to object. That argument was incorporated into the Nebraska bill itself, in the language which follows:

" 'It being the true intent and meaning of this act not to legislate slavery into any territory or state, nor to exclude it therefrom; but to leave the people thereof perfectly free to form and regulate their domestic institutions in their own way, subject only to the Constitution of the United States.'

"Then opened the roar of loose declamation in favor of 'squatter sovereignty,' and 'sacred right of self-government.' 'But,' said opposition members, 'let us amend the bill so as to expressly declare that the people of the territory may exclude slavery.' 'Not we,' said the friends of the measure; and down they voted the amendment.

"While the Nebraska bill was passing through Congress, a law case involving the question of a negro's freedom, by reason of his owner having voluntarily taken him first into a free state and then into a territory covered by the Congressional prohibition, and held him as a slave for a long time in each, was passing through the United States Circuit Court for the district of Missouri; and both Nebraska bill and lawsuit were brought to a decision in the same month of May, 1854. The negro's name was 'Dred Scott,' which name now designates the decision finally made in the case.

"Before the then next presidental election, the case came to, and was argued in the Supreme Court of the United States, but the decision of it was deferred until after the election.

Still before the election, Mr. Trumbull, on the floor of the Senate, requested the leading advocate of the Nebraska bill to state his opinion whether the people of a territory can constitutionally exclude slavery from their limits; and the latter answer.s: ·That is a question for the Supreme Court.'

"The election came. Mr. Buchanan was elected, and the endorsement, such as it was, secured. That was the second point gained. The endorsement, however, fell short of a clear popular majority of nearly four hundred thousand votes, and so, perhaps, was not overwhelmingly reliable and satisfactory. The outgoing President, in his last annual message, as impressively as possible echoed back upon the people the weight and authority of the indorsement. The Supreme Court met again; did not announce their decision, but ordered a re-argument. The presidential inauguration came, and still no decision of the court; but the incoming President in his inaugural address fervently exhorted the people to abide by the forthcoming decision, whatever it might be. Then, in a few days, came the decision.

"The reputed author of the Nebraska bill finds an early occasion to make a speech at this capital indorsing the Dred Scott decision, and vehemently denouncing all opposition to it. The new President, too, seizes the early occasion of the Silliman letter to indorse and strongly construe that decision, and to express his astonishment that any different view had ever been entertained.

VOTING IT UP OR DOWN.

"At length a squabble sprang up between the President and the author of the Nebraska bill, on the mere question of fact, whether the Lecompton Constitution was or was not, in any just sense, made by the people of Kansas; and in that quarrel the latter declares that all he wants is a fair vote for the people and that he cares not whether slavery be voted down or voted up. I do not understand his declaration that he cares not whether slavery be voted down or voted up to be intended by him other than an apt definition of the policy he would impress upon the pulic mind—the principle for which he declares he has suffered so much, and is ready to suffer to the end. And well may he cling. to that principle. If he has any parental feelings, well may he cling to it. That principle is the only shred left of his original Nebraska doctrine.

"Under the Dred Scott decision squatter sovreignty squatted out of existence, tumbled down like temporary scaffolding—like the mould at the foundry, served through one blast and fell back into loose sand—helped to carry an election and then was kicked to the winds. His late joint struggle with the Republicans, against the Lecompton Constitution, involves nothing of the original Nebraska doctrine. That struggle was made on a point—the right of a people to make their own constitution—upon which he and the Republicans have never differed.

"The several points of the Dred Scott decision, in connection with Senator Douglas' care not policy, constitute the piece of machinery, in its present state of advancement. This was the third point gained.

WORKING POINTS.

"The working points of that machinery are:

"First, That no negro slave, imported as such from Africa, and no descendant of such slave, can ever be a citizen of any state, in the sense of that term as used in the Constitution of the United States. This point is made in order to deprive the negro, in every possible event, of the benefit of that provision of the United States Constitution, which declares that 'The citizens of each state shall be entitled to all the privileges and immunities of citizens in the several states,'

"Secondly, That 'subject to the Constitution of the United States,' neither Congress nor a territorial legislature can exclude slavery from any United States territory. This point is made in order that indivinual men may fill up the territories with slaves, without danger of loosing them as property, and thus to enhance the chances of permanency to the institutions through all the future.

"Thirdly, That whether the holding the negro in actual slavery in a free state, makes him free, as against the holder, the United States courts will not decide, but will leave to be decided by the courts of any slave state the negro may be forced into by the master.

"This point is made, not to be pressed immediately, but, if acquiesced in for a while, and apparently indorsed by the people at an election, then to sustain the logical conclusion that what Dred Scott's master might lawfully do with Dred Scott, in the free state of Illinois, every other master may lawfully do with any other one, or one thousand slaves, or in any other free state.

"Auxiliary to all this, and working hand in hand with it. the Nebraska doctrine, or what is left of it, is to educate and mould public opinion, at least northern public opinion, not to care whether slavery is voted down or voted up. This shows exactly where we now are; and partially, also, whither we are tending.

A STRING OF HISTORICAL FACTS.

"It will throw additional light on the latter. to go back and run the mind over the string of historical facts already stated. Several things will now appear less dark and mysterious than they did when they were transpiring. The people were to be left 'perfectly free,' subject only to the Constitution.

What the Constitution had to do with it, outsiders could not then see. Plainly enough now, it was an exactly fitted niche, for the Dred Scott decision to afterward come in, and declare the perfect freedom of the people to be just no freedom at all. Why was the amendment, expressly declaring the right of the people voted down? Plain enough now; the adoption of it would have spoiled the niche for the Dred Scott decision Why was the court decision held up. Why even a senator's individual opinion withheld, till after the presidential election? Plainly enough now; the speaking out then would have damaged the perfectly free argument upon which the election was to be carried. Why the out-going President's felicitation on the indorsement? Why the delay of a re-argument? Why the incoming President's advance exhortation in favor of the decision? These things look like the cautious patting and petting of a spirited horse preparatory to mounting him, when it is dreaded that he may give the rider a fall. And why the hasty after-indorsement of the decision by the President and others?

"We cannot absolutely know that all these exact adaptations are the result of preconcert. But when we see a lot of framed timbers, different portions of which we know have been gotten out at different times and places and by different workman—Stephen, Franklin, Roger and James, for instance—and when we see these timbers joined together, and see they exactly make the frame of a house or a mill, all the tenons and mortices exactly adapted, and all the lengths and proportions of the different pieces exactly adapted to their respective places, and not a piece too many or too few—not omitting even scaffolding—or, if a single piece be lacking, we see the place in the frame exactly fitted and prepared yet to bring such a piece in—in such a case, we find it impossible not to believe that Stephen and Franklin and Roger and James all understood one another from the beginning and all worked upon a common plan or draft drawn up before the first blow was struck,

POWER OF A STATE.

"It should not be overlooked that, by the Nebraska bill, the people of a state as well as territory, were to be left 'perfectly free,' subject only to the Censtitution.' Why mention a state? They were legislating for territories, and not for or about states.

"Certainly the people of a state are or ought to be subject to the Constitution of the United States; but why is mention of this lugged into this merely territorial law? But why are the people of a territory and the pecple of a state therein lumped together, and their relation to the Constitution therein treated as being precisely the same? While the opinions of the court, by Chief Justice Taney, in the Dred Scott case, and the seperate opinions of all the concurring judges, expressly declare that the Constitution of the United States neither permits Congress nor a territorial legislature to exclude slavery from any United States territory, they all omit to declare whether or not the same Constitution permits a state, or the people of a state, to exclude it.

"Possibly, this is a mere omission; but who can be quite sure, if McLean or Curtis had sought to get into the opinion a declaration of unlimited power in the people of a state to exclude slavery from their limits, just as Chase and Mace sought to get such declaration, in behalf of the people of a territory, into the Nebraska bill; I ask, who can be quite sure that it would not have been voted down in the one case as it has been in the other.

"The nearest approach to the point of declaring the power of a state over slavery, is made by Judge Nelson. He approaches it more than once, using the precise idea and almost the language, too, of the Nebraska act. On one occasion his exact language is, 'except in cases where the power is restrained by the Constitution of the United States, the law of the state is supreme over the subject of slavery within its jurisdiction.

In what cases the power of the states is so restrained by the United States Constitution, is left an open question, precisely as the same question as to the restraint on the power of the territories was left open in the Nebraska act. Put this and that together, and we have another nice little niche, which we may, ere long, see filled with another Supreme Court decision, declaring that the Constitution of the United States does not permit a state to exclude slavery from its limits. And this may especially be expected if the doctrine of 'care not whether slavery be voted down or voted up,' shall gain upon the public mind sufficiently to give promise that such a decision can be maintained when made.

"Such a decision is all that slavery now lacks of being alike lawful in all the states. Welcome or unwelcome; such decision is probably coming, and will soon be upon us, unless the power of the present political dynasty shall be met and overthrown. We shall lie down pleasantly dreaming that the people of Missouri are on the very verge of making their state free, and we shall awake to the reality instead, that the Supreme Court has made Illinois a slave state. To meet and overthrow the power of that dynasty, is the work now before all those who would prevent that consumation. That is what we have to do. How can we best do it?

"A LIVING DOG IS BETTER THAN A DEAD LION."

"There are those who denounce us openly to their friends, and yet whisper us softly that Senator Douglas is the aptest instrument there is with which to effect that object. They wish us to infer all, from the fact that he now has a little quarrel with the present head of the dynasty; and that he has regularly voted with us on a single point, upon which he and we have never differed They remind us that he is a great man, and that the largest of us are very small ones. Let this be granted. But 'a living dog is better than a dead lion.' Judge Douglas, if not a dead lion, for this work, is at least a caged and toothless one. How can he oppose the advances of slavery? He don't care anything about it. His avowed mission is impressing the 'public heart' to care nothing about it.

A leading Douglas democratic newspaper treating upon this subject thinks Douglas' superior talent will be needed to resist the revival of the African slave trade. Does Douglas believe an effort to revive that trade is approaching? He has not said so. Does he really think so? But if it is, how can he resist it? For years he has labored to prove it a sacred right of white men to take negro slaves into the new territories. Can he possibly show that it is less a sacred right to buy them where they can be bought the cheapest? And unquestionably they can be bought cheaper in Africa than Virginia. He has done all in his power to reduce the whole question of slavery to one of a mere right of property: and as such, how can he oppose the foreign slave trade—how can he refuse that trade in that 'property' shall be 'perfectly free'—unless he does it as a protection to the home production? And as the home producers will probably not ask the protection, he will be wholly without a ground of opposition.

DOUGLAS IS NOT WITH US.

"Senator Douglas holds, we know, that a man may rightfully be wiser to-day than he was yesterday—that he may rightfully change when he finds himself wrong. But can we, for that reason, run ahead; and infer that he will make any particular change of which he himself has given no intimation? Can we safely base our actions upon any such vague reference? Now, as ever, I wish not to misrepresent Judge Douglas' position, question his motives, or do aught that can be personally offensive to him. Whenever, if ever, he and we can come together on principle so that our cause may have assistance from his great ability, I hope to have interposed no adventitious obstacle. But clearly, he is not now with us— he does not pretend to be — he does not pretend ever to be.

BUT WE SHALL NOT FAIL; THE VICTORY IS SURE.

"Our cause, then, must be intrusted to and conducted by its own undoubted friends—those whose hands are free, whose hearts are in the work—who do care for the result. Two years ago the Republicans of the nation mustered over thirteen thousand strong. We did this under the single impulse of resistance to a common danger, with every external circumstance against us. Of strange, discordant, and even hostile elements, we gathered from the four winds, and formed and fought the battle through, under the constant hot fire of a diciplined, proud and pampered enemy. Did we brave all then, to falter now? -now, when that same enemy is wavering, dissevered and belligerent? The result is not doubtful. We shall not fail—if we stand firm, we shall not fail. Wise counsels may accelerate, or mistakes delay it, but, sooner or later, the victory is sure to come."

MR. LINCOLN'S DEBATE WITH DOUGLAS.

His Celebrated Reply.

DELIVERED AT CHICAGO JULY 10, 1858.

MY FELLOW-CITIZENS: On yesterday evening, upon the occasion of the reception given to Senator Douglas, I was furnished with a seat very convenient for hearing him, and was otherwise very courteously treated by him and his friends, for which I thank him and them.

During the course of his remarks my name was mentioned in such a way as, I suppose, renders it at least not improper that I should make some sort of reply to him. I shall not attempt to follow him in the precise order in which he addressed the assembled multitude upon that occasion, though I shall perhaps do so in the main.

THE ALLEGED ALLIANCE.

There was one question to which he called the attention of the crowd, which I deem of somewhat less importance—at least of propriety for me to dwell upon—than the others, which he brought in near the close of his speech and which I think it would not be entirely proper for me to omit attending to, and yet if I were not to give some attention to it now, I should probably forget it altogether.

While I am upon this subject allow me to say that I do not intend to indulge in inconvenient modes sometimes adopted in pulbic speaking, of reading from documents; but I shall depart from that rule so far as to read a little scrap from his speech, which notices this first topic of which I speak—that is, provided I can find it in the paper.

[Examines the morning's paper and reads:]

"I have made up my mind to appeal to the people against the combination against me! the Republican leaders having formed an alliance, an unholy and unnatural alliance with a portion of unscrupulous federal office-holders. I intend to fight that allied army wherever I meet them.

I know they deny the alliance, but yet these men who are trying to divide the Democratic party for the purpose of electing a Republican Senator in my place, are just as much the agents and tools of the supporters of Mr. Lincoln. Hence I shall deal with this allied army just as the Russians deal with the allies at Sebastopol—that is, the Russians did not stop to inquire when they fired a broadside, whether it hit an Englishman, a Frenchman or a Turk.

Nor will I stop to inquire, nor shall I hesitate whether my blows shall hit these Republican leaders or their allies who are holding the Federal offices and yet acting in concert with them."

Well, now, gentlemen, is not that very alarming? Just think of it! right at the outset of his canvass, I, a poor, kind, amiable, intelligent gentleman, I am to be slain in this way. Why, my friends, the Judge is not only, as it turns out, not a dead lion, nor even a living one—he is the rugged Russian Bear!

[Laughter and applause.]

But if they will have it—for he says that we deny it—that there is any alliance, as he says there is— and I don't propose hanging very much upon this question of veracity —but if he will have it and there is such an alliance—that the admisistration men and we are allied, and we stand in the attitude of English, French and Turk, he occupying the position of the Russian, in that case, I beg that he will indulge us while we barely suggest to him that these allies took Sebastopol! [Great applause.]

Gentlemen, only a few more words as to this alliance. For my part I have to say, that whether there be such an alliance, depends, so far as I know, of what may be a right definition of the term alliance. If for the Republican party to see the other great party to which they are opposed divided among themselves, and not try to stop the division and rather be glad of it—if that is an alliance, I confess I am in; but if it is meant to be said that the Republicans formed an alliance going beyond that, by which there is contribution of money or sacrifice of principle on the one side or other, so far as the Republican party is concerned, if there be any such thing, I protest that I neither know anything of it, nor do I believe it.

I will, however, say—as I think this branch of the argument is lugged in—I would before I leave it state, for the benefit of those concerned, that one of those same

Buchanan men did once tell me of an argument that he made for his opposition to Judge Douglas.

He said that a friend of our Senator Douglas had been talking to him, and had among other things said to him: 'Why, you don't want to beat Douglas?" "Yes," said he, "'I do want to beat him, and I will tell you why. I believe his original Nebraska bill was right in the abstract, but it was wrong in the time it was brought forward. It was wrong in the application to a Territory in regard to which the question had been settled; it was tendered to the South when the South had not asked for it, but when they could not refuse it.

"And for this same reason he forced that question upon our party; it has sunk the best men all over the nation, everywhere, and now when our President, struggling with the difficulty of this man's getting up, has reached the very hardest point to turn in the case, he deserts him, and I am for putting him where he will trouble us no more."

Now, gentlemen, that is not my argumont at all. I have only been stating to you the argument of a Buchanan man. You will judge if there is any force in it.

WHAT IS POPULAR SOVEREIGNTY.

Popular sovereignty! everlasting popular sovereignty! Let us for a moment inquire into the vast matter of popular soverignty. What is popular sovereignty? We recollect that in an early period in the history of this struggle, there was another name for the same thing—Squatter Sovereignty. It was not exactly Popular Sovereignty but Squatter Sovereignty.

What do those terms mean? What do those terms mean when used now?

And vast credit is taken by our friend, the Judge, in regard to his support of it, when he declares the last years ot his life have been and all the future years shall be devoted to this matter of popular sovereignty. What is it? Why it is the sovereignty of the people! What was squatter sovereignty? I suppose if it had any significance at all it was the right of the people to govern themselves, to be sovereign in their own affairs while they had squatted

THE SQUATTER'S HOME.

on a Territory that did not belong to them, in the sense that a State belongs to the people who inhabit it—when it belonged to the nation—such right to govern themselves was called "Squatter Sovereignty."

Now I wish you to mark. What has become of that Squatter Sovereignty? What has become of it? Can you get anybody to tell you now that the people of a Territory have any authority to govern themselves in regard to this mooted question of slavery, before they form a State Constitution?

No such thing at all, although there is a general running fire, and although there has been a hurrah made in every speech on that side, assuming that policy had given the people of the Territory a right to govern themselves upon this question; yet the point is dodged. To-day it has been decided—no more than a year ago it had been decided by the Supreme Court of the United States, and is insisted upon to-day, that the people of a Territory have no right to exclude slavery from a Territory, and if any one man chooses to take slaves into a Territory, all the rest of the people have no right to keep him out.

This being so, and this decision being made one of the points that the Judge approved, and one in the approval of which he says he means to keep me down—put me down I should not say, for I have never been up, he says he is in favor of it, and sticks to it, and expects to win his battle on that decision which says there is no such thing as Squatter Sovereignty, but that any man may take slaves into a Territory, aud all the men may be opposed to it, and yet by reason of the Constitution they cannot prohiblt it.

When that is so, how much is left of this matter of Squatter Sovereignty, I should like to know?

[A voice—"It is all gone."]

When we get back, we get to the point of the right of the people to make a Constitution. Kansas was settled, for example, in 1854. It was a Territory yet, without having formed a Constitution, in a very regular way, for three years.

All this time negro slavery could be taken in by any few individuals, and by that decision of the Supreme Court, which the Judges approve, all the rest of the people cannot keep it out; but when they come to make a Constitution they may say they will not have slavery.

But it is there; they are obliged to tolerate it in some way, and all experience shows it will be so—for they will not take negro slaves and absolutely deprive the owners of them.

All experience shows this to be so. All that space of time that runs from the beginning of the settlement of the Territory until there is sufficiency of people to make a State Constitution—all that portion of time Popular Sovereignty is given up.

The seal is absolutely put down upon it by the Court decision, and Judge Douglas puts his own on the top of that, yet he is appealing to the people to give him vast credit for his devotion to popular sovereignty.

[Applause.]

Again, when we get to the question of the right of people to form a State Constitution as they please, to form with slavery or without slavery—if that is anything new, I confess I don't know it. Has there ever been a time when anybody said that any other than the people of a Territory itself should form a Constitution? What is now in it that Douglas should have fought several years of his life, and pledge himself to fight all the remaining years of his life for?

Can Judge Douglas find anybody on earth that said anybody else should form a Constitution for a people? [A voice—"Yes."] Well, I should like you to name him —I should like to know who he was [same voice—"John Calhoun

Mr. Lincoln—No, sir, I never heard of even John Calhoun saying such a thing. He insisted on the same principle as Judge Douglas; but his mode of applying it in fact, was wrong. It is enough for my purpose to ask this crowd, when ever a Republican said anything against it? They never said anything against it, but they have constantly spoken for it; and whosoever will undertake to examine the platform, and the speeches of responsible men of the party, and of irresponsible men, too, if you please, will be unable to find one word from anybody in the Republican ranks opposed to that Popular Sovereignty which Judge Douglas thinks that he has invented. [Applause.]

I suppose that Judge Douglas will claim in a little while that he is the inventor of the idea that the people should govern themselves; that nobody ever thought of such a thing until he brought it forward. We do remember, that in the old Declaration of Independence, it is said that "We hold these truths to be self-evident, that all men are created equal; that they are endowed by their Creator with certain inalienable rights; that among these are life, liberty, and the pursuit of happiness; that to secure these rights, governments are instituted among men, deriving their just powers from the consent of the governed." There is the origin of Popular Sovereignty.

[Loud applause.]

Who, then, shall come in at this day and say that he invented it?

[After referring, in appropriate terms, to the credit claimed by Douglas for defeating the Lecompton policy, Mr. Lincoln proceeds.]

I defy you to show a printed resolution passed in a Democratic meeting—I take it upon myself to defy any man to show a printed resolution of a Democratic meeting, large or small, in favor of Judge Trumbull, or any of the five to one Republicans who beat that bill. Everything must be for the Democrats.

They did everything, and the five to the one that really did the thing, they snub over, and they do not seem to remember that they have an existence upon the face of the earth.

A HOUSE DIVIDED AGAINST ITSELF CANNOT STAND.

THE OLD AND DIVIDED JERUSALEM WHICH FELL.

Gentlemen, I fear that I shall become tedious. I leave this branch of the subject to take hold of another. I take up that part of Judge Douglas' speech in which he respectfully attended to me.

Judge Douglas made two points upon my recent speech

at Springfield. He says they are to be the issues of this campaign. The first one of these points he bases upon the language in a speech which I delivered at Springfield, which I believe I can quote correctly from memory. I said there that " we are now far on in the fifth year when a policy was instituted for the avowed object, and with the confident promise of putting and end to slavery agitation; under the operation or that policy that agitation had not only not ceased, but had constantly augmented. I believe it will not cease until a crisis shall have been reached and passed.

A house divided against itself can not stand. I believe this government can not endure permanently half slave and half free.

I do not expect the Union to be dissolved—I am quoting from my speech—I do not expect the house to fall, but I do expect it will cease to be divided. It will come all one thing or the other. Either the opponents of slavery will arrest the spread of it, and place it where the public mind shall rest in the belief that it is in the course of ultimate extinction, or its advocates will push it forward until it shall have become alike lawful in all the States, North as well as South.

In this paragraph which I have quoted in your hearing, and to which I ask the attention of all, Judge Douglas thinks he discovered great political heresy. I want your attention particularly to what he has inferred from it. He says I am in favor of making all the States of the Union uniform. He draws this inference from the language I have quoted to you.

He says that I am in favor of making war by the North upon the South for the extinction of slavery; that I am

DEBATE WITH DOUGLAS. 371

also in favor of inviting, as he expresses it, the South to a war upon the North, for the purpose of nationalizing slavery. Now, it is singular enough, if you will carefully read the passage over, that I did not say that I was in fa-

HALF SLAVE AND HALF FREE.

vor of any such thing in it. I only said what I expected would take place.

I made a prediction only—it may have been a foolish one perhaps. I did not even say that I desired that slavery should be put in course of ultimate extinction. I do say so, now, however, so there need be no longer any difficulty about that. It may be written down in the next speech.

Gentlemen, Judge Douglas informed you that this speech of mine was probably carefully prepared. I admit that it was. I am not master of language; I have not a fine education; I am not capable of entering into a disquisition upon dialects, as I believe you call it; but I don't believe the language I employed bears any such construction as Judge Douglas puts upon it.

But I don't care about a quibble in regard to words. I know what I meant, and I will not leave this crowd in doubt, if I can explain it to them, what I really meant in the use of that paragraph.

I am not, in the first place, unaware that this government has endured eighty-two years half slave and half free. I know that. I am tolerably well acquainted with the history of the country, and I know that it has endured eighty-two years half slave and half free. I believe—and that is what I meant to allude to here—I believe it has endured, because during all that time, until the introduction of the Nebraska bill, the public mind did rest all the time in the belief that slavery was in the course of ultimate extinction.

That was what gave us the rest that we had during that period of eighty-two years; at least, so I believe. I have always hated slavery, I think, as much as any Abolitionist. I have been an old line Whig. I have always hated it, but I have always been quiet about it until this new era of the introduction of the Nebraska bill began. I have always believed that everybody was against it, and that it was in the course of ultimate extinction. [Pointing to Mr. Browning, who stood near by:] Browning thought so; the great mass of the nation have rested in the belief that slavery was in course of ultimate extinction. They had reason so to believe.

The adoption of the Constitution and its attendant history led the people to believe so; and that such was the belief of the framers of the Constitution itself.

Why did those old men, about the time of the adoption of the Constitution, decree that slavery should not go into the new territory, where it had not already gone? Why declare that within twenty years the African slave trade, by which slaves are supplied, might be cut off by Congress? Why were all these acts?

I might enumerate more of such acts; but enough.

What were they but a clear indication that the framers of the Constitution intended and expected the ultimate extinction of that institution? (Cheers.)

And now when I say, as I said in this speech that Judge Douglas has quoted from, when I say that I think the opponents of slavery will resist the further spread of it, and place it were the public mind shall rest with the belief that it is in the course of ultimate extinction. I only meant to say, that they will place it where the foundation of this Government originally placed it.

I have said a hundred times, I have no inclination to take it back that I believe there is no right, and ought to be no inclination of the people of the free States to enter into the slave States, and to interfere with the question of slavery at all. I have said that always. Judge Douglas has heard me say it, if not quite a hundred times, at least as good as a hundred times; and when it is said that

I am in favor of interfering with slavery where it exists, I know it is unwarranted by anything I have ever intended, and, as I believe, by anything I have ever used language which could be fairly so constructed (as, however, I believe I never have), I now correct it.

So much, then, for the inference that Judge Douglas draws, that I am in favor of setting the sections at war with one another. I know that I never meant any such thing, and I believe that no fair mind can infer any such thing, from anything I have ever said.

SELF-GOVERNMENT.

Now in relation to his inference that I am in favor of a general consolidation of all the various institutions of the various States, I will attend to that for a little while, and try to inquire, if I can, how on earth it could be that any man could draw such an inference from anything I said.

I have said, very many times, in Judge Douglas hearing, that no man believed more than I in the principle of self-government, from beginning to end. I have denied his use of that term applied properly. But for the thing itself, I deny that any man has gone ahead of me in his devotion to the principle, whatever he may have done in efficiency in advocating it.

I think that I have said in your hearing—that I believe each individual is naturally entitled to do as he pleases with himself and the fruit of his labor, so far as it in no wise interferes with any other man's rights--[applause] that each community, or a State, has a right to do exactly as it pleases with the concerns within that State that interfere with the right of no other State, and that the General Government, upon principle, has no right to interfere with anything other than that general class of things that does concern the whole. I have said that at all times.

I have said as illustrations, that I do not believe in the right of Illinois to interfere with the cranberry laws of Indiana, the oyster laws of Virginia, or the liquor laws of Maine. I have said these things over and over again, and I repeat them here as my sentiments.

So much then as to my disposition, my wish, to have all the State Legislatures blotted out, and a uniformity of domestic regulations in all the States; by which I suppose it is meant, if we raise corn here, we must make sugar-cane too, and we must make those which grow North grow in the South. All this I suppose he understands, I am in favor of doing.

Now so much for all this nonsense; for I must call it so. The Judge can have no issue with me on a question of established uniformity in the domestic regulations of the State.

DRED SCOTT DECISION.

A little now on the other point; the Dred Scott decision. Another of the issues he says that is to be made with me, is upon his devotion to the Dred Scott decision, and my opposition to it.

I have expressed heretofore, and I now repeat my opposition to the Dred Scott decision, but I should be allowed to state the nature of that opposition, and I ask your indulgence while I do so. What is fairly implied by the term which Judge Douglas has used, "resistance to the decision?" I do not resist it. If I wanted to take

Dred Scott from his master, I would be interfering with property, and that terrible difficulty that Judge Douglas speaks of, of interfering with property would arise.

But I am doing no such thing as that, but all that I am doing is refusing to obey it as a political rule. If I were in Congress and a vote should come up on a question whether slavery should be prohibited in a new Territory, in spite of the Dred Scott decision, I would vote that it should.

That is what I would do. Judge Douglas said last night, that before the decision he might advance his opinion, and it might be contrary to the decision when it was made; but after it was made he would abide by it until it was reversed. Just so! We let this property abide by the decision, but we will try to reverse that decision. (Loud applause.)

We will try to put it where Judge Douglas will not object, for he says he will obey it until it is reversed. Somebody has to reverse that decision, since it was made, and we mean to reverse it, and we mean to do it peaceably.

What are the uses of decisions of courts? They have two uses. As rules of property they have two uses. First; they decide upon the question before the court. They decide in this case that Dred Scott is a slave. Nobody resists that. Not only that, but they say to everybody else, that persons standing just as Dred Scott stands, is as he is. That is, that when a question comes up upon another person, it will be so decided again unless the court decides in another way, unless the court overrules its decision. (Renewed applause.) Well, we mean to do what we can to have the court decide the other way. That is one thing we mean to try to do.

The sacredness that Judge Douglas throws around this decision, is a degree of sacredness that has never been before thrown around any other decision. I have never heard of such a thing. Why, decisions apparently contrary to that decision, or good lawyers thought were contrary to that decision, have been made by that very court before. It is the first of its kind; it is an astonisher in legal history. It is a new wonder of the world. it is based on falsehoods in the main as to the facts; allegations of facts upon which it stands are not facts at all in many instances, and no decision made on any question; the first instance of a decision made under so many unfavorable circumstances; thus placed, has ever been held by the profession as law, and it has always needed confirmation before the lawyers regarded it as law. But Judge Douglas would have it that all hands must take this extraordinary decision, made under these extraordinary circumstances, and give their vote in congress in accordance with it, yield to it and obey it in every possible sense,

Circumstances alter cases. Do not gentlemen here remember the case of that Supreme Court, twenty-five or thirty years ago, deciding that a National Bank was Constitutional? I ask, if somebody does not remember that a National Bank was declared to be Constitutional? Such is the truth, whether it be remembered or not. The bank charter ran out, and a re-charter was granted. That re-charter was laid before General Jackson.

It was urged upon him, when he denied the constitutionality of the bank, that the Supreme Court had decided that it was constitutional; and that General Jackson then said that the Supreme Court had no right to lay down a rule to govern a co-ordinate branch of the Government, the members of which have sworn to support the Constitution; that each member had sworn to support that Constitution as he understood it.

I will venture here to say, that I have heard Judge Douglas say that he approved of General Jackson for that

act. What has now become of all his tirade about "resistence to the Supreme Court?"

THE DECLARATION OF INDEPENDENCE.

We were often; more than once, at least; in the course of Judge Douglas' speech last night, reminded that this Government was made for white men; that he believed it was made for white men. Well that is putting it into a shape in which no one wants to deny it; but the Judge then goes into his passion for drawing inferences that are not warranted.

I protest, now and forever, against that counterfeit logic which presumes that because I did not want a negro woman for a slave, I do not necessarily want her for a wife. My understanding is that I need not have her for either; but as God made us separate, we can leave one another alone, and do one another much good thereby.

There are white men enough to marry all the white women, and enough black men to marry all the black women, and in God's name let them be so married. The Judge regales us with the terrible enormities that take place by the mixture of races; that the inferior race bears the superior down. Why, Judge, if you do not let them get together in the Territories they won't mix there!

A voice; "Three cheers for Lincoln." (The cheers were given with a hearty good will.

Mr. L.—I should say at least that this is a self evident truth.

Now, it happens that we meet together once every year some time about the Fourth of July, for some reason or other. These Fourth of July gatherings I suppose have their uses. If you will indulge me, I will state what I suppose to be some of them.

A MIGHTY NATION.

We are now a mighty nation; we are thirty; or about thirty millions of people, and we own and inhabit about one-fifteenth part of the dry land of the whole earth.

We run our memory back over the pages of history for about eighty-two years, and we discover that we were then a very small people in point of numbers, vastly inferior to what we are now, with a vastly less extent of country, with vastly less of everything we deem desirable among men; we look upon the change as exceedingly advantageous to us and to our prosterity, and we fix upon something that happened away back, as in some way or other being connected with this rise of prosperity.

We find a race of men living in that day whom we claim as our fathers and grandfathers; they were iron men; they fought for the principle that they were contending for; and we understood that by what they then did it has followed that the degree of prosperity which we now enjoy has come to us.

We hold this annual celebration to remind ourselves of all the good done in this process of time, of how it was done and who did it, and how we are historically connected with it; and we go from these meetings in better humor with ourselves; we feel more attached the one to the other, and more firmly bound to the country we inhabit.

In every way we are better men in the age, and race, and country in which we live, for these celebrations. But after we have done all this, we have not yet reached the whole. There is something else connected with it.

We have, besides these; men descended by blood from our ancestors; those among us, perhaps half our people, who are not descendents at all of these men; they are men who have come from Europe; German, Irish, French and Scandinavian; men that have come from Europe themselves, or whose ancestors who have come hither and settled here, finding themselves our equals in all things. If they look back through this history to trace their connection with those days of blood, they find they have none, they cannot carry themselves back into that glorious epoch and make themselves feel they are part of us; but when they look through that old Declaration of Independence, they find that those old men say that "We hold these truths to be self evident, that all men are created equal," and then they feel that that moral sentiment, taught on that day, evidences their relation to those men, that it is the father of all moral principle in them, and that they have a right to claim it as though they were the blood of the blood and flesh of the flesh of the men who wrote that Declaration [loud and long continued applause], and so they were.

That is the electric cord in that Declaration that links the hearts of patriotic and liberty-loving men together, that will link those patriotic hearts as long as the love of freedom exists in the minds of men throughout the world. (Applause.)

RUBBING OUT THE SENTIMENT OF LIBERTY.

Now, sirs, for the purpose of squaring things with this idea of "don't care if slavery is voted up or voted down," for sustaining the Dred Scott decision, for holding that the Declaration of Independence did not mean anything at all, we have Judge Douglas giving his exposition of what the Declaration of Independence means and we have him saying that the people of America are equal to the people of England. According to his construction, you Germans are not connected with it.

Now I ask you in all soberness, if all these things, if

indulged in, if ratified, if confirmed and indorsed, if taught to our children and repeated to them, do not tend to rub out the sentiment of liberty in the country, and to transform this Government into a government of some other form.

These arguments that are made that the inferior race are to be treated with as much allowance as they are capable of enjoying; that as much is to be done for them as their condition will allow; what are these arguments? they are the arguments that Kings have made for enslaving the people in all ages of the world.

You will find that all arguments in favor of King-craft were of this class; they always bestrode the necks of the people, not that they wanted to do it. but because the people were better off for being ridden.

That is their argument, and this argument of the Judge is the same old serpent that says: You work and I eat; you toil and I will enjoy the fruits of it.

Turn it whatever way you will: whether it comes from the mouth of a King, an excuse for enslaving the people of his country, or from the mouth of men from one race as the reason for enslaving the men of another race, it is all the same old serpent, and I hold if that course of argumentation that is made for the purpose of convincing the public mind that we should not care about this, should be granted, it does not stop with the negro.

I should like to know, if taking this old Declaration of Independence, which declares that all men are equal upon principle, you begin making exceptions to it, where you will stop? If one man says it does not mean a negro, why not another man say it does not mean some other man! If that declaration is not the trnth, let us get the statute book, in which we find it, and tear it out? If it is not true, let us tear it out! [cries of "no, no"]; let us stick to it then; let us stand by it then. (Applause.)

It may be argued that there are certain conditions that make necessities and impose them upon us, and to the extent that a necessity is imposed upon a man, he must submit to it. I think that was the condition in which we found ourselves when we established this Government. We have slaves among us; we could not get our Constitution unless we permitted them to remain in slavery; we could not secure the good we did secure if we grasped for more: and having, by necessity, submitted to that much, it does not destroy the principle that is the charter of our liberties. Let that charter stand as our standard.

LET US STAND FIRMLY BY EACH OTHER.

My friend has said to me that I am a poor hand to quote Scripture. I will try it again, however. It is said in one of the admonitions of our Lord: "As your Father in Heaven is perfect, be ye also perfect."

The Savior, I suppose, did not expect that any human creature could be as perfect as the Father in Heaven; but He said: As your Father in Heaven is perfect, be ye also perfect.

He set that up as a standard, and he who did most toward reaching that standard, attained the highest degree of moral perfection. So I say in relation to the principle that all men are created equal, let it be as nearly reached as we can. If we cannot give freedom to every creature, let us do nothing that will impose slavery upon any other creature. (Applause.) Let us then turn this Government back into the channel in which the

OUR SAVIOR PERFORMING THE MIRACLE AT THE WEDDING IN CANA.

framers of the Constitution originally placed it. Let us stand firmly by each other. If we do not do so we are turning in the contrary direction, that our friend Judge Douglas proposes; not intentionally; as working in the traces tends to make this one universal slave nation. He is one that runs in that direction, and as such I resist him.

My friends, I have detained you about as long as I desire to do, and I have only to say, let us discard all this quibbling about this man and the other man; this race and that race and the other race being inferior, and therefore they must be placed in an inferior position—discarding our standard that we have left us. Let us discard all these things, and unite as one people throughout this land, until we shall once more stand up declaring that all men are created equal.

My friends, I could not, without launching off upon some new topic, which would detain you too long, continue to-night. I thank you for this most extensive audience that you have furnished me to-night. I leave you, hoping that the lamp of liberty will burn in your bosoms until there shall no longer be a donbt that all men are created free and equal.

———:o:———

DOUGLAS' SEVEN QUESTIONS.

Lincoln's Position Defined on the Questions of the Day.

[Delivered at Freeport, Ill., July, 1858.]

LADIES AND GENTLEMEN:—On Saturday last, Judge Douglas and myself first met in public discussion. He spoke one hour, I an hour and a half, and he replied for half an hour. The order is now reversed. I am to speak an hour, he an hour and a half, and then I am to reply for half on hour. I propose to devote myself during the first hour to the scope of what was brought within the range of his half hour speech at Ottawa. Of course there was brought within the scope of that half-hour's speech something of his own opening speech. In the course of that opening argument Judge Douglas proposed to me seven different interrogatories.

In my speech of an hour and a half, I attended to some other parts of his speech; and incidentally, as I thought, answered one of the interrogatories then. I then distinctly intimated to him that I would answer the rest of his interrogatories on condition only that he should agree to answer as many for me. He made no intimation at the time of the proposition, nor did he in his reply allude at all to that suggestion of mine. I do him no injustice in saying that he occupied at least half of his reply in dealing with me as though I had refused to answer his interrogatories. I now propose that I will answer any of the interrogatories, upon condition that he will answer questions from me not exceeding the same number, I give him an opportunity to respond. I now say that I will answer his interrogatories, whether he answers mine or not [applause]; and that after I have done so, I will propound mine to him. [Applause.]

I have supposed myself, since the organization of the Republican party at Bloomington, in May, 1856, bound as a party man by the platform of the party, then and since. If in any interrogatories which I shall answer I go beyond the scope of what is in these platforms, it will be perceived that no one is responsible but myself.

Having said this much, I will take up the Judge's interrogatories as I find them printed in the Chicago Times, and answer them seriatim. In order that there may be no mistake about it, I have copied the interrogatories in writing, and also my answers to them. The first one of these interrogatories is in these words:

Q. 1. "I desire to know whether Lincoln to-day stands, as he did in 1854, in favor of the unconditional repeal of the Fugitive Slave Law?"

A. I do not now, nor never did, stand in favor of the unconditional repeal of the Fugutive Slave Law.

Q. 2. I desire him to answer whether he stands pledged to-day, as he did in 1854, against any more slave States into the Union, even if the people want them?"

A. I do not now, nor never did, stand pledged against the admission of any more slave States into the Union.

Q. 3. "I want to know whether he stands pledged against the admission of a new State into the Union with such a Constitution as the people of that State may see fit to make?"

A. I do not stand pledged against the admission of a new State into the Union, with such a constitution as the people of that State may see fit to make.

Q. 4. "I want to know whether he stands to-day pledged to the abolition of slavery in the District of Columbia.

A. I do not stand to-day pledged to the abolition of slavery in the District of Columbia.

Q. 5. "I desire him to answer whether he stands pledged to the prohibition of the slave-trade between the different States?"

A. I do not stand pledged to the prohibition of the slave-trade between the different States.

Q. 6. "I desire to know whether he stands pledged to prohibit slavery in all the Territories of the United States, North as well as South of the Missouri Compromise line?"

A. I am impliedly, if not expressedly, pledged to a belief in the right and duty of Congress to prohibit slavery in the United States Territories. [Great applause.]

Q. 7. "I desire to know whether he is opposed to the acquisition of any new territory unless slavery is first prohibited therein?"

A. I am not generally opposed to honest acquisition of Territory; and, in any given case, I would or would not oppose such acquisition, accordingly as I might think such acquisition would or would not agitate the slavery question among ourselves.

Now, my friends, it will be perceived upon an examination of these questions and answers, that so far I have only answered that I was not pledged to this, that or the other. The Judge has not framed his interrogatories to ask me anything more than this, and I have answered in strict accordance with his interrogatories, and have answered truly that I am not pledged at all upon any of the points to which I have answered. But I am not disposed to hang upon the exact form of his interrogatory. I am rather disposed to take up at least some of these questions, and state what I really think upon them.

LINCOLN'S POSITION MORE FULLY DEFINED.

As to the first one, in regard to the Fugitive Slave Law, I have never hesitated to say, and I do not now hesitate to say, that I think, under the Constitution of the United States, the people of the Southern States are entitled to a Congressional slave law. Having said that, I have nothing to say in regard to the existing Fugitive Slave Law, farther than that I think it should have been framed so as to be free from some of the objections that pertain to it, without lessening its efficiency. And inasmuch as we are not now in agitation upon the general question of slavery.

In regard to the other question, of whether I am pledged to the admission of any more slave States into the Union, I state to you frankly that I would be exceedingly sorry ever to be put in a position of having to pass upon that question. I should be exceedingly glad to know that there would never be another slave State admitted into the Union; but I must add, that if slavery shall be kept out of the Territories during the Territorial existence of any one given Territory, and then the people shall, having a fair chance and a clear field, when they come to adopt the Constitution, do such an extraordinary thing as to adopt the Constitution, uninfluenced by the actual presence of the institution among them, I see no alternative if we own the country, but to admit them into the Union. [Applause.]

The third interrogatory is answered by the answer to the second, it being, as I conceive, the same as the second.

The fourth one is in regard to the abolition of slavery in the District of Columbia. In relation to that I have my mind very distinctly made up. I should be exceedingly glad to see slavery abolished in the District of Columbia. I believe that Congress has Constitutional power to abolish it. Yet as a member of Congress, I should not with my present views be in favor of endeavoring to abolish slavery in the District of Columbia, unless it would be upon these conditions. First, that the abolition should be gradual; second, that it should be on a vote of the majority of qualified voters of the District; and third, that compensation should be made to unwilling owners. With these three conditions, I confess I would be exceedingly glad to see Congress abolish slavery in the District of Columbia, and in the language of Henry Clay, "sweep from our Capital that foul blot upon our Nation."

In regard to the fifth interrogatory, I must say that as

to the question of abolition of the slave-trade between the different States, I can truly answer, as I have, that I am pledged to nothing about it. It is a subject to which I have not given that mature consideration that would make me feel authorized to state a position so as to hold myself entirely bound by it. In other words, that question has never been prominently enough before me to induce me to investigate whether we really have the Constitutional power to do it. I could investigate if I had sufficient time to bring myself to a conclusion upon that subject; but I have not done so, and I say so frankly to you here, and to Judge Douglas. I must say, however, that if I should be of the opinion that Congress does possess the Constitutional power to abolish slave-trading among the different States, I should not still be in favor of that power unless upon some conservative principle as I conceive it, akin to what I have said in relation to the abolition of slavery in the District of Columbia.

My answer as to whether I desire that slavery should be prohibited in all Territories of the United States, is full and explicit within itself, and cannot be made clearer by any comment of mine. So I suppose in regard to the question whether I am opposed to the acquisition of any more territory unless slavery is such that I could add nothing by way of illustration, or making myself better understood, than the answer, which I have placed in writing.

Now, in all this, the Judge has me, and he has me on the record. I suppose he had flattered himself that I was really entertaining one set of opinions for one place and another set for another place—that I was afraid to say at one place what I uttered at another. What I am saying here I suppose I say to a vast audience in the State of Illinois, and I believe I am saying that which, if it would be offensive to any persons and render them enemies to myself, would be offensive to persons in this audience.

———:o:———

LINCOLN'S GREAT COOPER INSTITUTE SPEECH.

Delivered at Cooper Institute, New York City, February 27, 1860.

[This speech, more than any other one, is supposed to have secured Lincoln the nomination for the Presidency.]

MR. PRESIDENT and Fellow-Citizens of New York:—
The facts with which I shall deal this evening are mainly old and familiar; nor is there anything new in the general use I shall make of them. If there shall be any novelty, it will be in the mode of presenting the facts, and the references and observations following that presentation.

OUR FATHERS AND THE CONSTITUTION.

In his speech last autumn at Columbus, Ohio, as reported in the New York Times, Senator Douglas said:

"Our fathers, when they framed the government under which we live, understood this question just as well and even better than we do now."

I fully indorse this, and I adopt it as a text for this discourse. I so adopt it because it furnishes a precise and agreed starting-point for a discussion between Republicans and that wing of Democracy headed by Senator Douglas. It simply leaves the inquiry: "What was the understanding those fathers had of the question mentioned?

What is the frame of government under which we live?

The answer must be: "The Constitution of the United States."

That Constitution consists of the original, framed in 1837 (and under which the present government first went into operation), and twelve subsequently framed amendments, the first ten of which were framed in 1789.

Who were our fathers that framed the Constitution? I suppose the "thirty-nine" who signed the original instrument may be fairly called our fathers who framed that part of our present government. It is almost exactly true to say they framed it, and it is altogether true to say they fairly represented the opinion and sentiment of the whole nation at that time. Their names being familiar to nearly all, and accessible to quite all, need not now be repeated.

I take these "thirty-nine" for the present, as being "our fathers who framed the government under which we live."

What is the question which, according to the text, those fathers understood just as well and even better than we do now?

THE GREAT ISSUE.

It is this: Does the proper division of local from Federal authority, or anything in the Constitution, forbid our Federal Government to control us as to slavery in our Federal Territories?

Upon this Douglas holds the affirmative, and Republicans the negative. This affirmative and denial form an issue; and this issue—this question—is precisely what the text declares our fathers understood better than we.

In 1784—three years before the Constitution—the United States then owning the North-western Territory, and no other—the Congress of the Confederation had before them the question of prohibiting slavery in that Territory; and four of the "thirty-nine" who afterward framed the Constitution were in that Congress, and voted on that question.

Of these, Roger Sherman, Thomas Mifflin and Hugh Williamson voted for the prohibition—thus showing that, in their understanding, no line divided local from Federal authority, nor anything else, properly forbade the Federal Government to control as to slavery in Federal territory.

The other of the four—James McHenry—voted against the prohibition, showing that, for some cause, he thought it improper to vote for it.

ORDINANCE OF 1787.

In 1787, still before the Constitution, but while the convention was in session framing it and while the Northwest Territory was the only territory owned by the United States, the same question of prohibiting slavery in the territory again came before the Congress of the Confederation and three more of the "thirty-nine" who afterward signed the Constitution were in that Congress and voted on that question.

They were: William Blount, William Few, and Abraham Baldwin, and they all voted for the prohibition—

thus showing that, in their understanding, no line dividing local from Federal authority, nor anything else, properly forbade the Federal Government to control as to slavery in Federal territory. This time the prohibition became a law, being a part of what is now known as the ordidance of '87.

The question of Federal control of slavery in the territories seems not to have been directly before the convention which framed the original Constitution; and hence it is not recorded that the "thirty-nine," or any of them, while engaged on that instrument, expressed any opinion on that precise question.

THE FIRST CONGRESS.

In 1789, by the first Congress which sat under the Constitution, an act was passed to enforce the ordinance of '87, including the prohibition of slavery in the Northwestern Territory. The bill for this act was reported by one of the "thirty-nine," Thomas Fitzsimmons, then a member of the House of Representatives from Pennsylvania.

It went through all its stages without a word of opposition, and finally passed both branches without yeas or nays, which is equivalent to a unanimous passage. In this Congress there were sixteen of the "thirty-nine" fathers who framed the original Constitution. They were:

John Langdon,	George Clymer,	Richard Bassett,
Nicholas Gilmad,	William Few,	George Read,
Wm. S. Johnson,	Abraham Baldwin,	Pierce Butler,
Roger Sherman,	Rufus King,	Daniel Carroll,
Robert Morris,	William Patterson,	James Madison.
	Thomas Fitzsimmons	

This shows that in their understanding no line divided local from Federal authority, nor anything in the Constitution properly forbade Congress to prohibit slavery in the Federal territory, else both their fidelity to correct principle and their oath to support the Constitution would have constrained them to oppose the prohibition.

GEORGE WASHINGTON.

Again, George Washington, another of the "thirty-nine," was then President of the United States, and, as such, approved and signed the bill, thus completing its validity as a law, and thus showing that in his understanding, no line dividing local from Federal authority, nor anything in the Constitution, forbade the Federal Government to control as to slavery in Federal territory.

THE FIRST TERITORIES.

No great while after the adoption of the original Constitution, North Carolina ceded to the Federal Government the country now constituting the State of Tennessee. and a few years later Georgia ceded that which now constitutes the States of Mississippi and Alabama. In both deeds of cession it was made a condition by the ceding States that the Federal Government should not prohibit slavery in the ceded country. Besides this, slavery was already in the ceded country. Under these circumstances, Congress, on taking charge of these countries, did not absolutely prohibit slavery within them. But they did interfere with it, take control of it, even there, to a certain extent.

In 1798, Congress organized the territory of Mississippi. In the act of organization they prohibited the bringing of slaves into the territories from any place without the United States, by fine, and giving freedom to slaves so brought.

This act passed both branches of Congress without yeas and nays. In that Congress were three of the "thirty-nine" who framed the original Constitution. They were John Langdon, George Read and Abraham Baldwin.

They all, probably, voted for it. Certainly they would have placed their opposition to it upon the record, if, in their understanding, any line dividing local from Federal authority, or anything in the Constitution properly forbade the Federal Government to control as to slavery in Federal territory.

THE LOUISIANA COUNTRY.

In 1803, the Federal Government purchased the Louisiana country. Our former territorial acquisitions came from certain of our own States; but this Louisiana country was acquired from a foreign nation. In 1804, Congress gave a territorial organization to that part of it which now constitutes the State of Louisiana. New Orleans, laying within that part, was an old and comparatively large city.

There were other considerable towns and settlements, and slavery was extensively and thoroughly intermingled with the people. Congress did not, in the territorial act, prohibit slavery; but they did interfere with it—take control of it—in a more marked and extensive way than they did in the case of Mississippi. The substance of the provision therein made, in relation to slaves, was:

First: That no slaves should be imported into the territory from foreign parts.

Second: That the slaves should be carried into it who had been imported into the United States since the first day of May, 1798.

Third: That no slave should be carried into it, except by the owner, and for his own use as a settler; the penalty in all the cases being a fine upon the violator of the law, and freedom to the slave.

This act, also, was passed without yeas and nays. In the Congress which passed it there were two of the "thirty-nine." They were Abraham Baldwin and Jonathan Dayton. As stated in the case of Mississippi, it is probable they both voted for it; they would not have allowed it to pass without recording their opposition to it, if, in their understanding, it violated either the line properly dividing local from Federal authority or any provision of the Constitution.

THE MISSOURI QUESTION.

In 1819-20 came, and passed, the Missouri question. Many votes were taken by yeas and nays, in both branches of Congress, upon the various phases of the general question.

Two of the "thirty-nine"—Rufus King and Charles Pinckney—were members of that Congress. Mr. King steadily voted for slavery prohibition and against all compromises. By this Mr. King showed that in his understanding, no line divided local from Federal authority, nor anything in the Constitution, was violated by Congress prohibiting slavery in Federal territory; while Mr. Pinckney, by his votes, showed that in his understanding, there was some different reason for opposing such prohibition in the case.

The cases I have mentioned are the only acts of the "thirty-nine," or any of them upon the direct issue, which I have been able to discover.

So enumerate the persons who thus acted, as being four in 1784, three in 1787, seventeen in 1789, three in 1798, two in 1804, and two in 1819-20, there would be thirty-one of them. But this would be counting John Langdon, Roger Sherman, William Few, Rufus King, and George Read, each twice, and Abraham Baldwin four times.

The true number of those of the "thirty-nine," whom I have shown to have acted upon the question, which, by the text, they understood better than we, is twenty-three, leaving sixteen not shown to have acted upon it in any way.

Here, then, we have twenty-three of our "thirty-nine" fathers who framed the government under which we live, who have, upon their official responsibility and their corporal oaths, acted upon the very question which the text affirms they "understood just as well, and even better than we do now; and twenty-one of them—a clear majority of the whole "thirty-nine"—so acting upon it as to make them guilty of gross political impropriety and wilful perjury, if, in their understanding, any proper division between local and Federal authority, or anything in the Constitution they had made themselves and sworn to support, forbade the Federal Government to control, as to slavery, the Federal territories. Thus the twenty-one acted: and, as actions speak louder than words, so actions under such responsibility speak still louder.

Two of the twenty-three voted against Congressional prohibition of slavery in the Federal territories, in the instances in which they acted upon the question. But for what reasons they so voted is not known. They may have done so because they thought a proper division of local from Federal authority, or some provision or principal of the Constitution stood in the way; or they may, without any such question, have voted against the prohibition on what appeared to them to be sufficient grounds of inexpediency.

No one who has sworn to support the Constitution can conscienciously vote for what he understands to be an unconstitutional measure however expedient he may think it; but one may and ought to vote against a measure which he deems constitutional, if, at the same time, he deems it inexpedient.

It, therefore, would be unsafe to set down even the two who voted against the prohibition, as having done so because, in their understanding, any proper division of local from Federal authority, or anything in the Constitution, forbade the Federal Government to control, as to slavery, in the territory.

The remaining sixteen of the the "thirty-nine," so far as I have discovered, have left no record of their understanding upon the direct question of Federal control of slavery in the Federal territories. But there is much reason to believe that their understanding upon that question would not have appeared different from that of their twenty-three compeers, had it been manifested at all.

For the purpose of adhering rigidly to the text, I have

purposely omitted whatever understanding may have been manifested, by any person, however distinguished, other than the "thirty-nine" fathers who framed the original Constitution; and, for the same reason I have also omitted whatever understanding may have been manifested by any of the "thirty-nine," even on any other phase of the general question of slavery. If we should look into their acts and declarations on these other phases, as the foreign slave trade, and the morality and policy of slavery generally, it would appear to us that on the direct question of Federal control of slavery in Federal territories, the sixteen, if they had acted at all, would probably have acted just as the twenty-three did. Among that sixteen were several of the most noted anti-slavery men of those times—as Dr. Franklin, Alexander Hamilton, and Governor Morris—while there is not one now known to have been otherwise, unless it may have been John Rutledge, of South Carolina.

SUMMARY

The sum of the whole is, that of our "thirty-nine" fathers who framed the original Constitution, twenty-one—a clear majority of the whole—certainly understood that no proper division of local from Federal authority, nor any part of the Constitution, forbade the Federal Government to control slavery in the Federal territories; while all the rest probably had the same understanding. Such, unquestionably, was the understanding of our fathers who framed the original Constitution; and the text affirms that they understood the question better than we.

AMENDMENT TO THE CONSTITUTION.

But, so far, I have been considering the understanding of the question manifested by the framers of the original Constitution. In and by the original instrument, a mode was provided for amending it; and, as I have already stated, the present frame of government under which we live consists of that original and twelve amendatory articles framed and adopted since.

Those who now insist that Federal control of slavery in Federal territories violates the Constitution, point us to the provisions which they suppose it thus violates; and, as I understand, they all fix upon provisions in these amendatory articles, and not in the original instrument. The Supreme Court, in the Dred Scott case, plant themselves upon the fifth amendment, which provides that "no person shall be deprived of property without due process of law;" while Senator Douglas and his peculiar adherents plant themselves upon the tenth amendment, providing that "the powers granted by the Constitution are reserved to the States respectively and to the people."

Now, it so happens that these amendments were framed by the first Congress which sat under the Constitution—the identical Congress which passed the act already mentioned, enforcing the prohibition of slavery in the Northwestern Territory. Not only was it the same Congress, but they were the identical same individual men who, at the same session, and at the same time within the session, had under consideration, and in progress toward maturity, these constitutional amendments and this act prohibiting slavery in all the territory the nation then owned. The constitutional amendments were introduced before and passed after the act enforcing the ordinance of 1787, so that during the whole pendency of the act to enforce the ordinanace, ·the constitutional amendments were also pending.

That Congress, consisting of all the seventy-six members, including sixteen of the framers of the original Constitution, as before stated, were pre-eminently our fathers who framed that part of the government under which we live which is now claimed as forbidding the Federal Government to control slavery in the Federal territories.

Is it not a little presumptous in any one at this day to affirm that the two things which that Congress deliberately framed, and carried to maturity at the same time, are absolutely inconsistent with each other? And does not such affirmation, from the same mouth, that those who did the two things alleged to be inconsistent understood whether they really were inconsistent better than we—better than he who affirms that they are inconsistent?

It is surely safe to assume that the "thirty-nine" framers of the original constitution, and the seventy-six members of the Congress which framed the amendments thereto, taken together, do certainly include those who may be fairly called our fathers who framed the government under which we live. And so assuming, I defy any man to show that any one of them ever in his whole life declared that, in his understanding, any proper division of local from Federal authority, or any part of the Constitution, forbade the Federal Government to control as to slavery in the Federal territories.

I GO A STEP FARTHER.

I go a step farther. I defy any one to show that any living man in the whole world ever did, prior to the beginning of the present century, (and I might almost say prior to the beginning of the last half of the present century,) declare that, in his understanding, any proper division of local from Federal authority, or any part of the Constitution, forbade the Federal Government to control as to slavery in the Federal territories.

To those who so now declare, I give, not only "our fathers who framed the government under which we live," but with them all other living men within the century in which it was framed, among whom to search, and they shall not be able to find the evidence of a single man agreeing with them.

LET THERE BE NO MISUNDERSTANDING.

Now, and here, let me guard a little against being misunderstood. I do not mean to say we are bound to follow implicitly in whatever our fathers did. To do so would be to discard all the lights of current experiences—to reject all progress—all improvement. What I do say is, that if we would supplant the opinions and policy of our fathers in any case, we should do so upon evidence so conclusive, and argument so clear, that even their great authority, fairly considered and weighed, can not stand; and most surely not in a case whereof we ourselves declare they understood the question better than we.

If any man, at this day, sincerely believes that a proper division of local from Federal authority, or any part of the Constitution, forbids the Federal Government to control as to slavery in the Federal territories, he is right to say so, and to enforce his position by all truthful evidence and fair argument which he can.

But he has no right to mislead others, who have less access to history and less lesiure to study it, into the false belief that "our fathers who framed the government under which we live," were of the same opinion—thus substituting falsehood and deception for truthful evidence and fair argument.

If any man at this day sincerely believes "our fathers who framed the government under which we live," used and applied principles, in other cases, which ought to have led them to understand that a proper division of local from Federal authority, or some part of the Constitution, forbids the Federal Government to control slavery in the Federal territories, he is right to do so.

But he should, at the same time, brave the responsibility of declaring that, in his opinion, he understands their principles better than they did themselves; and especially should he not shirk that responsibility by asserting that they "understood the question just as well, and even better, than we do now."

But enough. Let all who believe that "our fathers who framed the government under which we live, understood this question just as well, and even better, than we do now," speak as they spoke, and act as they acted upon it. This is all Republicans ask—all Republicans desire—in relation to slavery. As those fathers marked it, so let it be again marked, as an evil not to be extended, but to be tolerated and protected only because of and so far as its actual presence among us makes that toleration and protection a necessity. Let all the guarantees those fathers gave it be, not grudgingly, but fully and fairly maintained. For this Republicans contend, and with this, so far as I know or believe, they will be content.

A FEW WORDS FROM MR. LINCOLN TO THE SOUTHERN PEOPLE.

And now, if they would listen—as I suppose they will not—I would address a few words to the Southern people.

I would say to them: You consider yourselves a reasonable and just people, and I consider that in the general qualities of reason and justice you are not inferior to any other people. Still, when you speak of us Republicans you do so only to denounce us as reptiles, or, at the best, as no better than outlaws. You will grant a hearing to pirates or murderers, but nothing like it to "Black Republicans." In all your contentions with one another, each of you deems an unconditional condemnation of "Black Republicanism" as the first thing to be attended to. Indeed, such condemnation of us seems to be an indispensable prerequisite—license, so to speak —among you, to be admitted or permitted to speak at all.

Now, can you, or not, be prevailed upon to pause and to consider whether this is quite just to us, or even to yourselves?

"BRING FORWARD YOUR CHARGES."

Bring forward your charges and specifications, and then be patient long enough to hear us deny or justify.

You say we are sectional. We deny it. That makes

an issue; and the burden of proof is upon you. You produce your proof; and what is it? Why that our party has no existence in your section—gets no votee in your section. The fact is substantially true; but does it prove the issue. If it does, then, in case we should, without change of principle, begin to get votes in your section, we should thereby cease to be sectional.

You can not escape this conclusion; and yet, are you willing to abide by it? If you are, you will probably soon find that we have ceased to be sectional, for we shall get votes in your section this very year. You will then begin to discover as the truth plainly is, that your proof does not touch the issue.

The fact that we get no votes in your section is a fact ot your making and not of ours. And if there be fault in that fact that fault is primarily yours, and remains so until you show that we repel you by some wrong principle or practice.

If we do repel you by any wrong principle or practice, the fault is ours; but this brings you to where you ought to have started—to a discussion of the right or wrong of our principle. If our principle, put in practice, would wrong your section for the benefit of ours, or for any other object, then our principle, and we with it, are sectional, and are justly exposed and denounced as such. Meet us, then, on the question of whether our principle, put in practice would wrong your section; and so meet it as if it were possible that something may be said on our side.

Do you accept the challenge? No? Then you really believe the principle which "our fathers, who framed the government under which we live," thought so clearly right as to adopt it and indorse it again and again, upon their official oaths, is, in fact, so clearly wrong as to demand your condemnation without a moment's consideration.

COULD WASHINGTON SPEAK, WHAT WOULD HE SAY?

Some of you delight to flaunt in our faces the warning against sectional parties given by Washington in his Farewell Address. Less than eight years before Washington gave that warning, he had, as President of the United States, approved and signed an act of Congress enforcing the prohibition of slavery in the Northwestern Territory, which act embodied the policy of the government upon that subject, up to and the very moment he penned that warning; and about one year after he penned it, he wrote Lafayette that he considered that prohibition a wise measure, expressing, in the same connection, his hope that we should some time have a Confederacy of free States.

Bearing this in mind, and seeing that sectionalism has since arisen on this same subject, is that warning a weapon in your hands against us, or in our hands against you? Could Washington himself speak, would he cast the blame of that sectionilsm upon us, who sustain his policy, or upon you who repudiate it? We respect that warning of Washington, and we commend it to you, together with his example pointing to the right application of it.

WHAT IS CONSERVATISM?

But you say you are conservative—eminently conservative—while we are revolutionary, destructive or something of the sort. What is conservatism? It is not adherence to the old and tried, against the new and untried? We stick to contend for the identical old policy, on the point of controversy, which was adopted by our fathers who framed the government under which we live; while you with one accord reject, and scout, and spit upon that old policy, and insist upon subsituting something new. True, you disagree among yourselves as to what that substitute shall be. You have considerable variety of new propositions and plans, but you are unanimous in rejecting and denouncing the old policy of the fathers.

Some of you are for reviving the foreign slave trade; some for a congressional slave code for the territories; some for Congress forbidding the territories to prohibit slavery within their limits, some for maintaining slavery in the territories through the judiciary; some for the "gur-reat pur-rinciple" that "if one man would enslave another, no third man should object," fantastically called "popular sovereignty;" but never a man among you in favor of Federal prohibition of slavery in Federal territories, according to the practice of our fathers who framed the government under which we live.

Not one of all your various plans can show a precedent or an advocate in the century within which our government originated. Consider, then, whether your claim of conservatism for yourselves, and your charge of destructiveness against us, are based on the most clear and staple foundations.

WE DENY IT.

Again, you say we have made the slavery question more prominent than it formerly was. We deny it. We admit that it is more prominent, but we deny that we made it so. It was not we, but you, who discarded the old policy of the fathers. We resisted, and still resist, your innovation, and thence comes the greater prominence of the question. Would you have that question reduced to its former proportions? Go back to that old policy. What has been will be again, under the same conditions. If you would have the peace of the old times, readopt the precepts and policy of the old times.

You charge that we stir up insurrections among your slaves. We deny it; and what is your proof? Harper's Ferry! John Brown! John Brown was no Republican; and you have failed to implicate a single Republican in his Harper's Ferry enterprise.

If any member of our party is guilty in that matter, you know it or you do not know it. If you do know it you are inexcusable to not designate the man and prove the fact. If you do not know it, you are inexcusable to assert it, and especially to persist in the assertion after you have tried and failed to make the proof. You need not be told that persisting in a charge which one does not know to be true, is simply malicious slander.

"WE DO NOT BELIEVE IT."

Some of you admit that no Republican designedly aided or encouraged the Harper's Ferry affair, but still insist that our doctrines and declarations necessarily lead to such results. We do not believe it. We know we hold to no doctrines, and make no declarations which, were not held to and made by our fathers who framed the government under which we live. You never dealt fairly by us in relation to this affair. When it occurred some important state elections were near at hand, and you were in evident glee with the belief that by charging the blame upon us you could get an advantage of us in those elections. The elections came, and your expectations were not quite fulfilled. Every Republican man knew that, as to himself at least your charge was a slander, and he was not much inclined by it to cast his vote in your favor. Republican doctrines and declarations are accompanied with a continual protest against any interference whatever with your slaves, or with you about your slaves.

Surely this does not encourage them to revolt. True, we do, in common with our fathers who framed the government under which we live, declare our belief that slavery is wrong; but the slaves do not hear us declare even this. For anything we say or do the slaves would scarcely know there was a Republican party. I believe they would not, in fact, generally know it but for your misrepresentations of us in their hearing. In your political contests among yourselves, each faction charges the other with sympathy with Black Republicanism; and then, to give point to the charge, defines Black Republicanism to simply be insurrection, blood and thunder among the slaves.

INSURRECTION IMPOSSIBLE.

Slave insurrections are no more common now than they were before the Republican party was organized. What induced the Southampton insurrection, twenty-eight years ago, in which at least three times as many lives were lost as at Harper's Ferry? You can scarcely stretch your very elastic fancy to the conclusion that Southampton was got up by Black Republicanism. In the present state of things in the United States, I do not think a general or even a very extensive slave insurrection is possible. The indispensable concert of action cannot be attained. The slaves have no means of rapid communication; nor can incendiary free men, black or white, supply it. The explosive materials are everywhere in parcels; but there neither are, nor can be supplied, the indispensable connecting trains.

Much is said by Southern people about the affection of slaves for their masters and mistresses; and a part of it, at least, is true· A plot for an uprising could scarcely be devised and communicated to twenty individuals before some one of them, to save the life of a favorite master or mistress, would divulge it. This is the rule; and the slave revolution in Hayti was not an exception to it, but a case occurring under peculiar circumstances. The gunpowder plot of British history, though not connected with slaves, was more in point. In that case only about twenty were admitted to the secret; and yet one of them, in his anxiety to save a friend, betrayed the plot to that friend, and, by consequence, averted the calamity.

Occasional poisonings from the kitchen, and open or stealthy assassinations in the field, and local revolts extending to a score or so, will continue to occur as the natural results of slavery, but no general insurrection of slaves, as I think, can happen in this country for a long time. Whoever much fears, or much hopes, for such an event, will be alike disappointed.

In the language of Mr. Jefferson, uttered many years ago, "It is still in our power to direct the process of emancipation, and deportation peaceably, and in such slow degrees, as that the evil will wear off insensibly; and their places be, pari passu, filled up by free white laborers. If, on the contrary, it is left to force itself on, human nature must shudder at the prospect held up."

Mr. Jefferson did not mean to say, nor do I, that the power of emancipation is in the Federal Government. He spoke of Virginia; and as to the power of emancipation, I speak of the slave-holding states only.

The Federal Government, however. as we insist, has the power of restraining the extension of the institution —the power to insure that a slave insurrection shall never occur on any American soil which is uow free from slavery.

JOHN BROWN.

John Brown's effort was peculiar. It was not a slave insurrection. It was an attempt by white men to get up a revolt among slaves, in which the slaves refused to participate. In fact, it was so absurd that the slaves, with all their ignorance, saw plainly enough it could not succeed. That affair, in its philosophy, corresponds with the many attempts, related in history, at the assassinations of kings and emperors. An enthusiast broods over the oppression of a people till he fancies himself commissioned by Heaven to liberate them. He ventures the attempt, which ends in little else than in his own execution.

Orsini's attempt on Louis Napoleon, and John Brown's attempt at Harper's Ferry, were, in their philosophy, precisely the same. The eagerness to cast blame on old England in the one case, and on new England in the other, does not disprove the sameness of the two things.

And how much would it avail you if you could, by the use of John Brown, Helper's book, and the like, break up the Republican organization? Human action can be modified to some extent, but human nature cannot be changed. There is a judgment and a feeling against slavery in this nation, which cast at least a million and a half of votes! You cannot destroy that judgment and feeling—that sentiment—by breaking up the political organization which rallies around it.

You can scarcely scatter and disperse an army which has been formed into order in the face of your heaviest fire; but if you could, how much would you gain by forcing the sentiment which created it out of the peaceful channel of the ballot box into some other channel? What would that other channel probably be? Would the number of John Brown's be lessened or enlarged by the operation?

"RULE OR RUIN."

But you will break up the Union, rather than submit to a denial of your constitutional rights.

That has a somewhat reckless sound; but it would be palliated, if not fully justified, were we proposing, by the mere force of numbers, to deprive you of some right, plainly written down in the Constitution. But we are proposing no such thing.

When you make these declarations, you have a specific and well understood allusion to an assumed Constitutional right of yours, to take slaves into the Federal Territories, and to hold them there as property. But no such right is specifically written in the Constitution. That instrument is literally silent about any such right. We, on the contrary, deny that such a right has any existence in the Constitution, even by implication.

Your purpose, then, plainly stated, is, that you will destroy the government unless you be allowed to construe and enforce the Constitution as you please, on all points in dispute between you and us. You will rule or ruin in all events. This, plainly stated, is your language to us.

"NOT QUITE SO."

Perhaps you will say the Supreme Court has decided the disputed constitutional question in your favor. Not quite so. But, waiving the lawyers' distinction between dictum and decision, the court has decided the question for you in a sort of way. The court has substantially said it is your constitutional right to take slaves into the Federal territories, and to hold them there as property.

When I say the decision was made in a sort of way, I mean it was made in a divided court, by a bare majority of the judges, and they not quite agreeing with one another in the reasons for making it; that it is so made as that its avowed supporters disagree with one another about its meaning; and that it was mainly based upon a mistaken statement of fact—the statement in the opinion that "the right of property in a slave is distinctly and expressly affirmed in the Constitution."

An inspection of the Constitution will show that the right of property in a slave is not distinctly and expressly affirmed in it. Bear in mind the judges do not pledge their judicial opinion that such right is implicitly affirmed in the Constitution; but they pledge their veracity that it is distinctly and expressly affirmed there—"distinctly"—that is, not mingled with anything else—"expressly"—that is, in words meaning just that, without the aid of any inference, and susceptible of no other meaning.

If they had only pledged their judicial opinion. that such right is affirmed in the instrument by implication. it would be open to others to show that, neither the word "slave" nor "slavery" is to be found in the Constitution, nor the word "property" even, in any connection with language alluding to the things slave or slavery, and that wherever, in that instrument, the slave is alluded to, he is called "a person," and wherever his master's legal right in relation to him is alluded to, it is spoken of as "service or labor due," as a "debt" payable in service or labor.

Also, it would be open to show, by cotemporaneous history, that this mode of alluding to slaves and slavery, instead of speaking of them, was employed on purpose to exclude from the Constitution the idea that there could be property in man.

To show all this is easy and certain.

When the obvious mistake of the judges shall be brought to their notice, is it not reasonable to expect that they will withdraw the mistaken statement, and reconsider the conclusion based upon it?

And then it is to be remembered that "our fathers, who framed the government under which we live"—the men who made the Constitution—decided this same constitutional question in our favor, long ago—decided it without a division among themselves about the meaning of it after it was made, so far as any evidence is left, without basing it upon any mistaken statements of facts.

Under all these circumstances, do you really feel yourself justified to break up this government, unless such a court decision as yours is shall be at once submitted to as a conclusive and final rule of political action?

But you will not abide the election of a Republican President. In that supposed event, you say, you will destroy the Union; and then, you say, the great crime of having destroyed it will be upon us?

This is cool. A highwayman holds a pistol to my ear, and mutters through his teeth, "Stand and deliver, or I shall kill yon, and then you will be a murderer."

To be sure, what the robber demanded of me—my money—was my own, and I had a clear right to keep it; but it was no more my own than my vote is my own: and the threat of death to me, to extort my money and the threat of destruction to the Union, to extort my vote, can scarcely be distinguished in principle.

A FEW WORDS TO REPUBLICANS.

A few words now to Republicans. It is exceedingly desirable that all parts of this great confederacy shall be at peace, and in harmony, one with another. Let us Republicans do our part to have it so. Even though much provoked, let us do nothing through passion and ill temper. Even though the Southern people will not so much as listen to us, let us calmly consider their demands, and yield to them if, in our deliberate view of our duty, we possibly can. Judging by all they say and do, and by the subject and nature of their controversy with us, let us determine, if we can, what will satisfy them.

Will they be satisfied if the territories be unconditionally surrendered to them? We know they will not. In all their present complaints against us, the territories are scarcely mentioned. Invasions and insurrections are the rage now. Will it satisfy them if, in the future, we have nothing to do with invasions and insurrections? We know it will not. We so know because we know we never had anything to do with invasions and insurrections; and yet this total abstaining does not exempt us from the charge and the denunciation.

The question recurs, what will satisfy them? Simply this: We must not only let them alone, but we must, somehow, convince them that we do let them alone. This we know by experience is no easy task. We have been so trying to convince them from the very beginning of our organization, but with no success. In all our platform and speeches, we have constantly protested our purpose to let them alone; but this has had no tendency to convince them. Alike unavailing to convince them is the fact that they have never detected a man of us in any attempt to disturb them.

These natural and apparently adequate means all failing, what will convince them? This, and this only: Cease to call slavery wrong, and join them in calling it right. And this must be done thoroughly—done in acts as well as words. Silence will not be tolerated—we must place ourselves avowedly with them. Douglas' new sedition law must be enacted, and enforced, suppressing all declarations that slavery is wrong, whether made in politics, in presses, in pulpits, or in private. We must arrest and return their fugitive slaves with greedy pleasure. We must pull down our Free State Constitutions. The whole atmosphere must be disinfected from all taint of opposition to slavery, before they will cease to believe that all their troubles proceed from us.

I am quite aware they do not state their case precisely in this way. Most of them would probably say to us, "Let us alone, do nothing to us, and say what you please about slavery." But we do let them alone—have never disturbed them—so that, after all, it is what we say which dissatisfies them. They will continue to accuse us of doing until we cease saying.

I am also aware they have not, as yet, in terms, demanded the overthrow of our Free State Constitntions. Yet those constitutions declare the wrong of slavery with more solemn emphasis than do all other sayings against it; and when all other sayings shall have been silenced, the overthrow of these constitutions will be demanded, and nothing be left to resist the demand. It is nothing to the contrary that they do not demand the whole of this just now. Demanding what they do, and for the reason they do, they can voluntary stop nowhere short of this consummation. Holding as they do, that slavery is morally right and socially elevating, they can not cease to demand a full national recognition of it, as a legal right and a social blessing.

Nor can we justifiably withhold this on any ground, save our conviction that slavery is wrong. If slavery is right, all words, acts, laws and constitutions against it, are themselves wrong, and should be silenced and swept away. If it is right, we can not justly object to its nationality—its universality, if, it is wrong, they can not justly insist upon its extension—its enlargement. All they ask we could readily grant, if they thought slavery right; all we ask they could readily grant, if they thought it wrong.

Their thinking it right, and our thinking it wrong, is the precise fact upon which depends the whole controversy. Thinking it right, as they do, they are not to blame for desiring its full recognition, as being right; but thinking it wrong, as we do, can we yield to them? Can we cast our votes with their view and against our own? in view of our moral, social and political responsibility, can we do this?

Wrong as we may think slavery is, we can yet afford to let it alone where it is, because that much is due to the necessity arising from its actual presence in the nation; but can we, while our votes will prevent it, allow it to spread into the national territories, and to overrun us here in these free states?

If our sense of duty forbids this, then let us stand by our duty fearlessly and effectively. Let us be diverted by none of those sophistical contrivances wherewith we are so industriously plied and belabored—contrivances, such as groping for some middle ground between the right and the wrong, vain as the search for a man who should be neither a living man nor a dead man—such as Union appeals, beseeching true Union men to yield to disunionist, reversing the Divine rule, and calling, not the sinners, but the righteous to repentance—such as invocations of Washington—imploring men to unsay what Washington said—and undo what Washington did.

Neither let us be slandered from our duty by false accusations against us, nor frightened from it by menaces of destruction to the government, nor of dungeons to ourselves.

Let us have faith that right makes might; and in that faith let us, to the end dare do our duty as we understand it.

LINCOLN'S RAIL SPLITTING SPEECH.

[Delivered at the Republican State Convention in Decutur, Ill., May 9, 1860. Mr. Lincoln had been carried bodily upon the stage, and soon "Old John Hanks" (a democrat) came into the midst of the assemblage bearing on his shoulders "two small triangular heart rails" surmounted by a banner with this inscription:

"Two rails from a lot made by Abraham Lincoln and John Hanks, in the Sangamon bottom, in the year 1830." It is said that Lincoln blushed, but seemed to shake with inward laughter. Great were the shouts and calls for Lincoln.]

Gentlemen:— I suppose you want to know something about those things (pointing to old John and the rails). Well, the truth is, John Hanks and I did make rails in the Sangamon bottom. I don't know whether we made those rails or not; the fact is I don't think they are a credit to the maker (laughing as he spoke), but I do know this; I made rails then, and I think I could make better ones than these now.

FIRST TALK AFTER HIS NOMINATION.

[The telegram was received in the Journal office at Springfield. Immediately everybody wanted to shake his hand; and so long as he was willing, they continued to congratulate him.]

GENTLEMEN: (with a twinkle in his eye) you had better come up and shake my hand while you can; honors elevate some men, you know. * * * Well, gentlemen, there is a little woman at our house who is probably more interested in this dispatch than I am; and if you will excuse me, I will take it up and let her see it.

———:o:———

FIRST SPEECH AFTER HIS NOMINATION.

[To the Committee, Springfield, Ill., May 19, 1860.]

MR. CHAIRMAN AND GENTLEMEN OF THE COMMITTEE:—

I tender to you, and through you to the Republican National Convention, and all the people represented in it, my profoundest thanks for the high honor done me, which you now formally announce. Deeply and even painfully sensible of the great responsibility which I could wish had fallen upon some one of the far more eminent men and experienced statesmen whose distinguished names were before the convention, I shall by your leave consider more fully the resolutions of the Convention denominated the platform, and, without unnecessary and unreasonable delay, respond to you, Mr. Chairman, in writing, not doubting that the platform will be found satisfactory and the nomination gratefully accepted. And now I will not longer defer the pleasure of taking you, and each of you, by the hand.

GOOD-BYE SPEECH AT SPRINGFIELD.

[Delivered at Springfield, Ill., Feb. 11, 1861, the day on which Mr. Lincoln started for Washington.]

FRIENDS:—No one who has never been placed in a like position can understand my feelings at this hour, nor the oppressive sadness I feel at this parting. More than a quarter of a century I have lived among you, and during that time I have received nothing but kindness at your hands.

Here I have lived from my youth, until now I am an old man. Here the most sacred ties of earth were assumed. Here all my children were born, and here one of them lies buried. To you, dear friends, I owe all that I have, all that I am. All the strange checkered past seems to crowd now upon my mind. To-day I leave you. I go to assume a task more difficult than that which devolved upon Washington. Unless the Great God who inspired him, shall be with and inspire me, I must fail; but if the same Omniscient mind and Almighty arm that directed and protected him, shall guide and support me, I shall not fail—I shall succeed. Let us all pray that the God of our fathers shall not forsrke us now. To Him I commend you all. Permit me to ask that, with equal sincerity and faith, you will invoke His wisdom and guidance for me. With these few words I must leave you; for how long I know not. Friends, one and all, I must now bid you an affectionate farewell.

―――:o:―――

AT INDEPENDENCE HALL, PHILA.

The object of Lincoln's visit, Feb. 1, 1861, to Independence Hall, was to assist in raising the national flag

LINCOLN RAISING THE AMERICAN FLAG ON INDEPENDENCE HALL, PHILADELPHIA. FEB. 21, 1862.

over the hall. Arrangements had been made for the performance of this ceremony, and Mr. Lincoln was escorted to the platform prepared for the purpose, and was invited, in a brief address, to raise the flag. He responded in a patriotic speech, announcing his cheerful compliance with the request.]

LADIES AND GENTLEMAN:—The future is in the hands of the people. It is on such an occasion as this we can reason together, reaffirm our devotion to the country and the principles of the Declaration of Independence. Let us make up our minds that whenever we do put a new star upon our banner, it shall be a fixed one, never to be dimmed by the horrors of war, but brightened by the contentment and prosperity of peace. Let us go on to extend the area of our usefulness, and add star upon star until their light shall shine over five hundred millions of free and happy people.

[Then he performed his part in the ceremony, amidst a thundering discharge of artillery.

LINCOLN'S SPEECH IN WASHINGTON.

[Delivered Wednesday, Feb. 27, 1861, at his Hotel.]

[On Wednesday, the 27th, the Mayor and Common Council of the city waited upon Mr. Lincoln and tendered him a welcome. He replied to them as follows:]

MR. MAYOR:—I thank you, and through you the municipal authorities of this city who accompany you, for this welcome. And as it is the first time in my life since the present phase of politics has presented itself in this country, that I have said anything publicly within a region of country where the institution of slavery exists, I will take this occasion to say that I feel very much of the ill-feelings that has existed and still exists between the people in the sections from which I came and the people here, is dependent upon a misunderstanding of one another. I therefore avail myself of this opportunity to assure you, Mr Mayor, and all the gentlemen present, that I have not now, and never have had, any other than as kindly feelings towards you as the people of my own section. I have not now, and never have had, any dis-

[UNITED STATES CAPITOL.]

position to treat you in any respect otherwise than as my own neighbors. I have not now any purpose to withhold from you any of the benefits of the Constitution, under any circumstances, that I would not feel myself constrained to withhold from my own neighbors; and I hope, in a word, that when we shall become better acquainted —and I say it with great confidence—we shall like each other the more. I thank you for the kindness of this reception.

INAUGURATION OF PRESIDENT LINCOLN, WASHINGTON, 1861.

LINCOLN'S FIRST INAUGURAL ADDRESS.

Delivered March 4, 1861, at Washington.

FELLOW-CITIZENS OF THE UNITED STATES:—In compliance with a custom as old as the government itself, I appear before you to address you briefly, and to take, in your presence, the oath prescribed by the Constitution of the United States to be taken by the President before he enters on the execution of his office.

POSITION STATED.

I do not consider it necessary, at present, for me to discuss those matters of administration about which there is no special anxiety or excitement. Apprehension seems to exist among the people of the Southern states, that, by the accession of a republican administration, their property and their peace and personal security are to be endangered. There has never been any reasonable cause for such apprehension. Indeed, the most ample evidence to the contrary has all the while existed, and been open to their inspection. It is found in nearly all the published speeches of him who now addresses you. I do but quote from one of those speeches, when I declare that "I have no purpose directly or indirectly, to interfere with the institution of slavery in the states where it exists." I believe I have no lawful right to do so; and I have no inclination to do so. Those who nominated and elected me did so with the full knowledge that I had made this, and made many similar declarations, and had never recanted them. And more than this, they placed in the platform, for my acceptance, and as a law to themselves and to me, the clear and emphatic resolution which I now read:

"Resolved, That the maintenance inviolate of the rights of the states, and especially the right of each state to order and control its own domestic institutions according to its own judgement exclusively, is essential to that balance of power on which the perfection and endurance of our political fabric depend; and we denounce the lawless invasion by armed force of the soil of any state or territory, no matter under what pretext, as among the gravest of crimes."

I now reiterate these sentiments; and in doing so I only press upon the public attention the most conclusive evidence of which the case is susceptible, that the property, peace, and security of no section are to be in anywise endangered by the now incoming administration.

I add, too, that all the protection, which, consistently with the Constitution and the laws, can be given, will be given to all the states when lawfully demanded, for what ever cause, as cheerfully to one section as to another.

There is much controversy about the delivering up of fugitives from service or labor. The clause I now read is as plainly written in the Constitution as any other of its provisions.

"No person held to service or labor in one state under the laws thereof, escaping into another, shall, in consequence of any law or regulation therein; be discharged from such service or labor, but shall be delivered up on claim of the party to whom such service of labor may be due."

It is scarcely questioned that this provision was intended by those who made it for the reclaiming of what we call fugitive slaves; and the intention of the lawgiver is the law.

All members of Congress swear their support to the whole Constitution—to this provision as well as any other. To the proposition, then, that slaves whose cases come within the terms of this clause "shall be delivered up," their oaths are unanimous. Now, if they would make the effort in good temper, could they not, with nearly equal unanimity, frame and pass a law by means of which to keep good that unanimous oath?

There is some difference of opinion whether this clause should be enforced by national or by state authority; but surely that difference is not a very material one. If the slave is to be surrendered, it can be but of little consequence to him or to others by which authority it is done; and should any one, in any case, be content that this oath shall go unkept on a mere substantial controversy as to how it shall be kept?

Again, in any law upon this subject, ought not all the safeguards of liberty known in civilized and humane jurisprudence to be introduced, so that a free man be not, in any case, surrendered as a slave? And might it not be well at the same time to provide by law for the enforcement of that clause in the Constitution which guarantees that "the citizens of each state shall be entitled to all the privileges and immunities of citizens in the several states?"

NO MENTAL RESERVATION.

I take the official oath to-day with no mental reservations, and with no purpose to construe the Constitution or laws by any hypercritical rules; and while I do not choose now to specify particular acts of Congress as proper to be enforced, I do suggest that it will be much safer for all, both in official and private stations, to conform to and abide by all those acts which stand unrepealed, than to violate any of them. trusting to find impunity in having them held to be unconstitutional.

It is seventy-two years since the first inauguration of a President under our national Constitution. During that period fifteen different and very distinguished citizens have in succession administered the executive branch of the government. They have conducted it through many perils, and generally with great success. Yet, with all this scope for precedent, I now enter upon the same task for the brief constitutional term of four years, under great and peculiar difficulties.

"I HOLD THE UNION OF THESE STATES IS PERPETUAL."

A disruption of the Federal Union, heretofore only menaced, is now formidably attempted. I hold that in the contemplation of universal law and of the Constitution, the Union of these states is perpetual. Perpetuity is implied, if not expressed, in the fundamental law of all national governments. It is safe to assert that no government proper ever had a provision in its organic law for its own termination. Continue to execute all the express provisions of our national Constitution, and the Union will endure forever, it being impossible to destroy except by some action not provided for in the instrument itself.

Again, if the United States be not a government proper, but an association of states in the nature of a contract merely, can it, as a contract, be peaceably unmade by less than all the parties who made it? One party to a contract may violate it—break it, so to speak; but does it not require all to lawfully rescind it? Descending from these general principles, we find the proposition that in legal contemplation the Union is perpetual, confirmed by the history of the Union itself.

The Union is much older than the Constitution. It was formed, in fact, by the Articles of Association in 1774. It was matured and continued in the Declaration of Independence in 1776. It was further matured, and the faith of all the then thirteen states expressly plighted and engaged that it should be perpetual, by the Articles of the Confederation, in 1778; and, finally, in 1787, one of the declared objects for ordaining and establishing the Constitution was to form a more perfect union. But if the destruction of the Union by one or by part only of the states be lawfully possible, the Union is less perfect than before, the Constitution having lost the vital element of perpetuity.

It follows from these views that no state, upon its own mere motion, can lawfully get out of the Union; that resolves and ordinances to that effect are legally void. and that acts of violence within any state or states against the authority of the United States are insurrectionary or revolutionary, according to circumstances.

I therefore consider that, in view of the Constitution and the laws, the Union is unbroken, and to the extent of my ability, I shall take care, as the Constitution itself expressly enjoins upon me, that the laws of the Union shall be faithfully executed in all the states. Doing this, which I deem to be only a simple duty on my part, I shall perfectly perform it, so far as is practicable, unless my rightful masters, the American people, shall withhold the requisition, or in some authoritative manner direct the contrary.

I trust this will not be regarded as a menace, but only as the declared purpose of the Union that it will constitutionally defend and maintain itself.

In doing this there need be no bloodshed or violence, and there shall be none unless it is forced upon the national authority.

WHAT SHALL BE DONE?

The power confided to me will be used to hold, occupy, and possess the property and places belonging to the government, and collect the duties and imposts; but beyond what may be necessary for these objects there will be no invasion, no using of force against or among the people anywhere.

Where hostility to the United States shall be so great and so universal as to prevent competent resident citizens from holding federal offices, there will be no attempt to force obnoxious strangers among the people that object. While strict legal right may exist of the government to enforce the exercise of these offices, the attempt to do so would be so irritating, and so nearly impracticable withal, that I deem it best to forego for the time the uses of such offices.

"The mails, unless repelled, will continue to be furnished in all parts of the Union.

"So far as possible, the people everywhere shall have that sense of perfect security which is most favorable to calm thought and reflection.

"The course here indicated will be followed, unless current events and experience shall show a modification or change to be proper; and in every case and exigency my best discretion will be exercised according to the circumstances actually existing, and with a view and hope of a peaceable solution of the national troubles, and the restoration of fraternal sympathies and affections.

"That there are persons in one section or another, who seek to destroy the Union at all events, and are glad of any pretext to do it, I will neither affirm nor deny. But if there be such, I need address no word to them."

A WORD TO THOSE WHO LOVE THE UNION.

To those, however, who love the Union, may I not speak, before entering upon so grave a matter as the destruction of our national fabric, with all its benefits, its memories and its hopes? Would it not be well to ascertain why we do it? Will you hazard so desperate a step, while any portion of the ills you fly from have no real existence? Will you, while the certain ills you fly to are no greater than all the real ones you fly from? Will you risk the commission of so fearful a mistake? All profess to be content in the Union if all constitutional rights can be maintained. Is it true, then, that any right, plainly written in the Constitution, has been denied? I think not. Happily the human mind is so constituted that no party can reach to the audacity of doing this.

Think, if you can, of a single instance in which a plainly-written provision of the Constitution has ever been denied. If, by the mere force of numbers, a majority should deprive a minority of any clearly-written constitutional right, it might, in a moral point of view, justify revolution; it certainly would, if such right were a vital one. But such is not our case.

All the vital rights of minorities and of individuals are so plainly assured to them by affirmations and negations guarantees and prohibitions in the Constitution, that controversies never arise concerning them. But no organic law can ever be framed with provision specifically applicable to every question which may occur in practical administration. No foresight can anticipate, nor any document of reasonable length contain, express provisions for all possible questions. Shall fugitives from labor be surrendered by national or by state authorities? The Constitution does not expressly say. Must Congress protect slavery in the territories? The Constitution does not expressly say. From questions of this class, spring all our constitutional controversies, and we divide upon them into majorities and minorities.

THE MAJORITIES VS. THE MINORITIES.

If the minority did not acquiesce, the majority must, or the government must cease. There is no alternative for continuing the government acquiescence on the one side or the other. If a minority in such a case will secede rather than acquiesce, they make a precedent, which, in time, will ruin and divide them, for a minority of their own will secede from them whenever a majority refuses to be controlled by such a minority. For instance, why not any portion of a new confedracy a year or two hence, arbitrarily secede again, precisely as portions of the present Union now claim to secede from it? All who cherish disunion sentiments are now being educated to the exact temper of doing this. Is there such a perfect identity of interests among the States to compose a new Union as to produce harmony only and prevent renewed secession? Plainly, the central idea of secession is the essence of anarchy.

A majority held in check by constitutional check limitation, and always changing easily with deliberate changes of popular opinions and sentiments, is the only true sovereign of a free people. Whoever rejects it, does, of necessity, fly to anarchy or despotism. Unanimity is impossible; the rule of a minority, as a permanent arrangement, is wholly inadmissible. So that, rejecting the majority principle, anarchy or despotism, in some form, is all that is left.

I do not forget the position assumed by some that constitutional questions are to be decided by the Supreme Court, nor do I deny that such decisions must be binding in any case upon the parties to a suit, as to the object of that suit, while they are also entitled to a very high respect and consideration in all parallel cases by all other departments of the Government; and while it is obviously possible that such decision may be erroneous in any given case, still the evil following it, being limited to that particular case, with the chance that it may be overruled and never become a precedent for other cases, can better be borne than could the evils of a different practice.

At the same time the candid citizen must confess that,

if the policy of the government upon the vital question affecting the whole people is to be irrevocably fixed by the decisions of the Supreme Court, the instant they are made, as in ordinary litigation between parties in personal action, the people will have ceased to be their own masters, unless having to that extent practically resigned their government into the hands of that eminent tribunal.

Nor is there in this view any assault upon the court or the judges. It is a duty from which they may not shrink, to decide cases properly brought before them; and it is no fault of theirs if others seek to turn their decisions to political purposes. One section of our country believes slavery is right and ought to be extended, while the other believes it is wrong and ought not to be extended; and this is the only substantial dispute; and the fugitive slave clause of the Constitution and the law for the suppression of the foreign slave trade, are each as well enforced, perhaps, as any law can ever be in a community where the moral sense of the people imperfectly supports the law itself. The great body of the people abide by the dry legal obligation in both cases, and a few break over in each. This, I think, cannot be perfectly cured, and it would be worse, in both cases, after the separation of the sections than before. The foreign slave trade, now imperfectly suppressed, would be ultimately revived, without restriction in one section; while fugitive slaves, now only partially surrendered, wonld not be surrendered at all by the other.

WE CANNOT SEPARATE.

Physically speaking we cannot separate; we cannot remove our respective sections from each other, nor build an impassable wall between them. A husband and wife may be divorced, and go out of the presence and beyond the reach of each other, but the different parts of our country cannot do this. They can but remain face to face, and intercourse, either amicable or hostile, must continue between them. Is it possible, then, to make that intercourse more advantageous or more satisfactory after separation than before? Can aliens make treaties easier than friends can make laws? Can treaties be more faithfully enforced between aliens than laws can among friends? Suppose you go to war, you cannot fight always; and when, after much loss on both sides, and no gain on either, you cease fighting, the identical questions as to terms of intercourse are again upon you.

THE PEOPLE.

This country, with its institutions, belongs to the people who inhabit it. Whenever they shall grow weary of the existing government, they can exercise their constitutional right of amending, or their revolutionary right to dismember or overthrow it. I cannot be ignorant of the fact that many worthy and patriotic citizens are desirous of having the national Constitution amended. While I make no recommendation of amendment, I fully recognize the full authority of the people over the whole subject, to be exercised in either of the modes prescribed in the instrument itself, and I should, under existing circumstances, favor rather than oppose a fair opportunity being afforded the people to act upon it.

I will venture to add, that to me the convention mode seems preferable, in that it allows amendments to originate with the people themselves, instead of only permitting them to take or reject propositions originated by others not especially chosen for the purpose, and which might not be precisely such as they would wish either to accept or refuse. I understand that a proposed amendment to the Constitution (which amendment, however, I have not seen) has passed Congress, to the effect that the Federal Government shall never interfere with the domestic institutions of States, including that of persons held to service. To avoid misconstruction of what I have said, I depart from my purpose not to speak of particular amendments, so far as to say that, holding such a provision to now be implied constitutional law, I have no objection to its being made express and irrevocable.

THE ULTIMATE JUSTICE OF THE PEOPLE.

The chief magistrate derives all his authority from the people, and they have conferred none upon him to fix the terms for the separation of the States. The people. themselves, also, can do this if they choose, but the executive, as such, has nothing to do with it. *His duty is to administer the present government as it came to his hands, and to transmit it unimpaired by him to his successor. Why should there not be a patient confidence in the ultimate justice of the people? Is there any better or equal hope in the world? In our present differences is either party without faith of being in the right? If the Almighty Ruler of nations, with His eternal truth and justice, be on your side of the North, or on yours of the South, that truth and that justice will surely prevail by the judgment of this great tribunal, the American people. By the frame of the government under which we live, this same people have wisely given their public servants but little power for mischief, and have with equal wisdom provided for the return of that little to their own hands at very short intervals. While the people retain their virtue and vigilance, no administration, by any extreme wickedness or folly, can very seriously injure the government in the short space of four years.

MY COUNTRYMAN ONE AND ALL.

My countrymen, one and all, think calmly and well upon this subject. Nothing valuable can be lost by taking time.

If there be an object to hurry any of you, in hot haste, to a step which you would never take deliberately, that object will be frustrated by taking time; but no good can be frustrated by it.

Such of you as are now dissatisfied still have the old Constitution unimpaired, and, on the sensitive point, the laws of your own framing under it; while the new administration will have no immediate power, if it would, to change either.

If it were admitted that you who are dissatisfied hold the right side in the dispute, there is still no single reason for precipitate action. Intelligence, patriotism, Christianity, and a firm reliance upon Him who has never yet forsaken this favored land, are still competent to adjust, in the best way, all our present difficulties.

In your hands, my dissatisfied fellow-countrymen, and not in mine, is the momentous issue of civil war. The government will not assail you.

You can have no conflict without being yourselves the aggressors. You have no oath registered in heaven to destroy the government; while I shall have the most solemn one to preserve, protect and defend it.

I am loth to close. We are not enemies, but friends, We must not be enemies. Though passion may have strained, it must not break our bonds of affection.

The mystic cords of memory, stretching from every battle-field and patriot grave to every living heart and hearthstone all over this broad land., will yet swell the chorus of the Union, when again touched, as surely they will be, by the better angels of our nature.

———:o:———

THE EMANCIPATION PROCLAMATION.

Issued by President Lincoln, January 1, 1863, at Washington.

Whereas, on the twenty-second day of September, in the year of our Lord one thousand eight hundred and sixty-two, a proclamation was issued by the President of the United States, containing among other things, the following, to-wit:

"That on the first day of January, in the year of our Lord one thousand eight hundreed and sixty- three, all persons held as slaves within any state or designated part of a state, the people whereof shall then be in rebellion against the United States, shall be then, thenceforward, and forever free, and the Executive government of the United States, including the military and naval authority thereof, will recognize and maintain the freedom of such persons, and will do no act or acts to repress such persons, or any of them, in any efforts they may make for their actual freedom.

"That the Executive will on the first day of January aforesaid, by proclamation, designate the states and parts of states, if any, in which the people thereof respectively shall then be in rebellion against the United States; and the fact that any state or the people thereof shall on that day be in good faith represented in the Congress of the United States, by members chosen thereto at elections wherein a majority of the qualified voters of such state shall have participated, shall, in the absence of strong countervailing testimony, be deemed conclusive evidence that such state, and the people thereof, are not then in rebellion against the United States.

"Now, therefore, I, ABRAHAM LINCOLN, President of the United States, by virtue of the power in me vested as Commander-in Chief of the Army and Navy of the United States in time of actual armed rebellion against the authority and government of the United States, and as a fit and necessary war measure for suppressing said rebellion, do, on the first day of January, in the year of our Lord one thousand eight hundred and sixty-three, and in accordance with my purpose so to do, publicly proclaimed for the full period of one hundred days from the day first above mentioned, order and designate, as the states and parts of states wherein the people thereof respectively are this day in rebellion against the United States, the following, to-wit:

"Arkansas, Texas, Louisiana (except the parishes of St. Bernard, Plaquemine, Jefferson, St. John, St. Charles, St. James, Ascension, Assumption, Terre Bonne, Lafourche, St. Marie, St. Martin and Orleans, including the city of New Orleans), Mississippi, Alabama, Florida, Georgia, South Carolina, North Carolina and Virginia (except the forty-eight counties designated as West Virginia, and also the counties of Berkely, Accomac, Northampton, Elizabeth City, York, Princess Anne, and Norfolk, including the cities of Norfolk and Portsmouth), and which excepted parts are for the present left precisely as if this proclamation were not issued.

"And, by virtue of the power and for the purpose aforesaid, I do order and declare that all persons held as slaves within said designated States and parts of States, are, and henceforward shall be free; and that the Executive Government of the United States, including the military and naval authorities thereof, will recognize and maintain the freedom of said persons.

"And I hereby enjoin upon the people so declared to be free, to abstain from all violence, unless in necessary self-defense; and I recommend to them, that in all cases, when allowed, they labor faithfully for reasonable wages.

"And I further declare and make known that such persons of suitable condition will be received into the armed service of the United States, to garrison forts, positions, stations and other places, and to man vessels of all sorts in said service.

"And upon this act, sincerely believed to be an act of justice, warranted by the Constitution, upon military necessity, I invoke the considerate judgment of mankind, and the gracious favor of the Almighty God.

"In testimony whereof, I have hereunto set my name, and caused the seal of the United States to be affixed.

"Done at the City of Washington, this first day of January, in the year of our Lord one thousand eight [L. S.] hundred and sixty-three, and of the Independence of the United States the eighty-seventh.

ABRAHAM LINCOLN.

"By the President:
"WILLIAM H. SEWARD, Secretary of State."

———:o:———

A FOURTH OF JULY SPEECH.

Delivered at Washington, July, 1863, just after the victory at Vicksburg, Port Hudson, and other points.

FELLOW-CITIZENS:—I am very glad indeed to see you to-night, and yet I will not say I thank you for this call; but I do most sincerely thank Almighty God for the occasion on which you have called. How long ago' is it? eighty odd years since, on the Fourth of July, for the first time, in the history of the world, a nation, by its representatives, assembled and declared as a self-evident truth, "that all men are created equal." That was the birthday of the United States of America. Since then the Fourth of July has had several very popular recognitions.

The two men most distinguished in the framing and support of the Declaration were Thomas Jefferson and John Adams—the one having penned it, and the other sustained it the most forcibly in debate—the only two of fifty-five who signed it, and were elected Presidents of the United States. Precisely fifty years after they put their hands to the paper, it pleased Almighty God to take both from this stage of action. This was indeed an extraordinary and remarkable event in our history.

Another President five years after, was called from this stage of existence on the same day and month of the year, and now on this last Fourth of July, passed, when we have a gigantic rebellion, at the bottom of which is an effort to overthrow the principle that all men were created equal, we have the surrender of a most powerful position and army on that very day. And not only so, but in a succession of battles in Pennsylvania, near to us, through three days so rapidly fought that they might be called one great battle, on the first, second and third of the month of July; and on the fourth the cohorts of those who opposed the Declaration that all men are created equal, "turned tail" and run. [Long continued cheers.]

Gentlemen, this is a glorious theme, and the occasion for a speech, but I am not prepared to make one worthy of the occasion. I would like to speak in terms of praise due to the many brave officers and soldiers who have fought in the cause of the Union and liberties of the country from the beginning of the war. These are trying occasions; not only in success, but for the want of success. I dislike to mention the name of one single officer, lest I might do wrong to those I might forget. Recent events brings up glorious names, and particularly prominent ones; but these I will not mention. Having said this much, I will now take the music.

LINCOLN'S SPEECH AT GETTYSBURG.

Delivered at the dedication of the Gettysburg National Cemetery on the Gettysburg battle field, Nov. 19, 1863.

LADIES AND GENTLEMEN:—Fourscore and seven years ago our fathers brought forth upon this continent a new nation, conceived in liberty, and dedicated to the proposition that all men are created equal. Now we are engaged in a great civil war, testing whether that nation, or any nation so conceived and so dedicated, can long endure. We are met on a great battle-field of that war. We have come to dedicate a portion of that field as a final resting-place for those who here gave their lives that that nation might live. It is altogether fitting and proper that we should do this.

But in a larger sense we cannot dedicate, we cannot consecrate, we cannot hallow this ground. The brave men, living and dead, who struggled here, have consecrated it far above our power to add or detract. The world will little note, nor long remember, what we say here; but it can never forget what they did here.

It is for us, the living, rather to be dedicated here to the unfinished work which they who fought here have thus far so nobly advanced. It is rather for us to be here dedicated to the great task remaining before us, that from these honored dead we take increased devotion to that cause for which they gave the last full measure of devotion; that we here highly resolve that these dead shall not have died in vain; that this nation, under God, shall have a new birth of freedom, and *that the Government of the people, by the people, and for the people shall not perish from the earth.*"

"GOD BLESS THE WOMEN OF AMERICA."

On March 16, 1864, at the close of a fair in Washington, for the benefit of the sick and wounded soldiers of the army, President Lincoln was present, and in response to loud calls spoke as follows:

LADIES AND GENTLEMAN:—I appear to say but a word. This extraordinary war in which we are engaged falls heavily upon all classes of people, but the most heavily upon the soldiers. For it has been said, all that a man hath will be give for his life; and while all contribute of their substance, the soldier puts his life at stake, and often yields it up in his country's cause. The highest merit, then, is due to the soldier.

In this extraordinary war, extraordinary developments have manifested themselves, such as have not been seen in former wars; and among these manifestations nothing has been more remarkable than these fairs for the relief of suffering soldiers and their families. And the chief agents in these fairs are the women of America.

I am not accustomed to the use of language of eulogy; I have never studied the art of paying compliments to women; but I must say, that if all that has been said by orators and poets since the creation of the world in praise of women were applied to the women of America, it would not do them justice for their conduct during this war. I will close saying, God bless the women of America!

SPEECH AFTER THE BATTLE OF THE WILDERNESS.

Delivered in response to a Serenade May 9, 1864, at the White House.

FELLOW-CITIZENS:—I am very much obliged to you for the compliment of this call, though I apprehend it is owing more to the good news received to-day from the army than to a desire to see me. I am, indeed, very grateful to the brave men who have been struggling with the enemy in the field, to their noble commanders who have directed them, and especially to our Maker. Our cammanders are following up their victories resolutely and successfully. I think without knowing the particulars of the plans of General Grant, that what has been accomplished is of more importance than at first appears. I believe I know (and am especially grateful to know), that General Grant has not been jostled in his purpose; that he has made all his points; and today he is on his line, as he purposed before he moved his armies. I will volunteer to say that I am very glad of what has happened; but there is a great deal still to be done. While we are grateful to all the brave men and officers for the events of the past two days, we should, above all, be very grateful to Almighty God, who gives us victory.

There is enough yet before us requiring all loyal men and patriots to perform their share of the labor and follow the example of the modest General at the head of our armies, and sink all personal considerations for the sake of the country. I commend you to keep yourselves in the same tranquil mood that is characteristic of that brave and loyal man.

I have said more than I expected when I came before you. Repeating my thanks for this call, I bid you good-bye.

SPEECH ON THE WAR.

In June, 1864, the President attended a fair at Philadelphia, one of the largest that was held in all the country. At a supper given to him there, the health of the President having been proposed as a toast, the President said in acknowledgment:

LADIES AND GENTLEMAN:—I suppose that this toast is intended to open the way to me to say something. War at the best is terrible, and this of ours in its magnitude and duration is one of the most terrible the world has ever known. It has deranged business totally in many places and perhaps in all. It has destroyed property, destroyed life, and ruined homes. It has produced a national debt and a degree of taxation unprecedent in the history of this country. It has caused mourning among us until the heavens may almost be said to be hung in black. And yet it continues. It has had accompaniments never before known in the history of the world. I mean the Sanitary and Christian Commissions, with their labors for the relief of the soldiers, and the Volunteer Refreshment Saloons, understood better by those who hear me than by myself—(applause)—and these fairs, first begun at Chicago and next held in Boston, Cincinnati, and other cities. The motive and object that lie at the bottom of them is worthy of the most that we can do for the soldier who goes to fight the battles of his country. From the fair and tender hand of women is much, very much done for the soldier, continually reminding him of the care and thought for him at home. The knowledge that he is not forgotten is grateful to his heart. (Applause.) Another view of these institutions is worthy of thought. They are voluntary contributions, giving proof that the national resources are not at all exhausted, and that the national patriotism will sustain us through all. It is a pertinent question. When is the war to end? I do not wish to name a day when it will end, lest the end should not come at the given time. We accepted this war, and did not begin it. (Deafening applause.) We accepted it for an object, and when that object is accomplished the war will end, and I hope to God that it will never end until that object is accomplished. (Great applause.) We are going through with our task, so far as I am concerned, if it takes us three years longer. I have not been in the habit of making predictions, but I am almost tempted now to hazard one. I will. It is, that Grant is this evening in a position, with Mead and Hancock, of Pennsylvania, whence he can never be dislodged by the enemy until Richmond is taken. If I shall discover that General Grant may be greatly facilitated in the capture of Richmond, by rapidly pouring to him a large number of armed men at the briefest notice; will you go? (Cries of "Yes.") Will you march on with him? (Cries of "Yes, yes.) Then I shall call upon you when it is necessary. (Laughter and applause.)

———:o:———

LINCOLN'S SECOND INAUGURAL.

Delivered March 4, 1865, at Washington.

WITH MALICE TOWARD NONE, WITH CHARITY FOR ALL.

Fellow-Countrymen:—At this second appearing to take the oath of the Presidential office, there is less occasion for an extended address than there was at the first. Then a statement somewhat in detail of a course to be pursued seemed very fitting and proper. Now, at the expiration of four years, during which public declarations have been constantly called forth on every point and phase of the great contest which still absorbs the attention and engrosses the energies of the nation, little that is new could be presented.

"The progress of our arms, upon which all else chiefly depends, is as well known to the public as to myself; and it is, I trust, reasonably satisfactory and encouraging to all. With high hope for the future, no prediction in regard to it is ventuted.

"On the occasion corresponding to this four years ago, all thoughts were anxiously directed to an impending civil war. All dreaded it; all sought to avoid it. While the inaugural address was being delivered from this place, devoted altogether to save the Union without war, insurgent agents were in the city seeking to destroy it without war—seeking to dissolve the Union and divide the effects by negotiation. Both parties deprecated war;

but one of them would make war rather than let the nation survive, and the other would accept war rather than let it perish; and the war came.

"One eighth of the whole population were colored slaves, not distributed generally over the Union, but localized in the southern part of it. These slaves constituted a peculiar and powerful interest. All knew that this interest was somehow the cause of the war. To strengthen, perpetuate and extend this interest, was the object for which the insurgents would rend the Union even by war, while the government claimed no right to do more than to restrict the territorial enlargement of it.

"Neither party expected for the war the magnitude or the duration which it has already attained. Neither anticipated that the cause of the conflict might cease with, or even before, the conflict itself should cease. Each looked for an easier triumph, and a result less fundamental and astounding.

"Both read the same Bible and pray to the same God, and each invokes his aid against the other. It may seem strange that any man should dare to ask a just God's assistance in wringing their bread from the sweat of other men's faces; but let us judge not, that we be not judged. The prayers of both could not be answered. That of neither has been answered fully. The Almighty has his own purposes. 'Woe unto the world because of offense, for it must needs be that offenses come; but woe to that man by whom the offense cometh.' If we shall suppose that American slavery is one of these effenses, which in the providence of God must needs come, but which having continued through his appointed time, He now wills to remove, and that He gives to both North and South this terrible war as the woe due to those by whom the offense came, shall we discern therein any departure from those divine attributes which the believers in a living God always ascribe to Him? Fondly do we hope, fervently do we pray, that this mighty scourge of war may soon pass away.—Yet, if God wills that it continue until the wealth piled by the bondsman's two hundred and fifty years of unrequited toil shall be sunk, and until every drop of blood drawn with the lash shall be paid with another drawn with the sword; as was said three thousand years ago, so still it must be said, 'The judgments of the Lord are true and righteous altogether.'

"With malice toward none, with charity for all, with firmness in the right, as God gives us to see the right, let us strive on to finish the work we are in, to bind up the nation's wounds, to care for him who shall have born the battle and for his widow and orphans, to do all which may achieve and cherish a just and a lasting peace among ourselves and with all nations."

SPEECH TO 140th INDIANA REGIMENT.

Delivered at Washington, March 17, 1865.

Governor Morton had made a brief speech, in which he congratulated his auditors on the speedy approaching end of the rebellion, and concluded by introducing President Lincoln. The President addressed the assembly as follows:

FELLOW-CITIZENS:—It will be but a very few words that I shall undertake to say. I was born in Kentucky, raised in Indiana, and lived in Illinois; and now I am here, where it is my business to care equally for the good people of all the States. I am glad to see an Indiana regiment on this day able to present the captured flag to the Governor of Indiana. I am not disposed, in saying this, to make a distinction between the States, for all have done equally well.

There are but few views or aspects of this great war upon which I have not said or written something whereby my own opinions might be known. But there is one —the recent attempt of our erring brethren, as they are sometimes called, to employ the negro to fight for them. I have never written nor made a speech on that subject, because that was their business, not mine, and if I had a wish upon the subject, I had not the power to introduce it, or make it effective. The great question with them was whether the negro, being put into the army, will fight for them. I do not know, and therefore cannot decide. They ought to know better than me.

I have in my lifetime heard many arguments why the negroes ought to be slaves. but if they fight for those who would keep them in slavery, it will be a better argument than any I have yet heard. He who will fight for that, ought to be a slave. They have concluded, at last to take one out of four of the slaves and put them in the army, and that one out of the four who will fight to keep the others in slavery, ought to be a slave himself, unless he is killed in a fight. While I have often said that all men ought to be free, yet would I allow those colored persons to be slaves who want to be, and next to them those white people who argue in favor of making other people slaves. I am in favor of giving an appointment to such white men to try it on for these slaves. I will say one thing in regard to the negroes being employed to fight for them. I do know he cannot fight and stay at home and make bread, too. And as one is about as important as the other to them, I don't care which they do. I am rather in favor of having them try them as soldiers. They lack one vote of doing that, and I wish I could send my vote over the river so that I might cast it in favor of allowing the negro to fight. But they can not fight and work both. We must now see the bottom of the enemy's resources. They will stand out as long as they can, and if the negro will fight for them they must allow him to fight. They have drawn upon their last branch of resources, and we can now see the bottom. I am glad to see the end so near at hand. I have said now more than I intended, and will therefore bid you good-bye.

PRESIDENT LINCOLN'S LAST SPEECH.

A Carefully Worded, Wise and Memorable Production.

Delivered Tuesday Evening, April 11, 1865, in response to a serenade at the White House.

FELLOW-CITIZENS:—We meet this evening not in sorrow, but in gladness of heart. The evacuation of Petersburg and Richmond, and the surrender of the principal insurgent army, give hope of a righteous and speedy peace whose joyous expression cannot be restrained. In the midst of this, however, He from whom all blessings flow must not be forgotten. A call for a national thanksgiving is being prepared, and will be duly promulgated. Nor must those whose harder part give us the cause of rejoicing be overlooked. Their honors must not be parceled out with others. I myself was near the front, and had the high pleasure of transmitting much of the good news to you; but no part of the honor, for plan or execution, is mine. To Gen. Grant, his skillful officers and brave men, all belongs. The gallant navy stood ready, but was not in reach to take active part.

By these recent successes, the re-inauguration of the national authority, reconstruction, which has had a large share of thought from the first, is pressed much more closely upon our attention. It is fraught with great diffi-

[458]

culty. Unlike the case of a war between independent nations, there is no authorized organs for us to treat with. No one man has authority to give up the rebellion for any other man. We simply must begin with and mould from disorganized and discordant elements. Nor is it a small additional embarrassment that we, the loyal people, differ among ourselves as to the mode, manner and means of reconstruction.

As a general rule, I abstain from reading the reports of attacks upon myself, wishing not to be provoked by that to which I cannot properly offer an answer. In spite of this precaution, however, it comes to my knowledge that I am much censured from some supposed agency in setting up and seeking to sustain the new State Government of Louisiana. In this I have done just so much as, and no more than, the public knows. In the annual message of December, 1863, and accompanying proclamation, I presented a plan of reconstruction (as the phrase goes,) which I promised, if adopted by any state, should be acceptable to, and sustained by, the Executive Government of the nation. I distinctly stated that this was not the only plan which might possibly be acceptable; and I also distinctly protested that the Executive claimed no right to say whch or whether members should be admitted to seats in Congress from such States. This plan was, in advance, submitted to the then Cabinet, and distinctly approved by every member of it. One of them suggested that I should then, and in that connection, apply the Emancipation Proclamation to the heretofore excepted parts of Virginia and Louisiana: that I should drop the suggestion about apprenticeship for freed people, and that I should omit the protest against my own power, in regard to the admission of members of Congress, but even he approved every part and parcel of the plan which has since been employed or touched by the actions of Louisiana.

The new Constitution of Louisiana, declaring emancipation for the whole state, practically applies the proclamation to the part previously excepted. It does not adopt apprenticeship to freed people, and it is silent, as it could not well be otherwise, about the admission of members of Congress. So that, as it applies to Louisiana, every member of the Cabinet fully approved the plan. The message went to Congress, and I received many commendations of the plan, written and verbal; and not a single objection to it, from any professed emancipationist, came to my knowledge, until after the news reached Washington that the people of Louisiana had begun to move in accordance with it. From about July, 1862, I had corresponded with different persons, supposed to be interested seeking a reconstruction of a State Government for Louisiana. When the message of 1863, with the plan before mentioned, reached New Orleans, Gen. Banks wrote me he was confident that the people, with his military co-operation, would reconstruct substantially on that plan. I wrote him, and some of them, to try it. They tried it, and the result is known. Such only has been my agency in getting up the Louisiana government. As to sustaining it, my promise is out, as before stated.

But, as bad promises are better broken than kept, I shall treat this as a bad promise, and break it, whenever I shall be convinced that keeping it is adverse to the public interest. But I have not yet been so convinced.

I have been shown a letter on this subject, supposed be an able one, in which the writer expresses regret that my mind has not seemed to be definitely fixed on the question whether the seceded States, so-called, are in the Union or out of it. It would, perhaps, add astonishment to his regret to learn that, since I have found professed Union men endeavoring to make that question, I have purposely forborne any public expression upon it. As appears to me, that question has not been, nor yet is, a practically material one, and that any discussion of it, while it thus remains practically immaterial, could have no effect other than the mischievous one of dividing our friends.

As yet, whatever it may hereafter become, that question is bad, as the basis of a controversy, and good for nothing at all—a merely pernicious abstraction. We all agree that the seceded States, so-called, are out of their proper relation to the Union, and that the sole object of the Government, civil and military, in regard to those States, is to again get them into their proper practical relation. I believe it is not only possible, but in fact easier to do this without deciding, or even considering, whether these States have ever been out of the Union, than with it. Finding themselves safely at home, it would be utterly immaterial whether they had ever been abroad. Let us all join in doing the acts necessary to restoring the proper practical relations between these States and the Union, and each forever after innocently indulge his own opinion whether, in doing the acts, he brought the States from without into the Union, or only gave them proper assistance, they never having been out of it.

The amount of constituency, so to speak, on which the new Louisiana government rests, would be more satisfactory to all if it contained fifty, thirty, or even twenty thousand, instead of only about twelve thousand, as it really does. It is also unsatisfactory to some that the election franchise is not given to the colored man. I would myself prefer that it were now conferred on the very intelligent and those who serve our cause as soldiers. Still the question is not whether the Louisiana government, as it stands, is quite all that is desirable. The question is, "Will it be wiser to take it as it is, and help to improve it, or to reject and disperse it."

Can Louisiana be brought into proper practical relation with the Union sooner by sustaining or by discarding the new State government?

Some twelve thousand voters in the heretefore slave State of Louisiana have sworn allegiance to the Union, assumed to be the rightful political power of the State, held elections, organized a State government, adopted a free State constitution, giving the benefit of public schools equally to black and white, and empowering the Legislature to confer elective franchise upon the colored man. The Legislature has already voted to ratify the constitutional amendment passed by Congress, abolishing slavery throughout the nation. These twelve thousand persons are thus fully committed to the Union and to perpetual freedom in the States—committed to the very things, and nearly all the things the nation wants—and they ask the nation's recognition and its assistance to make good that committal.

Now, if we reject and spurn them, we do our utmost to disorganize and disperse them. We, in effect, say to the white men, "you are worthless, or worse, we will neither help you, nor be helped by you." To the blacks we say, "This cup of liberty which these, your old masters, hold to your lips, we will dash from you, and leave you to the chances of gathering the spilled and scattered contents in some vague and undefined when, where and how." If this course, discouraging and paralyzing both white and black, has any tendency to bring Louisiana into proper practical relations with the Union, I have, so far, been unable to perceive it. If on the contrary, we recognize and sustain the new government of Louisiana, the converse of all this is made true.

We encourage the hearts and nerve the arms of the 12,000 to adhere to their work, and argue for it, and proselyte for it, fight for it, and feed it, and grow it, and ripen it to a complete success. The colored, man, too, seeing all united for him, is inspired with vigilance, and energy, and daring the same end. Grant that he desires elective franchise, will he not obtain it sooner by saving the already advanced steps towards it, than by running backward over them? Concede that the new government of Louisiana is only as what it should be as the egg is to the fowl, we shall sooner have the fowl by hatching the egg than by smashing it. [Laughter.]

Again, if we reject Louisiana, we also reject one vote in favor of the proposed amendment to the National Constitution. To meet this proposition, it has been argued that no more than three-fourths of those States, which have not attempted secession, are necessary to validly ratify the amendment. I do not commit myself against this, further than to say that such a ratification would be questionable, and sure to be persistently questioned, while ratification by three-fourths of all the States would be unquestioned and unquestionable.

I repeat the question: "Can Louisiana be brought into proper practical relation with the Union sooner by sustaining or by discarding her new State Government?" What has been said of Louisiana will apply generally to other States. And yet so great peculiarities pertain to each State, and such important and sudden changes occur in the same State, and, withal, so new and unprecedented is the whole case, that no exclusive and inflexible plan can safely be prescribed as to details and collaterals. Such exclusive and inflexible plan would surely become a new entanglement. Important principles may, and must be inflexible.

In the present situation, as the phrase goes, it may be my duty to make some new announcement to the people of the South. I am considering, and shall not fail to act, when satisfied that action will be proper.

————:o:————

LINCOLN'S RELIGIOUS BELIEF.

Abraham Lincoln, says David P. Thompson, had the good fortune to be trained by a godly mother and stepmother. The two books which made the most impression upon his character were the Bible and Weem's "Life of Washington." The former he read with such diligence that he knew it almost by heart, and the words of scripture became so much a part of his nature that he rarely made a speech or wrote a paper of any length without quoting its language or teachings.

One of Mr. Lincoln's notable religious utterances was his reply to a deputation of colored people at Baltimore who presented him a Bible. He said: "In regard to the great book I have only to say it is the best gift which God has ever given man. All the good from the Savior of the world is communicated to us through this book. But for this book we could not know right from wrong. All those things desirable to man are contained in it."

Col. Rusling overheard the following conversation between President Lincoln and Gen. Sickels, just after the victory of Gettysburg: The fact is, General, said the President, in the stress and pinch of the campaign there, I went to my room, and got down on my knees and prayed Almighty God for victory at Gettysburg. I told Him that this was His country, and the war was His war, but that we really couldn't stand another Fredericksburg or Chancellorsville. And then and there I made a solemn vow with my Maker that if He would stand by you boys at Gettysburg, I would stand by Him. And He did, and I will! And after this I felt that God Almighty had taken the whole thing into His own hands. Mr. Lincoln said all this with great solemnity.

LINCOLN'S BURIAL AT OAK RIDGE CEMETERY, SPRINGFIELD, ILL. [466]

LINCOLN'S SAYINGS.

—All that I am, all that I hope to be, I owe to my angel mother.

—God must like common people or He would not have made so many of them.

—If all that has been said by orators and poets since the creation of the world in praise of women were applied to the women of America, it would not do them full justice for their conduct during the war. * * * God bless the women of America.

—That we here highly resolve that * * * this nation, under God, shall have a new birth of freedom, and that the government of the people, by the people and for the people shall not perish from the earth.

—This Government must be preserved in spite of the acts of any man or set of men.

—For thirty years I have been a temperance man, and I am too old to change.

—This country, with its institutions, belongs to the people who inhabit it.

—Let us have faith that right makes might; and in that faith, let us to the end dare to do our duty as we understand it.

—Nowhere in the world is presented a Government of so much liberty and equality.

—I am indeed very grateful to the brave men who have been struggling with the enemy in the field.

—Gold is good in its place; but living, brave and patriotic men are better than gold.

—The people, when they rise in mass in behalf of the Union and the liberties of their country, truly may it be said: The gates of hell cannot prevail against them.

—I have not willingly planted a thorn in any man's bosom.

—The reasonable man has long since agreed that intemperance is one of the greater, if not the greatest, of all evils among mankind.

—A house divided against itself cannot stand. I believe this Government cannot endure permanently, half slave and half free. I do not expect the Union to be dissolved; I do not expect the house to fall; but I do expect it will cease to be divided. It will become all one thing or all the other. Either the opponents of slavery will arrest the further spread of it and place it where the public shall rest in the belief that it is in the course of ultimate extinction, or its advocates will push it forward till it shall become alike lawful in all the States, old as well as new, North as well as South.

—Unless the great God * * * shall be with and aid me, I must fail; but if the same omniscient and almighty arm * * * shall guide and support me, I shall not fail; I shall succeed.

—Come what will, I will keep my faith with friend and foe.

—The purposes of the Almighty are perfect and must prevail, though we erring mortals may fail to accurately perceive them in advance.

978-3-33719-068-2

General U. S. Grant's Tour Around the World - Embracing His Speeches, Receptions, and Description of His Travels is an unchanged, high-quality reprint of the original edition of 1879.

Hansebooks is editor of the literature on different topic areas such as research and science, travel and expeditions, cooking and nutrition, medicine, and other genres. As a publisher we focus on the preservation of historical literature. Many works of historical writers and scientists are available today as antiques only. Hansebooks newly publishes these books and contributes to the preservation of literature which has become rare and historical knowledge for the future.

ISBN/EAN: 978-3-33719-068-2
www.hansebooks.com

hanse

—It is no pleasure to me to triumph over anyone.

—I do not impugn the motives of anyone opposed to me.

—I shall do my utmost that whoever is to hold the helm for the next voyage shall start with the best possible chance to save the ship.

—I appeal to you again to constantly bear in mind that with you (the people) and not with politicians, not with presidents, not with office-seekers, but with you, is the question, shall the Union, and shall the liberties of the country be preserved to the latest generation.

—So far as I have been able, so far as has came within my sphere, I have always acted as I believe was right and just, and have done all I could for the good of mankind.

—No men living are more worthy to be trusted than those who toil up from poverty—none less inclined to take or touch aught which they have not honestly earned.

—With malice toward none, with charity for all, with firmness in the right, as God gives us to see the right, let us strive on to finish the work we are in; to bind up the nation's wounds; to care for him who shall have borne the battle, and for his widow and orphans; to do all which may achieve and cherish a just and a lasting peace among ourselves and with all nations.

—I have never had a feeling politically that did not spring from the sentiments embodied in the Declaration of Independence.

———:o:———

LINCOLN'S TOMB AND MONUMENT, OAK RIDGE CEMETERY, SPRINGFIELD, ILL.

BRONZE CORNER PIECES—SARCOPHAGUS AND MEMORIAL ROOM.   [471]

LINCOLN ON LABOR AND CAPITAL.

In one of his messages to Congress President Lincoln spoke of the true relations of labor and capital. To the language then used by him he added a few sentences in March, 1864, when he replied to a workingmen's association that had made him an honorary member. The following is that part of the message bearing almost directly on the subject, with its later addendum:

"It is assumed that labor is available only in connection with capital; that no one labors, unless somebody else, owning capital, somehow by the use of it induces him to labor. Now there is no such relation between labor and capital as assumed; nor is there any such thing as a free man being fixed for life in the condition of a hired laborer. Labor is prior to and independent of capital. Capital is only the fruit of labor, and could never have existed if labor had not first existed. Capital has its rights, which are as worthy of protection as any other rights. Nor is it denied that there is, and probably always will be, a relation between labor and capital, producing mutual benefits. The error is in assuming that the whole labor of the community exists within that relation. A large majority neither work for others nor have others work for them. A considerable number mingle their own labor with capital; that is, they labor with their own hands, and also buy or hire others to labor for them; but this is only a mixed and not a distinct class. Property is the fruit of labor; property is desirable; it is a positive good in the world. That some should be rich shows that others may become rich, and hence it is a just encouragement to enterprise.

"Let not him that is houseless pull down the house of another, but let him work diligently and build one for himself; thus by example assuring that his own shall be safe from violence when built."

————:o:————

LINCOLN'S SADNESS.

"Lincoln was, in his fixed quality," says Mr. Usher, "a man of sadness. If he were looking out of a window alone, and you happened to be passing by and caught his eye, you would generally see in it an expression of distress.

"He was one of the greatest men who ever lived. It is now many years since I was in his Cabinet, and some of the things that happened there have been forgotten, and the whole of it is rather dreamy. But Lincoln's extraordinary personality is still one of the most distinct things in my memory. He was as wise as a serpent. He had the skill of the greatest statesman in the world. Everything he handled came to success. Nobody took up his work and brought it to the same perfection.

————:o:————

Standard Library, Cloth Edition

PUBLISHED BY

RHODES · & · McCLURE · PUBLISHING · CO.

CHICAGO, ILL.

· · · · · · · ·

ALL · HANDSOMELY · BOUND · IN · CLOTH,
With Gilt Side and Back Stamps.

· · · · · · · ·

Will be sent by Mail on receipt of the Price by the Publishers

· · · · · · · ·

Postage Stamps, Postal Notes, Postoffice Orders, or Express Money Orders may be sent to the Publishers by Mail at any time, and they will promptly forward the Books ordered.

- ....1—MOODY'S ANECDOTES AND ILLUSTRATIONS, $1.00
  210 pages. As related by D. L. Moody in his Revival Work.
- ....2—MOODY'S CHILD'S STORIES. Illustrated........ 1.00
  As related by D. L. Moody in his Revival Work.
- ....3—SAM JONES' SERMONS, Vol. I. 346 pages...... 1.00
- ....4—SAM JONES' SERMONS, Vol. II. 340 pages...... 1.00
- ....5—SAM JONES' ANECDOTES. 300 pages........... 1.00
  As related by him in his Revival Work.
- ....6—GREAT SPEECHES OF COL. R. G. INGERSOLL.
  Complete; 352 pages.................... .... 1.00
- ....7—WIT, WISDOM AND ELOQUENCE OF COL. R. G. INGERSOLL. 240 pages 1.00
- ..8—MISTAKES OF INGERSOLL. 600 pages......... 1.00
  Criticisms of the Clergy, and his Lectures, "Mistakes of Moses," "Skulls," "What Shall We Do to be Saved?" "Thomas Paine," "Funeral Oration at His Brother's Grave" appended.

STANDARD LIBRARY, CLOTH EDITION.

- **9—ABE LINCOLN STORIES.** English. 240 pages .. $1.00
- **10—ABE LINCOLN STORIES.** German. 240 pages ... 1.00
- **11—EDISON AND HIS INVENTIONS** 1.00
  Including sketch of his life, description of inventions, also a complete Electrical Dictionary, revised and complete. 264 pages. Illustrated.
- **12—CHICAGO:** History, Stories and Strangers' Guide. 400 pages. Illustrated................... 1.00
- **13—POETIC PEARLS.** Illustrated, gilt. 407 pages 1.50
- **14—POETIC PEARLS.** Illustrated, plain. 407 pages... 1.00
- **15—ENTERTAINING ANECDOTES.** 240 pages...... 1.00
  From all available sources. Illustrated.
- **16—BILL NYE'S CORDWOOD** 1.00
- **17—TEN YEARS A COW-BOY.** 471 pages............ 1.00
  Romances, Adventures, Life on the Plains, with experience as Cow-boy, Stock Owner and Rancher, with Descriptions of the Plains, Articles on Cattle and Sheep Raising, how to Make Money on the Plains. Illustrated.
- **18—GEMS OF TRUTH AND BEAUTY.** 300 pages... 1.00
  By Talmage, Moody, Beecher, Spurgeon, Guthrie and Parker.
- **19—STORIES, SKETCHES AND LIFE of GEN. GARFIELD,** from the Log Cabin to the White House, with a full account of his Assassination, Death and Burial. 228 pages. Illustrated................. 1.00
- **20—EVERY-DAY COOK BOOK** and Encyclopedia of Practical Recipes for Family Use. By Miss E. Neill. Economical, reliable and excellent. 324 pp. 1.00
- **21—GENERAL HANCOCK.** Including his early history, war record, public life, and all the interesting facts of his career..................................... .50
- **22—JETHRO WOOD,** Inventor of the Modern Plough. An account of his life, services and trials, together with the facts subsequent to his death and incident to his great invention. Illustrated................ .50
- **23—THE LORD'S PRAYER,** in the Principal Languages, Dialects and Versions of the World; printed in type and vernacular of the different nations. 200 pages.. 1.00
  This little book is placed before the public for the purpose of giving, in a concise form, an introductory view of the principal languages and dialects of the world as they appear in print, and at the same time to aid in the cultivation of religious thought and the adoration of the Supreme Being.
- **24—STORIES AND SKETCHES OF GEN. GRANT,** at Home, Abroad, in Peace and in War. 8vo, 216 pp. 1.00

FOR THE DEAF.

THE AUDIPHONE

An Instrument that Enables Deaf Persons to Hear Ordinary Conversation Readily through the Medium of the Teeth, and Many of those Born Deaf and Dumb to Hear and Learn to Speak.

INVENTED BY RICHARD S. RHODES, CHICAGO.

Medal Awarded at the World's Columbian Exposition, Chicago, 1893.

The Audiphone is a new instrument made of a peculiar composition, posessing the property of gathering the faintest sounds (somewhat similar to a telephone diaphragm), and conveying them to the auditory nerve, through the medium of the teeth. *The external ear has nothing whatever to do in hearing with this wonderful instrument.*

Thousands are in use by those who would not do without them for any consideration. It has enabled doctors and lawyers to resume practice, teachers to resume teaching, mothers to hear the voices of their children, thousands to hear their minister, attend concerts and theatres, and engage in general conversation. Music is heard perfectly with it when without it not a note could be distinguished. It is convenient to carry and to use. Ordinary conversation can be heard with ease. In most cases deafness is not detected.

Full instructions will be sent with each instrument. The Audiphone is patented throughout the civilized world.

: : PRICE : :

Conversational, small size, - - -	$5 00
Conversational, medium size, - - -	5 00
Concert size, - - - - -	5 00

The Audiphone will be sent to any address, on receipt of price, by

RHODES & McCLURE PUBLISHING CO.,

Agents for the World,

93 Washington St.,   CHICAGO, ILL.

WEBSTER'S
Unabridged Dictionary

REPRINT EDITION.

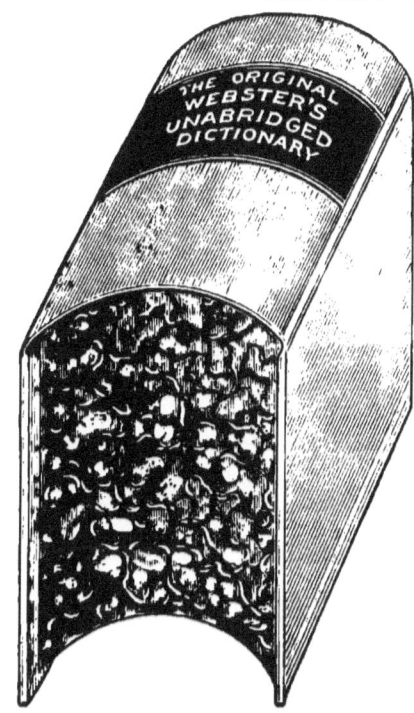

CLOTH, - - - $1.50
HALF MOROCCO, - 1.75
SHEEP, - - - - 2.00

Every School Child Should Have One of These Copies.

OVER 1300 PAGES.

Beautiful Frontispiece of the Flags of All Nations in Five Colors, Illustrated.

THE BEST ON THE MARKET TO-DAY FOR THE MONEY.

ADDRESS ALL ORDERS TO

Rhodes & McClure Publishing Co.,
93 Washington Street,
CHICAGO.

CONFIDENCE.   INTEGRITY.

DESPATCH.

UNION DETECTIVE SERVICE.

(ACKNOWLEDGED THE BEST IN THE WORLD.)

85 Dearborn St.,

Suits 201-2-3.   **Chicago, Ill.**

References:
　　Leading Banks,
　　Insurance Associations,
　　Mercantile Agencies,
　　Etc., Etc.

" ONLY SKILLED OPERATORS EMPLOYED."

J. H. LOBELL, Supt.

NERVOUS AND CHRONIC DISEASES

And all Poisoned Blood, Eruptions and all Unnatural Losses and Weakness caused by own indiscretions, cured quickly and surely under guarantee, without interference with business. Consultation personally or by mail FREE and SACRED. Medicines sent everywhere. Write for question list.

YOUNG MEN who suffer from Nervous Debility affecting Mind and Body, should consult the Celebrated Staff of Physicians and Surgeons at Chicago Medical Institute at once. Remember, nervous diseases or debility and loss of nerve power treated scientifically by new methods with never-failing success.

MIDDLE-AGED MEN who now find the penalty of their Transgressions or over Brain Work may consult with the assurance of Speedy Relief and a permanent Cure, if within the reach of Human Skill.

OLD MEN who suffer from weakness will find immediate relief and comfort, and in many cases a permanent cure.

All Blood and Skin Diseases Completely Eradicated without Mercury.

LADIES suffering from diseases or complaints peculiar to the female sex treated with utmost skill and experience

Call on or Address

Chicago Medical Institute, 157-159 S. Clark St., Chicago, Ill.

AGENTS WANTED in EVERY COUNTY to SELL OUR BOOKS

THEY ARE

HANDSOME,
POPULAR,
INSTRUCTIVE,
INTERESTING
AND AMUSING.

This is one of them; see partial list elsewhere in this volume. They sell readily. Liberal commissions given. For particulars address

RHODES & McCLURE PUBLISHING CO.
CHICAGO.

Knox & Stidger,

ATTORNEYS AT LAW,

612 Masonic Temple,

TELEPHONE MAIN 2196.   (Corner State and Randolph Sts.)

Admitted to practice in the Courts of England and Canada.

COMMUNICATIONS BY MAIL WILL RECEIVE PROMPT ATTENTION.

CATARRH **HAVE YOU GOT IT?** **If so, try my Medicine.** It is a sure cure. Try it and be convinced. You will never regret it. Sent by mail to any address. Price One Dollar. JOHN P. HORR, 125 Clark St., Chicago, Illinois. Send for Circular.

www.ingramcontent.com/pod-product-compliance
Lightning Source LLC
Chambersburg PA
CBHW051852300426
44117CB00006B/361